The Music Lover's Companion

Curarum Levamen

The Music Lover's Companion

Edited by
GERVASE HUGHES
and
HERBERT VAN THAL

LONDON
EYRE & SPOTTISWOODE

002587

SBN 413 27920 0

First published 1971
Copyright © 1971 Eyre & Spottiswoode (Publishers) Ltd
11 New Fetter Lane, EC4
Printed in Great Britain by
Cox & Wyman Ltd,
Fakenham, Norfolk

Contents

CONTENTS

PART III · OPERA

PART IV
INTERPRETERS AND INTERPRETATION

PART V · A MIXED BAG

PART VI · FICTION AND FANTASY

Illustrations

The Music Lover's Companion

Introduction

This collection of writings about music is divided into six sections, the first five of which are devoted to comment and criticism from many sources, together with personal reminiscences and extracts from private correspondence; the sixth and last section is given over to fiction and fantasy.

Part I concerns the pleasures that music can bring, the qualities which differentiate it from the other arts and the lessons that can be learnt from its history. In Part II some thirty-five composers are discussed, although those who distinguished themselves mainly in opera are more likely to be found in Part III, which deals specifically with that subject. Part IV concentrates on interpretation, and here some eminent interpreters put in an appearance, either as commentators or as topics for comment, while Part V gathers together a group of entries which do not fit neatly into any of the four preceding categories. The authors and poets represented in Part VI range from Peacock through Browning and Zola to writers of the present day.

A round dozen of the items in Parts I to V date from earlier than 1800, but the vast majority belong to the nineteenth and twentieth centuries, a period during which the outpouring of literature on music has been so prodigious that we cannot claim to have explored more than a small fraction of it. From that fraction we first chose some three hundred passages, varying in length from a single sentence to ten thousand words. When faced with the invidious task of reducing these three hundred 'possibles' to less than half that number of 'probables', we strove to maintain certain principles in making the selection.

A music lover's companion, we felt, should be based on sufficiently broad premises to admit controversial as well as authoritative points of view (controversy being the life-blood of shared enthusiasms), and partly for that reason our final choice incorporates contributions not only from acknowledged experts but also from writers outside the ranks of professional musicians and music critics. We thought it right to find room, too, for a few light-hearted *obiter dicta*, both pertinent and impertinent: an inclination to enjoy good music – and to read about it – does not involve abandonment of a sense of humour.

It must also be stressed that this anthology makes no pretence to be a substitute for a comprehensive and discriminating survey of music and musicians throughout the ages. That Beethoven is accorded fewer pages than Liszt, that Massenet finds a place while Palestrina is ignored, implies no editorial judgement on the relative historical importance of these composers. The criterion we adopted was not so much the stature of the musician as the quality of the enlightenment – or entertainment – provided by the writer, and since it was impracticable to allocate space to some of the most distinguished figures in musical history, we decided, in the interests of balance and variety, that *en principe* the maximum allowance for any musician, however great, should be one full-length essay – or its equivalent. (We later agreed between us to relax this restriction slightly in one or two special cases.)

By similar tokens, and after much heart-searching, we felt it best to limit each contributor to a single entry (with perhaps an occasional *obiter dictum* in addition). Even so – and despite Rollo H. Myers' opinion that 'there is so little first-class writing about music in existence' (see page 56) – we found an *embarras de richesses* at our disposal, and in the end we reluctantly had to pass over a number of eminent writers on music, of both yesterday and today, to whom we had originally hoped to give representation alongside their colleagues.

Warm thanks are due to the publishers for their many helpful suggestions, and to all those listed on pages 525–8, who have kindly allowed us to make use of copyright material; to any whose names are inadvertently omitted we offer our apologies.

Gervase Hughes
Herbert Van Thal

London 1971

PART I
The Scope of Music

The Pleasure to be derived from Music

W. H. HADOW

The immediate effect of music upon the nervous system is incontestable. It has often been noticed in animals other than man; it is a matter of common observation in children; it has been made the basis of a proposal to use the art as a medicinal agency. And as no two sets of nerves are exactly alike, it follows that in no two organisms will the same effect be produced. If the temperament be highly strung, and if there be no intellectual enjoyment of the art to divert attention, the nerve may be over-stimulated, and the result will be a feeling of pain. As the nerve strengthens, it will grow more tolerant; as education advances, the mind will be occupied with new interests. Questions of form and style will assert their pre-eminence over questions of tone. In a word, body will

> Get its sop and hold its noise,
> And leave soul free a little.

Théophile Gautier honestly defined music as 'le plus désagréable de tous les sons'. Charles Lamb rushed from the opera-house to solace his sufferings amid the rattle of the cab wheels. And equally the child Chopin cried with pain at the first sound of the pianoforte, and the child Mozart fainted under the intolerable blare of the trumpet. In all these cases the explanation is the same – a nerve too delicate to endure the stimulus, and an absence of any counter-acting influence that could inhibit the sensation.

It is thus wholly erroneous to suppose that there is a gulf fixed between the man who 'has no ear' and the trained musician: on the contrary, the two extremes shade into each other by a thousand varieties of graduation. And this is particularly true of these complex impressions which result from several notes combined in harmony. The stimulus which we receive from a chord is, for obvious reasons, more vehement and acute than that which we receive from any of its constituent notes taken separately; and hence it is in our appreciation of harmonies, more than in any other form of musical effect, that the sensuous side of the art becomes apparent. Now, there is not a single chord in common use at the present day which has not been at some time condemned as a dissonance. The major third was once held to be a discord; so, later, was the dominant seventh; so, within living memory, was the so-called dominant thirteenth. Fifty years ago [1845] Chopin's harmony was 'unendurable'; thirty years ago the world accepted Chopin, but shrank in terror from Wagner and Brahms; now, we accept all three, but shake our heads over Goldmark. And the inference to which all this points is, that the terms 'concord' and 'discord' are wholly relative to the ear of the listener. The distinction between them is not to be explained on any mathematical basis, or by any *a priori* law of acoustics; it is altogether a question of psychology.

At the same time, it may be held, fairly enough, that a composer is bound to write in a manner intelligible to his generation. Volapuk may be the language of the future, but a poet who, at the present day, should publish his epic in that tongue has only himself to thank if he finds no readers. True, but the composer, like the poet, is himself a part of his generation, and, if he writes simply and naturally, may be trusted not to pass out of touch with contemporary thought. He is a leader, but it is no part of a leader's business to lose sight of his army. And in Music, it is not the sensuous question which matters, but the intellectual; not the fact of concord or discord, but the way in which they are employed. We still find Monteverdi harsh and the Prince of Venosa crude, not because they use sharp dissonances and extreme modulations, but because they fail to justify them on any artistic grounds. They are in this matter children playing with edged tools. So, at the present day, a composer who should end a piece on a minor second would be deliberately violating the established language of the time;[1] and would be reprehensible, not because a minor second is ugly – for it will be a concord some day – but because, in the existing state of Music, it could not be naturally placed at the close of a cadence. Imagine Handel's face on being shown a song which finished on a dominant seventh out of the key. And, having imagined it, turn to Schumann's 'Im wunderschönen Monat Mai'.

[1] Paul Dukas did just that in his *Plainte, au loin, d'un faune* (1918). *Ed.*

Again, supposing that a generation has mainly agreed to find the climax of sensuous pleasure in certain chords – the augmented sixth, the diminished seventh and the like – it by no means follows that a composition is delightful because it contains those particular effects. Everything depends on their relation to their context, or the standpoint from which they are introduced, on the general style of the passage in which they appear. Any amateur purveyor of hymn tunes and waltzes can learn to write them; the difficulty is to present them fitly and properly, and to place them, as points of colour, where they will harmonize with the complete scheme of the work. Even more recondite effects, like the wonderful 'voca me cum benedictis' in Dvořák's *Requiem* are *qua* sensuous of secondary value. Their true importance lies in their intellectual side, in their function of exhibiting new key relationships or new methods of resolution. And if a chord does not fulfil some such duty, if it does not justify itself by bearing some definite organic part in the total plan, then it is not art but confectionery. Hearers, whose only delight in music arises from the perception of 'sweet' harmonies, are on a par with the schoolboy in Leech's picture, who suggests that the claret would be improved by a little sugar.

From this, two conclusions would seem to follow. First that Music can never be adequately criticized on sensuous grounds, partly because the receptivity of the nerve differs in different temperaments, partly because even where there is an agreement the sensuous side is wholly subordinate to the intellectual. Secondly, as a corollary from this, any musician who deliberately aims at sensuous effects alone, *ipso facto*, commits artistic suicide. He can be beaten on his own ground by the great masters, and he leaves untouched the whole of that field to the occupation of which they owe their greatness. Finally, it may be added, that sense notoriously grows tired, while mental activity endures. We very soon weary of the average drawing-room ballad, even if it gave us some animal pleasure at the first hearing; but we return again and again to the fugue of Bach or the sonata of Beethoven, because there we find the permanent expression of mind and intelligence. And thus the musical critic may virtually disregard the element of sensation, or at most may allude to it only so far as to show that it is, in Aristotle's phrase, 'obedient to reason'.

Music affects our emotional nature in two ways: partly through the nervous system, partly through the ordinary law of association. It is a commonplace of psychology that our emotions are largely conditioned by physical states in the body, and to this rule music assuredly offers no exception. Under certain circumstances, a current of energy, after passing from the ear to the brain, is transmuted into the nervous movements which constitute the material cause of the simple feelings, and thus we are roused or exhilarated or depressed by means as mechanical as those of any agency in external nature. Here, again, as in sensation itself, much depends upon the receptivity of the nerve. One hearer may be thrown into agitation by an impulse which leaves another comparatively cold, a strong temperament may be vehemently excited by conditions under which a weaker organism is stunned or paralysed. But all who are in any degree susceptible to the influence of music have experienced some measure of this emotional stimulus, poured into the brain through sensation, and then sublimated in a physical alembic. Among the most conspicuous existing causes may be noted the rapid tremolo of the strings, as in the death song at the end of *Tristan*, the beat of a recurring figure, as in the 'Ride to the Abyss' of Berlioz' *Faust*, the reiteration of high notes on the violin, as in much of Dvořák's chamber music, and the restlessness of frequent modulation or uncertain tonality. Any reader who is at the pains to analyse the effect produced upon him by these means of musical expression, will probably agree that they rouse first a particular kind of stimulus in the senses, and then without any conscious intervention on his own part, a corresponding state of emotional feeling.

Far more important is the influence of association. There is no reason *in rerum natura* why the minor mode should be sad, but our first ancestors noticed that a cry sank in tone as the power of its utterance failed, and hence established a connection between depression of note and waning strength. So began an association of ideas to which, by transmission and inheritance, the pathos of our minor keys is mainly due. Again, the bass naturally suggests gravity and earnestness, because that is the case with the speaking voice. "No man of real dignity," says Aristotle, "could ever be shrill of speech"; and similarly, when we look for serious or dignified music, we expect to find some prominence given to its lower register. Much, too, of this association is due to the motions of our ordinary life: the force that strikes like a blow in the first phrase of Beethoven's Fifth Symphony, the agitation so often expressed by rapid and irregular movement; the broken voices at the end of the Funeral March in the *Eroica*; and others of similar kind. Of course music cannot define any specific emotional state: it is far too vague and indeterminate to be regarded as an articulate language; but it undoubtedly can suggest and adumbrate general types of emotion, either by producing their sensuous conditions, or by presenting some form of phrase which we can connect by association with our own experience.

But it is not in this emotional influence that the truest laws of musical criticism are to be sought. Its criterion is nobler than that of sense, partly because it deals with an aspect of our nature which is less animal, partly because it implies a greater degree of skill in the artist; but it is too personal and intimate to afford a satisfactory basis for discussion, and taken by itself, it offers little or no opportunity for the exercise of the higher faculties. In the *Journal de Goncourt*, there is a well-known passage describing the effect of music on a roomful of highly-strung and unintelligent listeners. The picture is not a little degrading to our humanity: nervous emotion trembling on the verge of hysteria, sentiment that has passed out of rational control, an intoxication of feeling morbid in itself and dangerous in its inevitable reaction. The case may be extreme, the account may be rhetorically exaggerated, but it contains a salutary truth. If we look on music merely as a stimulus to our emotional nature, we are really disregarding all that makes it of permanent value as an art. We are lowering it to the level of sentimental romance or bloodthirsty melodrama. Grant that this form of indulgence is less gross than the direct gratification of the senses, it is not a whit more critical. While we are under its spell, we are as incapable of sane judgement as Rinaldo in Armida's garden; we have abrogated our manhood, we have drugged our reason, we are lying passive and inert at the mercy of an external will.

It is hardly necessary to point out that this state of mere recipience is altogether different from artistic appreciation. Art is no more a riot of the passions than it is a debauch of the senses: it contains, no doubt, sensuous and emotional elements, the importance of which there is no need to undervalue, but it is only artistic if it subordinate them to the paramount claims of reason. Even the purest and noblest emotions do not constitute a sufficient response. We are only in a position to criticize when we have passed through the emotional stage and emerged into the intellectual region beyond. To judge a composition simply from the manner in which it works upon our feelings, is no better than judging a picture or a poem merely from our sympathy with its subject.

To this conclusion two possible objections may be urged: first, that it takes an 'ascetic' view of art; second, that it places the criterion in a mere subservience to abstract and mechanical laws. Both of these rest on a misunderstanding of the position. True art is neither ascetic nor intemperate: it implies a full command of the sensuous and emotional factors in beauty, but it knows how to employ them. Its object is to make the whole work beautiful, not to elaborate this or that aspect at the expense of the rest; and such an object can only be achieved in virtue of certain intellectual principles. Beethoven's harmony is not less exquisite, or his passion less true and vital because he regards the requirements of style and structure as paramount. On the contrary, the sensuous and emotional beauties of his work are themselves enhanced by the unerring skill with which he places his effects and contrasts his colours. Again, whatever their intellectual laws may be they are not mechanical. They afford no excuse for *Kapellmeistermusik*, no justification for cold accuracy and dull correctness: so far from precluding genius, they pre-suppose it. They are not grammatical conventions which can be learned from text-books, they are the direct and spontaneous outcome of the human reason. Thus, in order to ascertain them, we must begin by discovering what is the broadest principle of formal beauty which can be deduced from the laws of mind, and use it as a provisional hypothesis with which to approach our problem. We shall then see how far this principle finds actual embodiment in the works of the great composers, and if there are exceptions or divergences, how far they can be explained. If our original hypothesis is confirmed by experience, we may reasonably conclude that it is true. If not, we must recognize that we are on the wrong line and we must retrace our steps.

In musical criticism, as in every other form of scientific investigation, it is not the function of man to anticipate facts, but to interpret them.

from STUDIES IN MODERN MUSIC *1894*

Three Kinds of Music and Three Classes of Musicians

ANICIUS MANLIUS SEVERINUS BOETHIUS[1]

There are three kinds of music: the first, the music of the universe; the second, human music; the third, instrumental music.

The first, the music of the universe, is especially to be studied in the combining of the elements and the variety of the seasons which are observed in the heavens. How indeed could the swift mechanism of the sky move silently on its course? Although no sound reaches our ears, the extremely rapid motion of such great bodies could not be altogether without it. Unless a certain harmony united the differences and contrary powers of the four elements, how could they form a single body and mechanism? Just as there is a measure of sound in low strings lest the lowness descend to inaudibility, and a measure of tenseness in high strings lest they be broken by the thinness of the sound, being too tense, so we perceive that in the music of the universe nothing can be excessive, but each part brings its own contribution or aids others to bring theirs.

What human music is, anyone may understand by examining his own nature. For what is that which unites the incorporeal activity of the reason with the body, unless it be a certain mutual adaptation and as it were a tempering of high and low sounds into a single consonance?

The third kind of music is that which is described as residing in certain instruments. This is produced by tension, as in strings,

[1] Boethius was a Roman statesman who also distinguished himself as a philosopher and theologian. *Ed.*

or by blowing, as in the tibiae or in those instruments activated by water, or by some kind of percussion, as in instruments which are struck upon certain bronze concavities, by which means various sounds are produced.

There are three classes concerned with the musical art. One class has to do with instruments, another invents songs, a third judges the work of instruments and songs. But that class which is dedicated to instruments and there consumes its entire efforts, consists of those who are separated from the intellect of musical science, since they are servants, nor do they bear anything of reason, being wholly destitute of speculation. The second class having to do with music is that of the poets, which is borne to song not so much by speculation and reason as by a certain natural instinct. Thus this class also is to be separated from music. The third is that which assumes the skill of judging, so that it weighs rhythms and melodies and the whole of song. And seeing that the whole is founded in reason and speculation, this class is rightly reckoned as musical, and that man as a musician who possesses the faculty of judging, according to speculation or reason, appropriate and suitable to music, of modes and rhythms and of the classes of melodies and their mixtures and of the songs of the poets.

from DE INSTITUTIONE MUSICA *515*

A Dangerous Aspect of Music

JOHN CALVIN

Among the things proper to recreate man and give him pleasure, music is either the first or one of the principal, and we must think that it is a gift of God deputed to that purpose. For which reason we must be the more careful not to abuse it, for fear of soiling and contaminating it, converting it to our condemnation when it has been dedicated to our profit and welfare. Were there no other consideration than this alone, it might well move us to moderate the use of music to make it serve all that is of good repute, and

that it should not be the occasion of our giving free rein to dis-
soluteness or of making ourselves effeminate with disordered
pleasures, and that it should not become the instrument of
lasciviousness or of any shamelessness. But there is still more, for
there is hardly anything in the world with more power to turn
and bend, this way or that, the morals of men. And in fact we
find by experience that it has a secret and almost incredible power
to move our hearts in one way or another.

Wherefore we must be that more diligent in ruling it in such a
manner that it may be useful to us and in no way pernicious. For
this reason the early doctors of the Church often complain that the
people of their times are addicted to dishonest and shameless
songs, which not without reason they call Satanic poison for the
corruption of the world. Now in speaking of music I understand
two parts, namely, the letter, or subject and matter, and the song,
or melody. It is true that every evil word corrupts good manners,
but when it has the melody with it, it pierces the heart much more
strongly and enters within; as wine is poured into the cask with a
funnel, so venom and corruption are distilled to the very depths
of the heart by melody. Now what is there to do? It is to have
songs not merely honest but also holy, which will be like spurs
to incite us to pray to God and to praise Him, and to meditate
upon His works in order to love, fear, honour and glorify Him.
Now no one can sing things worthy of God save what he has
received from Him, wherefore, although we look far and wide and
search on every hand, we shall not find better songs nor songs
better suited to that end than the Psalms of David which the Holy
Spirit made and uttered through him. Then we must remember
what Saint Paul says – that spiritual songs cannot be well sung
save with the heart. Now the heart requires the intelligence, and
therein, says Saint Augustine, lies the difference between the
singing of men and the singing of birds. For a linnet, a nightingale, a parrot will sing well, but it will be without understanding.
Now the peculiar gift of man is to sing knowing what he is saying.
After the intelligence must follow the heart and the affection,
which cannot be unless we have the hymn imprinted on our
memory in order never to cease singing.

May the world be so well advised that instead of the songs that
it has previously used, in part vain and frivolous, in part stupid

and dull, in part foul and vile and consequently evil and harmful,
it may accustom itself hereafter to sing these divine and celestial
hymns with the good King David.

from THE GENEVA PSALTER *1543*

An Innovation

CLAUDIO MONTEVERDI

I have reflected that the principal passions or affections of our
mind are three: namely, anger, moderation, and humility combined with tenderness. So the best philosophers declare, and the
very nature of our voice indicates this in having high, middle and
low registers. In all the works of former composers I have indeed
found examples of the 'tender' and 'moderate', but never of the
'angry', a genus nevertheless described by Plato as "harmony that
would fittingly imitate the utterances and the accents of a brave
man engaged in warfare". And since I was aware that it is contraries
which greatly move our mind and that this is the purpose which
all good music should have, I have applied myself with no small
diligence and toil to rediscover this genus. I took the divine Tasso,
as a poet who expresses with the greatest propriety and naturalness the qualities which he wishes to describe, and selected his
description of the combat of Tancred and Clorinda as an opportunity of describing in music contrary passions, namely, warfare
and entreaty and death. This composition was received by the best
citizens of the noble city of Venice with much applause and praise.

After the apparent success of my first attempt to depict anger,
I proceeded with greater zeal to make a fuller investigation, and
composed other works in that kind, both ecclesiastical and for
chamber performance. Further, this genus found such favour with
the composers of music that they not only praised it by word of
mouth, but, to my great pleasure and honour, they showed this
by written work in imitation of mine. For this reason I have
thought it best to make known that the investigation and the first
essay of this genus, so necessary to the art of music, came from

me. It may be said with reason that until the present, music has been imperfect, having been only 'tender' or 'moderate'. My rediscovery of the warlike genus has given me occasion to write certain 'angry' madrigals which I have called *guerrieri*. Although I know that this work will be imperfect, for I have but little skill (particularly in that warlike genus which is something quite new in our music). I pray the benevolent reader to accept my good will, which will await from his learned pen a greater perfection in the same style.

from MADRIGALI GUERRIERI ED AMOROSI *1638*

Harmonies, Melodies and so forth

JEAN PHILIPPE RAMEAU

It is certain that harmony can arouse in us different passions. There are harmonies that are sad, despairing, tender, gay and striking; and there are certain successions of harmonies for the expression of these passions. Consonant harmonies should be employed most frequently in music expressing gaiety and magnificence; and, since we cannot avoid intermingling some dissonant harmonies, we must contrive that these arise naturally. On the other hand despair and all passions having to do with anger or which have anything striking about them require dissonances of every kind; yet the ear must not be offended by too great a disproportion, for if we do nothing but pile dissonance on dissonance wherever there is a place for it, it will be a much greater fault than allowing only consonance to be heard. Dissonance, then, is to be employed with considerable discretion and, when we feel that its harshness is not in agreement with the expression, we ought to suppress it adroitly; for one ought always to bear in mind that a dissonant sound does not at all destroy the basis of the harmony and may always be suppressed when we think it appropriate.

Melody has not less force than harmony in expression, but it is almost impossible to give rules for it, since good taste is here more influential than any other considerations. Hence we leave to happy geniuses the pleasure of distinguishing themselves in this particular, for our limited intelligence does not permit us to rival them in this last degree of perfection, without which the most beautiful harmony becomes insipid and through which they are always in a position to excel. We would remind them, however, that it is only when one knows how to arrange a series of harmonies appropriately that one can derive a melody suited to the subject.

For the rest, a good musician ought to surrender himself to all the characters he wishes to depict and, like a skilful actor, put himself in the place of the speaker, imagine himself in the localities where the different events he wishes to represent occur, and take in these the same interest as those most concerned. He will then be able to adapt to circumstances his melody, his harmony, his modulation, and his movement.

from TRAITÉ DE L'HARMONIE *1722*

Sound

JOHN TYNDALE

Were our organs sharp enough to see the motions of the air through which an agreeable voice is passing we might see stamped upon that air the conditions of motion on which the sweetness of the voice depends. In ordinary conversation, also, the physical precedes and arouses the psychical; the spoken language, which is to give us pleasure or pain, which is to rouse us to anger or soothe us to peace, existing for a time, between us and the speaker, as a purely mechanical condition of the intervening air.

Noise affects us as an irregular succession of shocks. We are conscious while listening to it of a jolting and jarring of the auditory nerve, while a musical sound flows smoothly and without asperity or irregularity. How is this smoothness secured? *By rendering the impulses received by the tympanic membrane perfectly periodic.* A periodic motion is one that repeats itself. The motion of a common pendulum, for example, is periodic, but its vibrations

are far too sluggish to excite sonorous waves. To produce a musical
tone one must have a body which vibrates with the unerring
regularity of the pendulum, but which can impart much sharper
and quicker shocks to the air.

Imagine the first of a series of pulses following each other at
regular intervals, impinging upon the tympanic membrane. It is
shaken by the shock; and a body once shaken cannot come instan-
taneously to rest. The human ear, indeed, is so constructed that
the sonorous motion vanishes with extreme rapidity, but its
disappearance is not instantaneous: and if the motion imparted
to the auditory nerve by each individual pulse of our series continue until the arrival of its successor, the sound will not cease at
all. The effect of every shock will be renewed before it vanishes,
and the recurrent impulses will link themselves together to a
continuous musical sound. The pulses, on the contrary, which
produce noise are of irregular strength and recurrence. The action
of noise upon the ear has been well compared to that of a flickering
light upon the eye, both being painful through the sudden and
abrupt changes which they impose upon their respective nerves.

The only condition necessary to the production of a musical
sound is that the pulses should succeed each other in the same
interval of time. No matter what its origin may be, if this condition
be fulfilled the sound becomes musical. If a watch, for example,
could be caused to tick with sufficient rapidity – say one hundred
times a second – the ticks would lose their individuality and blend
to a musical tone. And if the strokes of a pigeon's wings could be
accomplished at the same rate, the progress of the bird through the
air would be accompanied by music. In the humming-bird the
necessity of rapidity is attained; and when we pass on from birds
to insects, where the vibrations are more rapid, we have a musical
note as the ordinary accompaniment of the insects' flight. The
puffs of a locomotive at starting follow each other slowly at first,
but they soon increase so rapidly as to be almost incapable of
being counted. If this increase could continue up to fifty or sixty
puffs a second, the approach of the engine would be heralded by an
organ peal of tremendous power.

from SOUND *1875*

Characterization in Music

CHARLES VILLIERS STANFORD

It is not necessary, in order to depict an ugly character or a horrible situation, to illustrate it with ugly music. To do so is the worst side of bad art. Ugly music is bad music. No great painter would paint even a Caliban badly. He draws the line at characterization. When Beethoven wrote music for one of the greatest villains in opera, Pizarro, he did not pen an ugly or even a crude bar, and yet it is a masterpiece of delineation. Nor did Weber for the characters of Lysiart and Eglantine in *Euryanthe*. No composer of inherent nobility will so sacrifice that most noble of the arts. For music stands alone among the arts in one respect: it is incapable without association with words or action of being in itself indecent or obscene. The faults of which it can be guilty, as absolute music, are only faults of taste, not of morals. It can be vulgar and trivial, priggish and flippant, but not offensive or grossly suggestive. On the other hand, the moment action or words come into play in combination with it, it can put a magnifying glass over every detail, and can accentuate to the most appalling extent the suggestions which they give. The torture scene in Sardou's *Tosca*, which in itself is horrible enough, becomes ten times more so when Puccini dots the i's and crosses the t's with his vivid score. So great can be its power for good or ill that it can make a revolutionary poem egg on a mob to the wildest excesses, or a patriotic one stir a whole nation, even when the literary value of the words is of the poorest. Great and far-reaching, therefore, is the responsibility of the man who holds the musician's pen. . . . It is the old fight between idealism and materialism; and when music ceases to be ideal, it will abrogate its chief duty, the refinement and elevation of public taste.

from MUSICAL COMPOSITION *1911*

Music as a Language

EDWARD J. DENT

We find ourselves confronted with the fundamental question, what is music? The best answer that has yet been given is M. Jules Combarieu's definition: *'La musique est l'art de penser avec les sons.'* The usual attempts to explain the meaning of music on the analogy of painting or other arts are merely confusing and misleading. The art which comes nearest to music is naturally that of poetry, but it must be clearly understood that poetry and music are now entirely separate things, although in the remote past they may have been undifferentiated. Primitive man experienced certain feelings, and desired to express them by means of his voice; as his feelings became more complex and he himself more skilful in conveying them to others, he distinguished speech from song, and employed each for its special purpose. That music has developed continuously into what we now possess is surely proof that it has fulfilled an important human need, and that men have always experienced in a greater or less degree certain feelings for which music, and music alone, can provide expression. Music has in fact become a separate language subject only to its own laws of construction, and available only for the expression of its own ideas.

When we first begin to learn a foreign language, French for example, we are taught to regard certain French words as being exact equivalents of certain English words. For a long time too, we habitually think in English, and laboriously translate that English – which is not our thought, but only the arbitrary symbol of it – into French. A moment arrives eventually at which we are actually able to think in French, and as we make further progress with the language, we find that there are many French words and expressions which we cannot translate into English, because they represent ideas so essentially French that a normal Englishman does not understand them, and consequently has no words to express them. The better we know French, the more we shall be conscious of the difference between the French and English mentalities; and supposing that we study other languages as well, the further we go geographically from our own country, the more impossible will it become to translate any ideas except those which are common to all human beings, civilized or uncivilized. Yet we have no doubt that Chinese, for instance, is a perfectly reasonable language, adapted to the needs of those who live in China. It is then only a short step further to conceive of a language of music, logical and adapted to quite complex needs for those who understand it, yet absolutely untranslatable into English, because the language of music and the language of daily life deal with two different worlds which have practically nothing in common.

Most people have without study picked up a rough smattering of the language of music, as one picks up a rough smattering of French by living in France. But the language of music is less consciously acquired than French, because no one ever finds himself in a position where an understanding of music is an absolute necessity for social intercourse. Similarly a man might go through life happily enough without ever discovering what swimming means. He knows that walking is the usual mode of progression on dry land, and up to a certain depth walking is practicable in water, though not always very convenient. But if he is to progress in deeper water, he must learn a totally different method of locomotion, a method too which it is impossible for him to learn completely on dry land, and which is absolutely useless except in water.

There is no short cut to the real understanding of music, any more than there is to a knowledge of a foreign language, or to the mastery of the art of swimming. The process involves the acceptance of a definite attitude of mind to begin with, and constant, and indeed lifelong, practice in the element itself. Nor have I any argument with which to demonstrate that this knowledge is worth acquiring, any more than I could find arguments to demonstrate to a casual Frenchman that English was worth studying for the sake of understanding what our poets have written. If he viewed English as many people seem to view music, he might say that he knew how to pronounce the words and liked the sound, but that he was convinced that, being totally ignorant of English grammar or syntax, he understood the essential poetry of Shakespeare a great deal better than any Englishman.

The first effect of music (I mean the first in time) upon us is a purely physiological stimulus, which affects us merely in the same way as a pleasant (or unpleasant) taste in the mouth, a pleasant (or unpleasant) touch to the skin. There are possibly some people whose appreciation of music never gets beyond this, and although the amount and character of the physiological stimulus varies in different cases, the most cultivated musician is always susceptible to it, and if he be honest he will admit that it forms an essential part, though by no means the whole part, of his pleasure in music. Between this appreciation and full intellectual appreciation there is a borderland, which for many people is their principal musical territory. They feel subconsciously that there is something in music beyond the physiological stimulus of mere loudness or softness and of pleasant or unpleasant quality of tone, but they are unable to analyse it logically, and therefore fall back upon the nonsensical vapourings which are sold for countless shillings and sixpences in our principal concert halls. They like to encourage themselves in the belief that this borderland is the domain of all noble emotions, and that beyond it there is only the arid desert of 'mathematics'. There are even composers who seem to hold the same belief, and to encourage it in their listeners. To them music is not a subject on which to use one's brains, but a sort of drug. What would our opinion be of a foreigner who, understanding no English, had Shakespeare read aloud to him to send him to sleep, or George Meredith's poems to stimulate his passions? If these victims of the musical drug-habit would make up their minds to listen to music with the same amount of intellectual energy that they are willing to expend on such 'relaxations' as chess or bridge, they would discover fairly soon that their appreciation of the essential poetry of great music, so far from being ruined, would on the contrary be deepened to an ever-increasing extent.

from MOZART'S OPERAS *1913*

The Plain Man and his Music

FRANCIS TOYE

A decade ago, according to our modern Lacaedemonians, the next war, like all wars, was to bring countless benefits – mental, moral and physical – to a decadent and peace-sodden community. Strange to tell, however, this gospel does not appear so popular now that we have experienced these benefits in practice. In fact, there is, perhaps, only one benefit that might still command universal assent: the 1914–18 war did effect an unprecedented mixing up of classes and cliques.

Owing to this salutary and not too unpleasant operation the writer himself was thrown into many and various societies which, speaking generally, had in common only one characteristic: a complete ignorance of and indifference to the musical values that he and, in all probability, his present readers are accustomed to take for granted. Isolated individuals, perhaps, could be found who liked the classics and Wagner – especially Wagner; one or two eccentrics had patronized recitals by Kreisler or Plunket Greene. But these were, most emphatically, the exceptions. And no one at all was interested in modern composers or composition. Names of men like Vaughan Williams, Ravel, Skriabin, so familiar to all of us, meant nothing at all to any of them. As an illustration, the following dialogue is perhaps worth recording. It took place between the writer, when he joined up with a certain unit in 1916, and his major – not an ordinary major, either, but a major who, in private life, was responsible for the entertainments at a popular seaside resort.

MAJOR: I hear you are a musical nut.

WRITER: ? ?

MAJOR: Well, anyhow, you know all about music. I like classical music, too; I like Mendelssohn's *Spring Song* and *The Bee's Wedding* awfully.

WRITER: ! !

MAJOR: Yes, I do. And one of the most famous composers in England lives at my place.

WRITER: Really, and who may that be?

MAJOR (naming a very well-known composer of ballads): "Mr Smith Robinson".

WRITER (momentarily reverting to type): But he's not a composer at all.

MAJOR: Oh come, my dear chap. *He makes four thousand a year.*

Now, it is obviously ridiculous to classify musical worth in terms of income, but much reflection, induced by the still felt shock of this announcement, has led me to believe the major was not altogether wrong . . . in theory. After all, by what standard other than success can the plain man judge a composer's worth? Is he to be involved in musicians' quarrels over the respective merits of Elgar and Stanford, Bax and Ireland, Vaughan Williams and Goossens? How shall he believe aright when one party is continually preaching that the god of the other party is a fraudulent idol? Who shall guide him when one pundit relegates the classics to the rubbish heap and another consigns all music written since the nineteenth century to the waste-paper basket? 'A plague on both' – and all – 'your houses' is his natural retort, and he turns to golf and the cinema, whereat merit and success are practically synonymous. He suffers; music suffers; it is all most unsatisfactory and unhealthy. Let us diagnose the disease a little more precisely.

Writing with considerable experience of continental Europe I should judge that in no other country did there exist a gap between music and 'popular' music so wide as in England. True, there seems to be in France between the adherents of the modern school and the conventional *bourgeois* a gap even wider – a world-famous violinist recently on a visit to London put the total number of 'modernists' in France as not more than 10,000 all told – but this phenomenon is very special and not altogether relevant to the point. In no other country, so far as I can judge, would it have been possible for our major to have made the remark he did, or for me to have received it with such disgust and incredulity. Ask the average middle-class Frenchman not only who is the most famous but the most popular French composer; he will answer, according to his temperament, Gounod or Massenet. Ask an Italian; he will certainly reply, Puccini. Ask a German; he will in all probability vote for Beethoven or Wagner. Now the reader may not approve of some of these composers, but they are, at any rate, respectable musicians. They are not 'possibles'. They are none of them like 'Mr Smith Robinson', who is, musically, neither respectable nor possible.

The reasons for this phenomenon are, I think, three. Firstly, the especial power in England of the interests that control the 'shop-ballad'. How great this is will only be apparent to one who has talked to foreign amateurs – not specialists – about English music. They are still inclined to believe that our music begins and ends with the ballad concert. Admittedly music of this class is, alas!, a *specialité de la maison*. Moreover, I am inclined to think that its characteristics do, in fact, reflect the emotions and sentiments of the majority of that middle-class which lives in and around our great cities. Aesthetically, these people have no emotion that is anything but superficial; their sentiment is sentimentality. To them beauty is synonymous with prettiness, and as for passion, the mother of all art, it is just bad form. Nevertheless, granted that the ballad represents truthfully a certain phase of our civilization, there can, I think, be no doubt but that its appeal has been artificially emphasized. Alone, among the chaos of English music, the ballad-monger is efficiently, even aggressively, organized. His wares are skilfully pushed and attractively handled. No excuse need be made for these commercial metaphors; the whole matter is one of business pure and simple. From the publisher who commissions the ballad, through the composer who writes it, down to the singer who sings it, everybody is concerned for one purpose; to make as much money as possible. Now money-making needs discipline and organization; art, though the better for these qualities, can, and usually does, dispense with them. What chance, when it comes to a battle for popular favour, have the ragged levies of English composers against the trained army of Chappell and Boosey?

Secondly, the lack of English opera deprives English musicians of the best means of attracting public attention to themselves. Opera, far from being the ideal of musical accomplishment, as our Victorian forebears used to think, is probably the least elevated of all forms of musical expression. Neither aesthetically nor intellectually can it compare with the symphony or the quartet. But it does serve one great purpose in that its very blatancy attracts the attention of that portion of the public whom the more modest claims of other music might otherwise have left unmoved. And, the introduction of music once effected, friendship, even love, sometimes ensues. How many have learned devotion to music through the mediation of Wagner and Verdi, even of Gounod and Puccini?

Lastly, English composers have to some extent themselves to thank for the public indifference to them and their works. Till quite recently, at any rate, they adopted a priggish, superior attitude that effectually cut them off from any fellowship with the normal community. The academics sinned especially in this respect. Their Beckmesserian pretensions sent a chill down the public spine, and Elgar, who first dared to break the tradition, incurred the displeasure of the orthodox *because* some of his music was at one time popular. Yet the younger men, the revolutionaries, were scarcely better. Writing dreary and lengthy works for enormous orchestras, they seemed to aim only at making performance of their compositions as difficult and expensive as possible. Any attempt to meet current musical requirements appeared to be beneath their dignity. Small wonder, then, that the public knew nothing of the more serious composers, contenting itself with a rigid boycott of the few concerts where their works were produced. In fairness, however, it must be said that there has been a change for the better during the last few years. English compositions though they may not fill, no longer empty the Queen's Hall; and it is most significant and hopeful that at the time of writing one of the best songs of one of our best composers is sung every night in a popular entertainment with very great success.

Such then, are, in my opinion, the reasons for the exceptional cleavage that exists in England between music and 'popular' music. But there are general causes, operating here as elsewhere, that must also be considered.

Foremost of these is the very rapid development of the art of music. We are too apt to forget the extreme youth of music as we know it. The father of modern composition, Johann Sebastian Bach, died not two hundred years ago; Beethoven scarcely one hundred; Mozart was born in 1756; Haydn in 1732. Now compare with these dates the dates of a few of the great masters of painting.

Raphael has been dead more than three hundred years; Titian nearly two hundred and fifty. Velazquez was born in 1599; Rembrandt in 1606. Yet it is, I think, true to say that even to modern eyes – the professional revolutionaries, of course, excepted – the Old Masters of Painting do not appear particularly old-fashioned. It is at any rate indubitable that they seem less old-fashioned than their musical compeers who flourished a century or more later. Even the studiously perverse who hail Bach as a modernist will do well to remember that Greco, who has also been hailed as 'typically modern', was dead seventy years before Johann Sebastian was born.

There is surely nothing in painting to compare with the rapid evolution of the means of expression that has taken place in music. Mozart and Ravel may be endeavouring to express approximately similar thoughts, but their vocabulary is quite different; whereas, speaking generally, Sargent and Franz Hals use the same language. Indeed the art of music has shot up like a beautiful hot-house flower; its growth and variety have been amazing. But hot-house flowers are not renowned for their hardiness, nor does remarkable growth tend to stability. Music is always outstripping her contemporaries, and there is some danger that, sooner or later, her contemporaries may decide to give up the race in disgust. All art, ultimately considered, must be judged as a relaxation for mankind. And how can there be relaxation when there is no breathing space? Man, by nature excessively rather than insufficiently conservative, will not endure for ever the chase after a will-o'-the-wisp who becomes more elusive every year, an Egeria whose radicalism appears more pronounced every decade.

Especially, I think, are the relations of the plain man to Music becoming strained at the present time. We live in an age of supreme restlessness, often dignified by the name of revolution, which is particularly noticeable in all intellectual and artistic movements. Any sense of the importance of tradition is scoffed at; any doubt of the value of the new for its own sake is regarded as akin to blasphemy. Indeed it is the modern blasphemy.

Now the plain man, who has many other interests in life, usually regards the function of music as one of solace, of inducing dreams and of banishing the sordid facts of drab everydayness. What, in fact, does he now find? An aggressive, rather minx-like

Muse, inclined to practical joking, decked out with tinsel and most insistent and loud in manner. Instead of ministering to his soulful if slightly absurd yearnings, she chucks him under the chin, digs him in the ribs, and generally belabours him for a sentimental idiot. Moreover, having (exceptionally) just acquired an admiration and even a love for the classic form he is now told that everything classical is as dead as mutton – and duller; that modern Russian or French aesthetic should be his only joy. Beethoven and Brahms sleep with their fathers. Stravinsky and Schmitt reign in their stead. Schumann . . . pooh! ("So badly shown up by the *Sacre du Printemps*", as one authority confided to me at the Prince's Theatre the other evening.) Verdi . . . ha! ha! Three cheers for Poulenc, Berners and Schoenberg! Whereupon the plain man, who has, perhaps, just succeeded in raising his musical culture to the level of Beethoven, Brahms and Schumann and is rather pleased with himself for the accomplishment, finds himself quite at sea again, his sense of values jettisoned, his scale of judgement once more thrown overboard.

Needless to say it is the fashion among musicians to pour scorn upon the plain man and his limitations. Nor has anybody suffered more from them than the writer, who is himself addicted to pedantry, even to modernist pedantry. But, in common fairness, it should be pointed out that the plain man has a legitimate defence. Why should we always expect him to admire everything that is new? Why should he, having once settled down to enjoy one particular musical convention, be scoffed at because he will not join in our last-born admiration for another? Half-unconsciously we have got into the habit of thinking that whatever comes latest in point of time is highest in point of merit – like women's fashions. Yet there are sufficient historical instances to give us pause. There was, let us remember, a time when Mendelssohn was rated as a composer far more profound and worthy than Mozart. The chromatic banalities of Spohr were hailed as 'the last word' in musical boldness. Meyerbeer, in France, was acclaimed as a fulfilment of, if not an improvement upon, Beethoven. Even a sage of the calibre of Samuel Butler could prefer Handel to Bach. And, outside music, the instances are even more glaring. For how many years was not Raphael acclaimed as the ideal painter? Did not Europe once unite in ranking Victor Hugo before Voltaire? In our own time is not an Edwardian Piccadilly Hotel voted an improvement on a Georgian Piccadilly?

The truth is that all aesthetic values, especially contemporary aesthetic values, fluctuate almost as violently and far more unreasonably than securities on the Stock Exchange. So that the plain man has some excuse for not taking the latest fashion in composers at the composer's, still less at the partisan's, valuation of his own merit. Especially, if so be the plain man have a trifle of philosophy, must he feel deliciously sceptical as to the quality of contemporary enthusiasms. Let him observe a fashionable Queen's Hall audience agape before Stravinsky. Not one in ten can play a five-finger exercise; not one in fifty can read, not one in a hundred can write a note of music. Yet how they shout, how they applaud! All they ask is to be allowed to worship 'the latest thing', for the less they understand the more they admire it. And the audience of the Russian Ballet, completely bamboozled by the strange cacophonies of M. Ansermet's newest importations from Paris, is like unto them. Terrible, insincere, pretentious, ignorant people, whose praise and blame is equally insulting, how much to be preferred to you is the rankest Philistine who really enjoys the refrain of a ballad or the lilt of a fox-trot!

But, someone may say, if the plain man is not to be expected to appreciate contemporary music, how are contemporary musicians to survive? Any art that does not create is a dead art, and our music must reflect our civilization. Which is all perfectly true, but what is not true is that this or any other doctrine is the better for being pushed to its logical conclusion. μηδὲν ἄγαν, the epitome not only of the philosopher's, but of all Greek wisdom, is a motto that should adorn every concert-room in Europe. It is a mistake to play too much old music; it is a mistake to play too much new music; everything 'too much' is a vice. Now, we moderns, restless and rather unbalanced, suffer particularly in this respect. We seem to love extremes for their own sake, almost hating moderation. It is just this characteristic – the good side of it, for every evil has a corresponding and inherent good – that leads us to lay so much stress on the value of originality. Yet we should reflect that the most artistic nations in the world's history, the Chinese, the Greeks, even the French, have been precisely those which emphasized firstly the importance of tradition, and only secondly the

importance of originality. In my view it is especially this failure
to appreciate the importance of tradition which has led to the
divorce that undoubtedly exists in England between contemporary
music and contemporary life. We have not woven our modern
experiments into the general and accepted fabric of our music.
Or, rather, when we have attempted so to do, the result has been
a failure owing to defective musical education and other causes.
Wherefore, to short circuit the difficulty, we have recourse to
'stunts'. We do not like programmes with one modern piece of
music. We like programmes that are all modern – if possible more
than modern – music, so that we can rave about them and treat
them as a nine-days' wonder. Which is surely the quintessence
of the 'stunt' philosophy. By this we accelerate artificially the
already too rapid evolution of music and increasingly widen the
gap between the music of the many and the music of the few. Or,
in other words, to revert to our original nomenclature, we
differentiate even more sharply the plain man from the specialist.

Now, this is a serious matter. In an age of increasing democracy
an art that tends to appeal more and more to the few is in danger of
sudden collapse. Yet this is precisely what our 'stunt' policy is
doing. The supporters of 'stunts' are fashionable ladies, would-be
patrons of the arts, parasites, conscious or unconscious, and
persons whose jaded senses need continual titillations. Emphatically they are not the class of people who view, or who would
even wish to view, music as a normal ingredient of everyday life.
They are primarily excitement-hungry. Yet it seems clear that this
class must, if only from economic pressure, gradually grow less.
At present Lady X, with an income of ten thousand a year, is a
very valuable friend of music, worth a hundred clerks and small-
shopkeepers. But when rising prices, income tax, and a possible
capital levy have reduced Lady X's income to five or even three
thousand, her musical value begins to appear less striking. Yet
Lady X and others like her are the very backbone – if the metaphor
be not too complimentary – of the 'stunt'-loving class. What will
happen to music if Lady X disappears and music has not made
friends with the clerk and the small-shopkeeper?

Especially in England is the question urgent, for in England
the upper and upper-middle classes are noticeably the least
musical of the community. And, unlike many of their brethren in

America and continental Europe, the English plutocrats, perhaps from a snobbish desire to emulate the class they have so successfully dispossessed, seem disposed to patronize the racing-stable rather than the concert-hall. A few of their women condescend to music, it is true. But they are fickle folk, only fortuitously interested. One day their passion is opera, the next a hat shop or aviation. The house built on sand would be stability itself compared with music founded on their support.

St Cecilia herself, as a writer recently urged in a weekly review, may not be democratic. But her supporters in England most emphatically are not aristocrats either of birth, position or money. The only constant music-loving public here comes from the middle-class. It is full of glaring and unpleasant vices; its musical education is bad; its worship of soloists of all descriptions is ludicrous; its very tolerance makes the enthusiast and the fanatic burn with rage. But it has two great virtues: it loves music and it has an infinite capacity for loyalty. When, as in the case of the Sullivan operettas, it discovers something it really likes, its support is so constant, so enthusiastic, as to be positively phenomenal. Yet I am convinced that this support can be had for other music also. Persons responsible for musical entertainments to the armies during the war are agreed that music of the most serious and exacting character was immensely popular – provided the interpretation of it were really of the highest order. But the proviso is essentially important, as musicians whose good intentions are more remarkable than their talents have often discovered to their cost.

Nevertheless, the public is there, and I submit that the capture of it is worth more to music and musicians than all the 'stunt' successes of a London season. Moreover, the probability is that these successes do actually alienate it from music as a whole. For the public feels, not unreasonably, that the 'stunt' is an exploitation of itself by the musicians, whereas its object is to make use of the musicians to satisfy a need of its daily life. At any rate I am sure that music in England, if it fails to satisfy a need and only attempts to turn itself into a luxury, is economically doomed; for, as a luxury trade, it cannot compete. The choice, speaking broadly, lies between Sir Henry Wood and his promenade concerts on the one hand, and M. Diaghilieff and his musical interludes on the other. The ideal solution, of course, is to keep both. But, if the success of one means the extinction of the other – and I am inclined to fear that it does – can any sane man hesitate which of the two to choose?

from Music and Letters *1921*

The Lesson of History

ARTHUR W. POLLITT

Many people maintain that art in general has seen its best days; that we live in a degenerate age; that the wealth of colouring of a Titian, the singleness of eye of an Apelles, the mighty intellect of a Da Vinci, the keen insight and power of a Shakespeare are manifestations which the world cannot hope to see repeated. This may or may not be true, but if we grant that drawing, painting, carving, designing, sculpture, and all their offshoots have seen their best days, it is no logical reason why the same can be said of music. It may be urged that intellectual activity runs in cycles, and affects all the crafts and arts in turn. How then can an exception be made in the case of music which has existed for thousands of years, and cannot have been ignored in the many upheavals and continued efforts towards a higher and purer medium of expression? We know, for instance, that good Bishop Ambrose, of Milan, concerned himself with the development of Church music in the fourth century A.D., and that Pope Gregory followed his example 200 years later. We know further, our critic will say, that such men as Andrea Gabrieli and his nephew Giovanni, Di Lasso, Willaert, Palestrina, Monteverdi, Scarlatti, Lully, Gluck, Bach, Haydn, Mozart and Beethoven, all concerned themselves in the advancement of musical art; that its advancement did not by any means end with Beethoven; that the work of Chopin, Berlioz, Wagner, Brahms and others, has carried music yet another step towards its goal, if not indeed to its ultimate.

All these objections may be freely granted. But what are the efforts of these men and a hundred others, in the thousands of years which have elapsed since music had its origin in the utterance of joy or sorrow on the part of primeval man? Truly it is a far cry to the beginnings of music; nay, it is even a far cry to the time when sounds were first systematized; but it is not yet 500 years since music as we know it began to develop: and it is certain that more progress has been made in the last 150 years [1770–1920] than in all the centuries since its inception.

It is interesting, and instructive, to compare the growth of architecture, painting and music. In the first case we find that the imperishable pyramids date from at least 3000 B.C.; and in recent years palaces have been excavated in Assyria and Persia dating from 884 B.C., and Greek temples erected in the period 650–324 B.C. Its development through Byzantine, Romanesque, Saxon, Norman, Early English, Decorated, Perpendicular and Flamboyant, culminated in the sixteenth century, and represents a magnificent record of imagination and skill. The pinnacle of beauty was reached hundreds of years ago; the science and craft of 5,000 years ago is a closed book to us, and the best modern work is merely adapted from one or other of the aforementioned styles, and, more often than not, is of a decadent character.

As regards painting – there are extant today examples of Egyptian and Assyrian mural art, though of a primitive and formal kind, dating as far back as the palmy days of Babylon's prosperity. In Egypt, painting and sculpture were intimately combined: we may say that the Egyptians enlivened every work of art with colour. Colour was everywhere! The Greeks advanced the art by the introduction of chiaroscuro; and Polygnotus, who lived during the fifth century B.C., established painting as an independent art, on an equal footing with architecture. Pamphilus – fourth century B.C. – insisted that every kind of knowledge was necessary to form a perfect artist. The revival of painting, in the thirteenth century, marked a great step forward; and the next two centuries saw the introduction of oil painting, and a tremendous advance in knowledge of perspective and chiaroscuro, as well as in earnestness, devotion, and general development. The works of Bellini, Giorgioni, Carpaccio, Perugino, Da Vinci, Michaelangelo, Raphael, and, greatest of all, Titian, represent a standard of achievement which no man has been able to surpass. It is generally agreed, therefore, that Italian painting of the fifteenth and sixteenth centuries is the supreme effort of the human mind in that direction.

How does music compare with these records? It would be useless to assert that it had not its origin as far back as human knowledge has penetrated: but how slow has been its growth; how tardy have been its votaries to make any improvements upon the conditions as they found them. Unlike the sister arts of architecture and painting, we do not find evidence of a steady growth which reached full flower centuries ago; but we do find evidence of a torpidity – a blight – which made men and women satisfied with bald successions of notes as the highest expression in music.

The sixteenth century saw the climax of painting, but only the beginning of music as we know it. One can only conclude that the portion of the human brain which responds to music had lain dormant for centuries. It is an arresting thought, because, logically pursued, it suggests that a future generation may regard our generation as being in quite a rudimentary stage of development. It is within the bounds of possibility that new faculties, of which we now know nothing, may spring into being. Applied to music, it suggests that a fuller and deeper significance for the whole human race may be found in its practice; a comprehension deeper than appreciation; in fact a spiritual force, which, because of its universal appeal, may easily succeed where religions have so lamentably failed.

To return to our comparisons of the three forms of art: we know that the ancient Egyptians found in music food for speculation and thought; it offered a ready medium in all their emotional expressions; and it is true that some attempt was made to systematize musical sounds, and to explain the relationship of one note to another; but we look in vain for any indications of progress in other directions. In spite of all their marvellous accumulated knowledge and scientific skill, the ancient Egyptians left music in much the same condition as they found it. The brains which conceived and carried out the erection of the Pyramids, the Sphinx, and other colossal works which still continue to perplex the specialist of our day, had no conception of music beyond a bare succession of notes, and those of restricted range.

The Israelites used music to a great extent at religious as well as at social functions. They were fond of effects conceived on a grand scale; indeed, they frequently employed choirs numbering four or five thousand voices; but there is no evidence that they ever attempted to sing in parts. Probably all the voices sang the same succession of notes, and the instruments merely doubled the voices, and supplied interludes.

The Greek era was responsible for the union of poetry and music, upon a system which aimed at the development of the principles underlying the natural inflections of the human voice in speech. Gregorian plainsong is a descendant of the Greek system, and shares with it the honour of occupying the serious attention of musicians and scholars, to the exclusion of any other form of development, for a period of 1,600 years!

The art of setting down music upon paper was not mastered until the tenth century, and it was not until the thirteenth century that musicians began to realize that more than one tune could be sung at the same time.

Then began the development of that Counterpoint (the art of combining melodies, or of writing melodious parts), which reached its culmination in the works of the Elizabethan madrigal school in this country, and of Palestrina and his school in Italy. Thus the coping-stone was added to the great polyphonic choral school of the sixteenth and seventeenth centuries. Bach added that to the polyphonic instrumental school, Beethoven and Brahms to the symphonic school, and Wagner to the dramatic school.

What is there left?

The year 1830 roughly marks the starting point of a new path in musical composition, the practical outcome of which, at the present time, is the music we denominate: (*a*) atmospheric, (*b*) realistic. They are both branches of the same tree, and indicate in no uncertain manner the general trend of modern music, which is the result of a striving against convention, and the often painful obviousness which permeated so much of the work of the old schools.

Whatever the final verdict may be with regard to the artistic permanence of the work of such men as Stravinsky, Debussy, Delius, and others, they deserve, at least, consideration, as well as for the special gifts which raise them above their contemporaries. We are at the present time experiencing the difficulties – which others have experienced in the past – of trying to gauge the ten-

dency of the newest phases of musical thought. For the seekers after
new light have had in the past, and as far as we can foresee will
always have, to give rise to much in the way of heart-burnings and
solemn finger shakings, and waggings of heads; but if the past is
to be allowed to teach us anything, it should teach us the folly of
hasty conclusions.

Unlike the other forms of art, music is always changing; it is
in a perpetual state of transition; and it is as impossible to control
the minds of music-makers as it is to foretell where their efforts
will eventually take us. Painters – and sculptors and architects –
turn to the great masterpieces of the past for guidance and inspiration; and they consider themselves fortunate indeed if they can
catch some echoes of their past glories, or, by much labour and
experiment, light upon a medium that will be the means of
preserving their work for posterity.

But for the modern composer there is no such Mecca; there are
no achievements in the past that can make him wring his hands in
despair that such a secret, or such a medium, has passed beyond the
ken of man. We are still in the laboratory of music; fresh colours
are constantly being invented; new schemes for music's advancement are still being put to the test. After mastering his mode of
expression, the modern writer has unlimited scope for the play
of his imagination. The shackles of conventionality and pedantism
have been broken down; the domain of the art has expanded to
an unconscionable degree; what it will eventually reach is more
than any man can say.

At any rate let us see that we all realize the true condition of
things, and let us resolve to keep open minds. No real progress is
unaccompanied by failure; there have been, and there will be,
mistakes – errors of judgement – that is inevitable. But that which
was incomprehensible to a past generation is now an open book:
in fact, it has already begun to sound a little old-fashioned; so,
in spite of stupid censures, and with the incontrovertible lesson of
history before us, we may hesitate before we presume to dog-
matize as to what is right, or wrong, with music.

I would plead very earnestly for the cultivation of a catholic
taste in art, because I find that the people who dislike new music
also dislike old music; in fact their sympathies are generally confined to the small groups of composers that flourished during the

early part of the nineteenth century. A spirit of tolerance, and the desire to see beauty in all phases of music, would open the door to unknown joys. There is a profound significance in the old promise, 'Seek, and ye shall find', for the real beauties of music must be sought; they are not revealed to the merely casual listener; indeed, they can only be found by those whose emotions and senses are alert, and yet under the control of their intelligence.

'As Wagner grew from the classic tongue of the late sonatas and ninth symphony of Beethoven to *Tristan*, *The Ring*, and *Parsifal* – as Strauss traversed the circumscribed paths of the symphonists only to quit them for a land of freedom and fecundity, so may we, if we will,' says Edmunstone Duncan, 'go forward in the sun and breeze of the passing day, leaving artificial lights and vaulty airs behind us. After all, the great things of the past are always within reach, when wanted. Music has become more conscious of her powers. And although we do not make the mistake of supposing that because the language is developing and changing, that therefore modern masters are greater men than their predecessors, let it be clearly asserted that their work is worthy of our best sympathies. The ultra-modernists are unrolling a new vision before our eyes. If all we see does not please us, that is only conformity with life and experience. Let us travel then in this new country, striving after the good, the true, and the beautiful. The good is that which uplifts and purifies. The beautiful rivets attention by its inherent compelling force. Its spell, its aroma, charms the soul through the senses. But what is *truth* in music? The answer to that question is the quest of history. And we need not attempt to anticipate it.'

from THE ENJOYMENT OF MUSIC *1921*

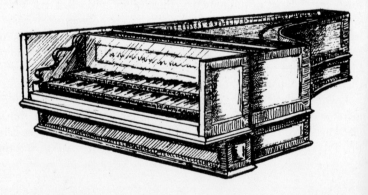

The Possibilities of Musical Criticism

ROLLO H. MYERS

It is a well-known fact that musical critics – and for that matter all critics – are generally despised by musicians and by creative artists in any sphere, and are looked upon by the public as a more or less necessary evil. In the popular eye they are gentlemen who have failed in the particular art of which they now set up to be well-qualified judges; and the public does not stop to think whether such a position is really as ridiculous as it may at first sight appear. Granted that ninety-nine per cent of art critics are either ignorant or pretentious, or probably both, and that the instinctive prejudice against them on the part of the creative artist and the public alike is in nine cases out of ten justified – there still remains the case of the one per cent, and that is important enough not to be ignored.

The notion that because a critic may have failed in the particular art of which he now claims to be a connoisseur he is, *ipso facto*, a bad critic, obviously reposes upon a confusion of ideas. A moment's thought will suffice to show that the contrary conclusion may be – and indeed quite often is – the true one. A man may fail as a creative artist owing to his critical faculty being stronger than his creative. The greatest creative artists, indeed, are generally devoid of the critical faculty in a more or less marked degree. In the nature of things creation must be egotistical, impulsive, self-centred, but not self-analytical. Criticism is cautious, seeking for 'grounds', and concerned with methods, style, and all the details of the actual execution of an idea. The creative impulse may be caught in the critical net, and before it escapes from those meshes, its original glitter and glamour may have departed for ever. But are we to conclude that one whose critical faculty has been too strong for his creative is therefore an ignoramus, and ought not to pretend to know anything about the art at which he is reputed to have failed? Is it not more probable that his own experience will have rendered him particularly well-qualified to judge, and when necessary, to sympathize with the achievements of others? The actual technical knowledge that our '*raté*' will necessarily have acquired on his road to failure will in itself prove a greater asset than all the theorizing of some armchair critic. Nevertheless it will be found that the latter gentleman's lack of practical experience will, in some quarters, actually be counted as a qualification rather than the reverse, and will be held to invest the judgements of this personage with a kind of Olympian aloofness and impartiality.

The fact is that both critics and public are generally wrong in their estimate of the proper function of criticism. The critic, or rather nine critics out of ten (the tenth, of course, is the perfect one whom we doubt has ever existed) is apt to think that when he has delivered himself of an opinion about a given work he has done his duty, and may go home and sleep the sleep of the just. He is a critic, he argues – therefore he certainly knows more about art than the man in the street who reads his criticisms, and possibly more than the artist whom he criticizes. The public, for its part, is inclined to take the same view (as far as the public ever bothers its head about such matters) and is content to take the critic at his own valuation, or else, more probably, ignore him altogether. The result in either case is hardly conducive to the raising of either the standard of criticism or the standard of appreciation.

That all art criticism fulfils some useful function is the basic assumption of this essay, the *raison d'être* of which would otherwise be non-existent. The problem, as it seems to the writer, is to discover (*a*) What this function is; and (*b*) What critical method, applied to music in particular, is likely to yield the most fruitful results?

The chief function of all art-criticism in general is no doubt to introduce clarity into a region of man's intellectual activity which at first sight seems to be the most obscure because the least subjected to any but an individual – i.e. self-inflicted – discipline, and therefore seemingly refractory to general laws. It is, nevertheless, the function of criticism to make the laws which govern this seemingly lawless activity, the exercise of the artistic faculties, apparent, by deducing from concrete results – i.e. works of art – the nature of the impulse which called them into being.

Criticism proper, I think, should confine itself to this role; it should not seek to lay down laws itself to govern art, which would then be reduced to the status of a craft. The technique of any craft (and even of any art, to a certain extent) can, of course, be taught; but no one can be taught 'art'. The reason for this is that art is a movement of the soul, and such movements have an unlimited capacity of creating new and adequate forms for themselves which can no more be taught theoretically than we can teach the clouds what forms they must assume. An observer may do useful work in classifying forms which clouds have been known to assume, but he is powerless to formulate any hard and fast rules governing cloud-formation in the future, as there will always be an infinite variety of exceptions to any rules he may have been able to deduce from his observations.

The art-critic is in much the same position in regard to the phenomena of art. While he is able to codify and note the recurrence of certain art-forms (just as the recurrence of certain cloud-formations may be noted) he is ultimately forced to approach every separate manifestation of art with a mind unbiased by preconceived conceptions, and to treat it as if it were unique.

To state in these terms the function of the ideal critic is not, of course, to deny the reality of art-forms, nor to minimize the value of a rational critical method. But it is perhaps necessary to emphasize the element of elasticity and even caprice in artistic phenomena, if only to guard against the error of thinking all such phenomena can ultimately be reduced to formulae.

This much granted with regard to the function of criticism in general, it remains to be seen how these principles can be best adhered to in the domain of musical criticism – admittedly one of the most difficult branches of the art, and generally the worst served by its practitioners. In no other department of criticism is the need for a rational method more apparent, and in none is it more difficult of application. One of the reasons for this, no doubt, is that the critic of music has, on the whole, less data of a precise nature to work on than the critic of painting or literature, while his task is as often as not complicated by the necessity of judging performers and performances in addition to music *per se*. I say as often as not, having in mind the lot of the newspaper critic and the host of chroniclers whose business it is, not only to keep the public informed about the production of new works and musical performances of all kinds, but also to relate the exploits of this or that executant, and incidentally contribute to the making or marring of the reputations of virtuosi. This is only one of the results of the ever-increasing commercialization of music – a complaint from which, by its very nature, it is condemned to suffer to a far greater extent than either literature or the plastic arts.

Musical criticism proper, however, may be considered to lie outside the sphere of the fevered and superficial reporting that fills the columns (or rather the out-of-the-way corners) of the daily press. And yet most musical criticism is actually done under these conditions, if we except the task of the musicographer, whose field of work lies rather in the library and study than in the concert-room. In any case the fact remains that if what may be called a musical literature can be said to exist at all, it is both scanty in volume and of decidedly unequal value.

And here we come to the crux of the whole problem – namely, why it should be harder to write about music satisfactorily than about any other subject. The answer, no doubt, is that owing to the very nature of music – its texture, its subject-matter – sound – and its extremely slender connection with what we call 'reality', it is almost impossible to talk about it at all – still less to do so intelligently, or even intelligibly. This aspect of music – its remoteness from reality – is well brought out in the following passage taken from Julien Benda's *Dialogue d'Eleuthère*:

> L'idée propre à la musique, celle qu'elle donne et que les autres arts ne sauraient donner, c'est l'idée d'existences irréelles. D'abord une phrase musicale semble un être irréel – je veux dire, exempt des principales conditions de l'existence réelle: elle semble n'être pas dans l'espace, et elle semble n'être pas – ou presque pas – extérieure à la conscience où elle apparaît, mais venir comme du fond même de cette conscience.

It is no doubt on this account that there is so little first-class writing about music in existence. One can recall no 'purple passages' by a writer on music comparable to, say, Pater's description of La Giaconda, which may or may not be good art-criticism, but which is, at any rate, a piece of memorable prose bearing the stamp of an authentic emotional reaction in the presence of a masterpiece. There has been no musical Ruskin – no

Coleridge, no Sainte-Beuve to lend to music the support and prestige of literary appreciation. Writers on music there have always been, but apart from works on the history of music, studies of individual composers, theoretical treatises and the like, the subject has rarely been treated in a universal way: and as for literary descriptions of musical works, save for a few exceptions (Proust, for example) the less said about them the better.

It is here that we are most conscious of the seemingly impassable barrier between the art of sounds and the art of words – the absence of any common factor. Anyone who has tried to describe a piece of music in words must at one stage or other have been convinced of the impossibility of ever being able to do so adequately. What he ultimately produces can only be a compromise – the freest of free translations from a text imperfectly apprehended into a language only partially familiar.

There can be no doubt, then, that the emotions aroused by music are of a different order from those aroused by the other arts, which, after all, are ultimately anchored somewhere in the 'real', and built of material with which we are familiar. Thus literature uses the words and sounds of ordinary human intercourse, and the plastic arts, however abstract, yet reflect the colours and forms of the visible universe. But the whole fabric of music is entirely built up by the imagination of man, and exists in a world as remote as possible from the physical world in which we live, and whose sense impressions we receive.

For, though it is evident that sound in the raw exists in the physical world, the connection between this raw material and what we call music is far slighter than the connection between the raw material of the other arts and the finished product. The green of grass, the contours of a hill, or of the human body, are there ready-made for the painter or sculptor to use, however much he may transform them in the process; and the poet does not have to invent the words he uses. But it would be foolish to pretend that sounds as they exist in nature afford any material whatsoever to the musician who, alone of artists, has had literally to invent *de toutes pièces* a purely artificial language of his own. Plastic form exists in nature, but not even the elements of what might be called tonal form. Natural sounds, on the contrary, are usually completely incoherent, and entirely lacking in what we call 'pitch', and even rhythm. Animal cries, thunder, and the noises caused by wind and water are, in fact, the only sounds in nature; and with the possible exception of the sea, which seems to observe an elementary kind of rhythm (and perhaps the song of certain birds), the rhythmic element is almost absent from these sounds.[1] Hence it is truer to say that a musician will be more readily inspired by the noise of machinery (which at least is rhythmic, having been made by man) than by the sounds which nature puts at his disposal.

Granted, then, that the emotions aroused by music are of a special kind, *sui generis*, what is the proper line of approach for a critic of music, bearing in mind the fact that he has only words in which to express what is suggested to him by an art which has, so to speak, no terms of reference, and is jealously self-contained?

He may, of course, attempt the impressionistic method, and try to re-create the musical work in terms of the impression made on his own imagination; but this method is hardly to be recommended, if we assume that the object of criticism is not only to convey the critic's enthusiasm to the reader, but to give him definite information as well. Indeed, for such critical method to carry any weight at all we must assume that it is possible for two people to receive identical impressions from the same piece of music. It is true that several listeners will often agree as to the *general character* of a given piece of music – as to whether it is cheerful or sad, tragic or comic, and so forth – but, after all, the emotions aroused by music are really irrelevant; it is the music itself that counts.

Take the following example. Baudelaire, in his essay on 'Richard Wagner et Tannhäuser' (*L'Art Romantique*) wishing to prove that music can 'suggérer des idées analogues dans des cerveaux différents' gives an illustration of the impressionistic, subjective method of criticism in comparing his own impressions of the Prelude to *Lohengrin* with those of Liszt and Wagner himself (by whom he seems to assume that the programme notes

[1] I am aware that I have omitted to mention the human voice; but it seems to me a debatable point whether the 'singing' voice can be considered a 'natural' sound; and as for the human 'speaking' voice, it is clearly not very far removed in kind from the chattering of apes or twittering of sparrows. To test the truth of this one has only to listen to the sounds made by a number of people talking together at the same time – during the entracte at the theatre, or in a crowded salon, for example.

from which he quotes were written). Liszt and Wagner, then, both indulge in a great deal of verbiage about sensations of 'espaces infinies', 'béatitude', 'beauté ineffable', 'lumineuse apparition', etc.; but while Wagner makes the music at its culminating point resolve itself into the apparition of a 'troupe miraculeuse des anges', Liszt, after giving a detailed description of the building material used in the Grail sanctuary ('portes d'or, solives d'asbeste, colonnes d'opale, parvis de cymophane', etc.) describes the climax as an 'éclat éblouissant de coloris' in which the holy building seems to glow 'dans toute sa magnificence lumineuse et radiante'. Baudelaire then relates his own impressions on hearing the Prelude for the first time (and before reading either of the above descriptions) and notes that he, too, experienced a sensation of being freed from the laws of gravitation, and of contemplating 'un immense horizon', and 'une large lumiére diffuse'. His own main impression was one of ever-increasing light – 'un surcroît toujours renaissant d'ardeur et de blancheur'.

He then calls attention to the differences between these three impressions, his own, it will be seen, being less concrete and precise than those of Wagner and Liszt. All, however, agree in their impression of physical and spiritual beatitude, and an immensity of space and intensity of light.

But it is clear that these same impressions might also have been suggested by any other piece of music of similar character; and although a person ignorant of *Lohengrin* reading these descriptions might obtain a general idea of the *sort* of music he was going to hear, it is evident that what is quite individual and unique in the Prelude – what, in fact, marks it off from any other piece of music of similarly spiritual and mystic character – cannot be conveyed in words, but must be experienced in terms of sound, and sound alone. Although no two people may feel music in exactly the same way, each individual's impression will be the true one for him, and must always be more or less uncommunicable to another.

The impressionistic, subjective method, then, may be the easiest way for the critic to avoid his difficulty, but such criticism is, in the long run, useless, in so far as it fails to give any real information about its subject-matter. The references to music in the works of Proust are an example of the subjective method pushed to its extremest limits; but in the passages, for example, dealing with the sonata of Vinteuil, what interests us most is not the music, but the reactions it provokes in the mind of the narrator, or, rather, the extraordinarily precise and subtle way in which these reactions are described. But here, of course, we are outside the field of musical criticism proper, and definitely within the realms of psychology. As an illustration of Proust's method it is interesting to note that Proust himself informs us that 'la petite phrase' in the Vinteuil sonata was taken from a sonata by Saint-Saëns – a composer he did not like – and that the rest of the sonata was made up from reminiscences of *Parsifal*, the Franck violin sonata, the Prelude to *Lohengrin*, something by Schubert, and a piano piece of Fauré's.

It is interesting, as a contrast in critical methods, to compare with the above-going appreciations of the Prelude to *Lohengrin* the remark which Berlioz (*A Travers Chants*) makes on the same subject. His approach is very different from that of either Wagner (if we are really to suppose that the programme notes quoted by Baudelaire were written by Wagner), Liszt, or Baudelaire himself. Berlioz, indeed, does not even seek to discover what relationship there may be between the form of this overture and the dramatic idea of the opera; he treats it simply and solely as a symphonic piece, confining himself to a more or less technical appreciation of the lines on which it is constructed. 'On pourrait,' he says, 'en donner une idée en parlant aux yeux par cette figure ——. C'est, en réalité, un immense crescendo lent qui . . . retourne au point d'où il était parti. . . .' He then praises the harmonic progressions, the instrumentation ('une merveille') etc., but does not even suggest that it possesses any mystical or spiritual significance.

This is a good example of strictly objective criticism. Another piece of objective criticism, also from the pen of Berlioz (rightly praised, and quoted in full by Mr Calvocoressi in his book on *Musical Criticism*), is the description of the transition from the Scherzo to the Finale in Beethoven's Fifth Symphony. This passage contains a certain amount of technical terms, but, as Mr Calvocoressi points out, it is such a faithful description of what actually takes place that 'stripped of its technicalities . . . its significance will remain'.

As far as the *describing* of music is concerned, this is probably the ideal method, though here again its limitations are obvious. It is at all events safer than the rhapsodic, subjective style, which though it may have the effect of kindling enthusiasm in the reader, and filling him with a desire to know and appreciate the work in question, can obviously only be valuable in proportion as the reader is already familiar with the general views and tastes of the critic, and knows whether he is likely to be a trustworthy guide.

Mr Clive Bell (*Since Cézanne*), lays down that 'the immediate object of criticism is to put readers in the way of appreciating fully a work or works in the merit of which the critic believes . . .', and again 'the critic has got to convince, he has got to persuade. . . .' Evidently this is one part of a critic's function, but I venture to doubt whether it is the whole. To 'jump for joy', which is the utmost that any critic, according to Mr Clive Bell, can ever hope to do in the presence of a work of art, may be an excellent thing in itself (excellent for the critic); but how often is a critic's joy transmitted to his readers without losing something on the way, or at any rate, causing some deception? And here again the personal factor plays a predominant part. It all depends on who the critic is. As long as I know, for example, that it is Mr Clive Bell who is jumping for joy, I shall probably be ready to jump with him; but if I see Mr X., Y. or Z. (unknown to me as critics) jumping for joy in the presence of a work also unknown to me, the value of such criticism will be, for me, exactly nil.

It is, of course, useless (and not even desirable) for a critic to aim at complete impartiality; if he had no personal predilections he could not be a critic – or, at all events, would be a very dull one. But at the same time he should always try to give some reasons for his preferences, and be able to point to some concrete feature on which he bases his appreciations. For if the critic can tell me some facts about the work which has moved him to enthusiasm, clearly I shall be in a better position to know whether I am likely to share his enthusiasm.

One must not, of course, attach too much importance to questions of procedure, tendencies, schools, and so forth, but a critical method which would exclude all such considerations cannot be considered complete, and will always be lacking in what may be called documentary value. Music, as we have seen, is in its essence sufficiently vague: like a balloon it is always threatening to escape into the higher strata of our emotional atmosphere. If only for this reason, it should be the object of musical criticism to provide it with strong guide-ropes, and endeavour to keep at least within hailing distance.

It is impossible (and again not desirable) to lay down canons of criticism, and the perfect critic is probably only a Chimera, but granted that criticism has a useful function to fulfil (a function I attempted to define at the outset of this essay) the equipment of the critic is obviously of some importance. Cocksureness, for example, may be a good, but is certainly a dangerous quality in a critic. In the case of one who defends in the face of universal reprobation a composer who is later universally admired, it carries its own justification; but when the reverse is the case – i.e. the critic attacks a composer universally acknowledged as a master – his cocksureness is then apt to look like silliness.

The chief fault into which all critics tend to fall is probably that of being led by their personal predilections to minimize the importance of works which to them personally are antipathetic. No critic should fail to recognize greatness, even when manifested in a form that may be distasteful to him; and he should know how to pay tribute to it as such. In general, then, the critic should avoid as far as possible the *terrain* of personal predilections, and endeavour to give his judgements a more substantial backing. Discernment will be his most useful quality; knowledge of his subject and sensibility will form a necessary part of his equipment; and above all the ability to consider any given work of art as far as possible from the creator's point of view so as to be able to judge results with a full comprehension of all the problems involved – in other words, to appraise an artist in proportion as he seems to have succeeded in achieving what he intended, or what it was possible for him, under given circumstances, to achieve. It would be unreasonable to demand of criticism more than this.

from The Musical Quarterly *1928*

"It is not the lot of music critics to be long remembered." *Oliver Edwards.*

Sex and Music

CECIL GRAY

A streak of homosexuality, and even a big fat slice of it, is probably present in every great artist, every outstandingly intelligent person; but it is only when it exceeds fifty per cent that we can legitimately call him homosexual.

Actually there is probably no such thing as a hundred-per-cent male, or female for that matter. Even those specimens of the human race who are as much as ninety per cent male or female are generally intolerable, and extremely stupid and insensitive. Homosexuality, indeed, appears to be a kind of leaven mitigating the monstrosity of the absolute male and the absolute female. It is only when the foreign element, so to speak, preponderates, that the trouble starts. For while a certain proportion of homosexuality is not merely desirable, but essential in an artist, it is an unmitigated disaster if it amounts to an overplus. After all, sexual relationships are among the most important things in life, and the source of all great art, however sublimated – perhaps most of all when sublimated. If this root is twisted and distorted, if this source is turned back on itself, the result must inevitably be an unnatural growth. No fifty-per-cent or more homosexual can ever be a great artist. It will always and inevitably come out in his work in the form of a lack of balance or proportion, a false perspective. In the whole history of music there is up to the present time only one male homosexual of eminence, namely Tchaikovsky, who wrote some very good ballet music. Ballet is the homosexual art-form *par excellence*, and if the numerous homosexual composers at work in this country at the present time would take a word of kindly advice, they would confine their energies to the cultivation of this form, for it is the only one in which they can hope to succeed.

from CONTINGENCIES, AND OTHER ESSAYS *1947*

The Social Foundations of Music

RALPH VAUGHAN WILLIAMS

We must not suppose that composers invent their music out of the blue, without forerunners or surroundings. The innovators are the small men who set the ball rolling. The big men come at the end of a period and sum it up. The period of Haydn and Mozart, not to speak of the smaller people like Cherubini and Hummel, led the way to the supreme master, Beethoven. We can trace the art of Wagner through the early *Singspiele* of Adam Hiller and his contemporaries in the eighteenth century, through Weber and Marschner, to find its culmination in *Die Meistersinger* and *Tristan*. These were the right men coming at the right time and under the right circumstances; that is what enabled them to be great. Sometimes the potentially right man comes at the wrong time. Purcell, for example, was a bit too early for his flower to bloom fully; Sullivan, who in other circumstances might have written a *Figaro*, was thwarted by mid-Victorian inhibitions: the public thought that great music must be portentous and solemn, an oratorio, or a sacred cantata at the least, and that comic opera was beneath notice as a work of art.

The great example of the right man, at the right time, in the right place is Johann Sebastian Bach. He was not a biological sport: he came from a long line of musical ancestors. And what is more, the musical gift did not die out with him, for he had several sons who would have shone brightly in the musical firmament if they had not been partly eclipsed by their great father. Johann Sebastian's first musical ancestor appears to have been Veit Bach, by profession a baker and miller, who used to spend his spare time playing on his beloved zither. Veit had a son who became a *Spielmann*, or professional musician; and from that time onward the tribe of family musicians grew until nearly every town in Thuringia had a Bach as its 'town piper', as the official musicians were called. They held a humble enough position; their duty was to provide music for all civic occasions as well as for weddings, banquets, and funerals. Doubtless some little thing of their own was often played on these occasions. Then came 1685: the time was ready, the place was ready, and the circumstances were ready for the man who, to my mind, is the greatest musician of all time. J. S. Bach's position was, nominally, not much more important than that of his numerous cousins and uncles. True, Leipzig is a comparatively large town, and he was dignified by the name of 'cantor', but his duties included teaching not only music, but also Latin, to the boys at the public school. He had to play the organ, either himself or by deputy, in two churches, and to conduct the services. Every week he had to provide a little thing of his own for performance on Sunday. It happened that these compositions included the *St Matthew Passion* and the *B minor Mass*.

from THE MAKING OF MUSIC *1954*

The Rape of St Cecilia

JOHN CULSHAW

Almost everything obvious about music on television has already been said, and most of it is negative. There are evidently nine reasons for not liking it, just as some years ago there were equivalent, or nearly equivalent, reasons for not liking music on the gramophone or the radio. The difference is that in bygone days the pedants blew their pea-shooters against the target of mass communications – the actual means of communication was secondary. Today, the idea of mass communication in music is no longer under fire, and the forces of reaction are having another go at the latest means and methods. Music at its simplest is sound, almost any sound: television, by definition, involves a picture whose composition has been dictated by a director or a cameraman: therefore, it is argued, the two are irreconcilable. The vehemence of the condemnation varies according to the period and the composer's reputation if he is already dead. The critics don't protest much about visual applications to Boulez or Bernstein or very late Stravinsky, but they might get a little cross about Schoenberg or

Webern; they get quite angry about Debussy, hot about Holst, furious about Beethoven and quite apoplectic if anyone puts pictures to Monteverdi. Their vision of an ideal musical world in the mid-twentieth century consists of clusters of people, not more than 200 at a time, sitting in village halls up and down the country night after night listening rapturously to string quartets with nothing to distract them save the draught, the smell of neighbouring socks and the atrocious acoustics.

The anti-music-on-television brigade get some support from the researchers of figures. The audience for a 'serious' music programme is depressingly small in relation to the total viewing population, and miserably so in relation to the figures for a Miss World contest or a Royal Variety Show. These, however, are idiot comparisons. By such a standard there would be no outlet in any medium for anything except frivolity. What does matter is that a 'poor' figure of, say, one million for a televised performance of a Beethoven symphony represents an audience ten times larger than the average cup final crowd, or the equivalent of 500 performances of the same symphony to capacity audiences in concert halls seating an average 2,000 people. The means of communication is therefore almost certainly working. Why, then, is it so deplored? Why is it supposed that poor St Cecilia is being raped *again*?

The trouble is that our critics love any opportunity to display their puritanism, and since most of us share it we enjoy being pleased or annoyed by what they say. We resist all change, but nowhere with more vehemence than in the *presentation* of the arts. We like to be comfortable, and listen to what we know performed by familiar artists in agreeable surroundings. We have learned, by means of the radio and the gramophone, to accept the sound of a full symphony orchestra in the living-room; but we still resist the sight. The clichés roll out – it's unreal, it's unnatural, it's not like being there. But by saying this sort of thing, we are trying to turn musical television into what it can never be – a near-identical copy of the concert hall.

We have somehow accustomed ourselves to the idea of television drama as something different from drama on the stage, and television has all but abandoned relays of dramatic works from the theatre. The critical squawks were exhausted years ago when the cinema had to make a similar breakthrough and, against a great deal of unwanted advice, proved that no theatrical work was so inviolable that it could be excused the radical changes in form, style and pace demanded by the new medium. Olivier put *Hamlet* and *Richard* and *Henry* on the big screen, and Mike Nichols did the same for *Virginia Woolf*.

A similar act of translation must apply to music in a visual medium, though to do it will take time and a lot of courage. After all, it took the gramophone something like half a century to grasp the utter idiocy of its claim to bring 'concert hall realism' into the home, and to understand that its strongest quality was that it could produce a sound which was at its best in home conditions, at its worst in a relay in a large hall, and had in any case nothing whatsoever to do with what one hears in a concert. The current pop music situation has arisen directly from this, and in some cases it is literally impossible to re-create the recorded sound under live performance conditions. Records therefore can be said to have grown up from the moment they realized they were records, and not a slightly shamefaced substitute for something else. Leaving aside the vexed subject of the quality of television sound reception, which must certainly be improved, there is no major problem in the presentation of music on television apart from television's own reticence – evident only now and then – to use its visual facilities to the full.

Not that the critics have failed in producing suggestions, although I have to admit that after a very short time in television I already find their proposals slightly less helpful than those of the lunatic public fringe who write daily letters of praise or complaint to Shepherd's Bush. My personal prize of the year goes to Anthony Burgess for a blinding ray of illumination in the *Listener* a week or two ago. When music is being played, he wants the *score* on the screen. The short answer is that this has been done, is being done and will be done – whenever it is specifically relevant, as it was, for example, in *Boulez on Boulez*. The idea has no general validity. The score, as such, is merely an aid to musical communication for the professional whose job it is to communicate. It is a sort of blueprint for performance and nothing more, except perhaps for the trained musician who can read the notes without the aid of an instrument; and there is no reason to suppose that to fill the screen with crotchets and quavers would in any way enhance musical communication to those who don't read music.

I suspect that my plumber enjoys hearing the *Eroica* on television, although he would not, as yet, pay to go to the Festival Hall to hear it. He enjoys watching other professionals practising their trade as instrumentalists. At this stage, my plumber hasn't got anywhere near the heart of the *Eroica*, but whereas he would have turned it off the radio, he is inclined to *watch* it on television, although he would certainly answer the telephone if it rang in the middle of the slow movement. And I hope he would go on to discuss the question of drain blockage while the funeral went on its way, because by doing so *he'd* be professional, which is the most ambitious thing any of us can ever hope to be. In an age when a million people, in their own homes, can simultaneously see and hear a fine performance of the *Eroica*, or listen to Nadia Boulanger holding a class, I don't think any critic has any right to complain that music is a failure on television.

It can, and must, be improved. Improvement can only come through experiment, and experiment requires that rules be broken. It is grudgingly granted that some images, sensitively handled by a good director, can be an agreeable adjunct to some music – so we need more images, more music and more directors. Nobody doubts for a moment that sins will be committed along the way; nobody supposes that the birth pangs of a new form of musical communication will be less than severe. The B.B.C. has already established a firm foundation in musical documentary, by which I mean that it is building a regular public for a type of programme which more often than not contains – and therefore communicates – more music than most people realize. Mr Burgess had a good old grumble about *The Golden Ring* ('this musical programme was really all eye'). For his information, the running time of the programme was ninety minutes, of which just over fifty minutes was music without commentary and included such long sections from *Götterdämmerung* as the complete final trio from Act II, the death of Siegfried and the Funeral March, and the latter half of the Immolation scene from Act III. Is this really 'all eye'?

Criticism can help, especially if it manages to grow up. It is simply too late to protest that St Cecilia's virginity has been violated. The offspring may be a bastard, but he's alive and strong, and potentially the biggest musical communicator the world has ever known. (*P.S.* Mother's not doing badly, either.)

from The Listener *1968*

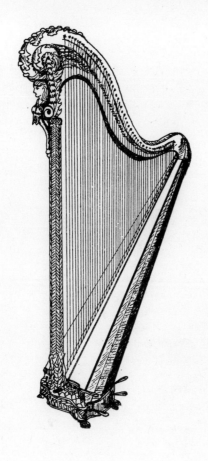

PART II

Composers

The Composer

PERCY M. YOUNG

The history of music shows that those who have become composers have been those who, possessing interest and talent, have applied themselves to the craft of musical composition more assiduously than those who have not become composers. This is the beginning of an answer to any who feel an urge in that direction.

It is possible to read accounts of the lives of the greater composers in which fiction plays a rather too powerful part in the establishment of causes. 'Fancifully speaking, I believe' – this is a quotation from a forty-year-old essay on Chopin – 'that at some secret moment of his childhood, a fairy, or a good genie, or some powerful member of the elfish aristocracy, gave him a piano and said, "My boy, here is a magic piano; when you are in any difficulty or doubt rub lightly upon its ivories, and you will find it ready with assistance."' That is doubtful – even 'fancifully speaking'.

Failing fairies – or other supernatural agents – there is heredity to fall back on. "Of course," says the visitor to the mother of the prodigy, "it runs in the family." By which he or she means to explain away a not always exceptional skill, that had been acquired, by flattery.

It is none the less tempting to look at the careers of some musicians and use them as proof of one theory or another. Those who enjoy speculation along the supernatural line instance such cases as those of Henry Purcell, Wolfgang Mozart, Felix Mendelssohn, or even William Crotch and Samuel Wesley. That they were all teenage composers is true: indeed Wesley – nephew of John Wesley – composed parts of an oratorio, *Ruth*, at the age of eight. That these composers arrived so apparently early was due rather to opportunity and much practice than to unnatural genius. In every case the boy had been thoroughly instructed in how to write music, just as others are taught mathematical problems. In no case can it be accepted that the creative musical work of extreme youth, however promising or even beautiful, is in any

73

absolute sense of the first order, nor without signs that more time might be profitably devoted to study. That applies to those mentioned above – all of whom did pursue their studies relentlessly throughout life.

But Purcell, Mozart, and Bach and Beethoven, were the children of practising musicians of some eminence. Is it not likely that their genius was inherited? In specific terms a particular skill is not inherited. Certain physical attributes which may lead towards that skill may be – but those are too general to be of much service in explaining what is called genius. In any case there is a long list of those composers descended from not particularly musical families to counter any easy theorizing: among composers of this class are Handel, Haydn, Mendelssohn, Sibelius, Vaughan Williams. Sometimes the enthusiastic biographer solves the problem of proving the creative artist to be essentially from other people by either claiming that the parents were amateur musicians (e.g. William Crotch's father was a carpenter 'with an ear for music' – whatever that means) or else by proposing, as in the case of Handel, that the genius – arrived by magic – was so strong as to overcome every obstacle.

There is, let it be said, something in the necessity for overcoming obstacles – especially in the modern world. The farther away from the centre of material life any vocation appears to be, the less will be the encouragement to embrace it and the more meagre the rewards. The place of an artist in the community depends, therefore, to some extent on the value which the community places on the art. The existence of an artist depends naturally on the existence of art itself and on his opportunities for close acquaintance with it. Thus we find at certain times and certain places the growth of schools of composers, of Church music, of opera, of symphonic music, of ballet, of jazz, for these kinds of musical expression developed only in a special social context in the first place.

The important word, then, is opportunity. This goes some way to explaining the special cases of Purcell, of the Bachs, of Mozart, and of a number of other father-son relationships within the field of composition. In every case there was a musical environment. Music was heard and practised. What is more, because music occupied a central position in the societies to which those composers belonged, the career prospects were as good as any others open to boys in the class to which they were born.

The cases of certain composers may be looked at to illustrate the points so far made.

Henry Purcell (1659–95) was the son of a singer in the Chapel Royal of Charles II. Since he was able to sing, the family connection ensured him a place as a chorister also in the Chapel Royal. As a choirboy Purcell lived with his companions in the choir school and was given a rigorous training in general musicianship. This included singing – and the great advantage of daily services was that sight-reading, by which one comes quickly to terms with new music, was an essential qualification; harpsichord and organ-playing; the tuning of musical instruments; and the elements of composition. So far as composition was concerned, the seventeenth-century student must, above all, know how to harmonize a bass at the keyboard; for accompaniments in those days were not 'written out', but left to the performer to work out himself. In the Chapel Royal anthems must be composed to meet the King's demand for gayer music than was performed in former times – for Charles II had acquired a taste for the brilliant music of the French court when he was in exile. Urged on by the presence of French musicians in England, and by Pelham Humfrey who had studied in France, Purcell imbibed certain French characteristics, especially rhythmic, and was regarded as at least very promising.

Later duties as a copyist at Westminster Abbey reminded Purcell of the fine contrapuntal tradition of the English school of the Tudor period, and he was able to follow the contrapuntal principles of Byrd and Gibbons but to combine them with the harmonic methods that were contemporary. As organist of Westminster Abbey, Purcell had many opportunities to write Church music, particularly since there were numerous royal occasions demanding music as a matter of course during the reigns of Charles II, James II, and William and Mary.

As a royal musician (he was also organist at the Chapel Royal) Purcell also provided works for many secular occasions. A seventeenth-century monarch approved such musico-poetic works as complimentary Odes because these were helpful in creating what is now called an 'image'. Purcell's Odes happen to be good, possibly great, because he was an exceptional craftsman. Other composers wrote Odes that served their purpose well enough (Jeremiah Clarke, for instance), but of a musical quality less distinguished than those of Purcell, whose more comprehensive style was to prove more durable.

Purcell's London was distinguished by tremendous activity in the theatre, and plays with music were fashionable. It was not unprofitable for Purcell to turn his hands to the songs and incidental pieces that were most often required, and the amount of theatre music he left was very considerable. Among it, of course, were such major works as *King Arthur* (written in conjunction with John Dryden), *The Fairy Queen* (a kind of 'musical' based on Shakespeare's *A Midsummer Night's Dream*) and *Dido and Aeneas* (commissioned by the proprietors of a dancing school for young ladies, in Chelsea).

There were many other works written for domestic music-making, songs, chamber music, and even catches designed for appreciation in taverns.

Purcell composed a vast amount of music. Most 'great' composers do: first of all because they live (or hope to live) by composition, and therefore do their best to supply the demand, which used to be considerable; second, because fluency in writing comes only from regular practice.

Purcell was an opportunist. In the free-for-all of post-Restoration England, he matched himself against his contemporaries and took every chance of improving his fortunes (even by hiring out seats in his organ-loft at Westminster at Coronation times). In a smart, volatile society, he did this by reflecting the characteristics of that society in his music: thus gaiety (in melodic outline and rhythmic vitality), wit and humour (in dramatic scenes), scientific adventurousness (exemplified in daring modulations and counterpoint), and a European outlook (in addition to studying French music, Purcell also looked profitably at what he could obtain from Italy), are evident. There are many other qualities also; but those that are taken to belong to the period in which he lived Purcell endeavoured to reflect by adjustments to his own musical idiom.

A composer of Purcell's time, and for most of the century following, was fortunately circumstanced so long as he enjoyed liberal patronage. As a beneficiary of the Church (albeit a Reformed Church), Purcell inherited the traditions of a medieval composer, and the contrapuntal texture of his works – as those of Bach and indeed Handel in the next generation – showed the imprint of medievalism. As a royal servant he enjoyed the privileges brought to the profession of composer by the Renaissance. Further he had a close relationship with the middle-class society that was increasingly exerting its power in the realm of the fine arts.

The picture is concise, co-ordinated, and satisfying. Purcell was a highly professional composer and once his talents had matured and he was placed in the right environment he could, in a moderate way, prosper. In general, however, the professional composer of that period must do what he was told. To question commissions was not done.

A hundred years or so later the case was different. The composer, particularly if his general education put him on terms of relative equality with other educated men, is less inclined to accept orders without question. He is apt to let it be known that he is the best judge of his own case. Purcell did not set out deliberately to express the 'spirit of the age'. He would have thought this irrelevant, and not the job of a composer (the nearest he got to a 'missionary' spirit was to encourage patriotism through *King Arthur*). Bach and Handel would have agreed with him. None the less, because true composers are bound by style, by libretti, by the instrumental and vocal resources, they did mirror their age – if for no other reason, because in retrospect their music, in a material sense, is seen to be limited; in a spiritual sense it is otherwise. The mere fact that their works are found to be of present-day importance is witness to that, but, once again, it is doubtful whether those craftsmen-composers considered that point either.

Handel and Bach were German composers. The former, of course, became a British subject. But in neither case was nationality of major importance, not in so far as music was concerned anyway. Handel cheerfully mixed together German, Italian and English ingredients to produce his individual style; while Bach, who stayed at home, cultivated Italian and French habits which are not difficult to distinguish. When, however, we catch up with Carl Maria von Weber (1786–1826), also a great German composer, we notice another attitude. Weber wished to be a German composer – but on his own terms.

Like Purcell, Weber was a member of a family in which there were many professional musicians. His father, Franz Anton – whose cousin Constanze was Mozart's wife – had a varied career as military musician, as soldier (he was wounded while fighting against Frederick the Great in 1756), as court functionary, as peripatetic violin and viola player, and as musical director at various theatres. The elder Weber not only wished his sons (Carl Maria was the third) to become musicians but also wished for at least one of them to show talents appropriate to a connection of the great Mozart.

Carl Maria learnt music in the first place from his father, but made such slow progress that his brother Fritz is reported to have said "Carl, you may become anything else you like, but you will never be a musician." But Fritz was wrong.

Franz Anton moved from theatre to theatre, taking his family with him, and Carl Maria was enchanted by the whole theatrical atmosphere. He learnt all that he could about the theatre from observation. In the meantime he began to develop skill in composition, having had lessons from various teachers of whom the most notable was Michael Haydn – brother of the more famous Joseph. Before he was fourteen Weber had written fughettas (little fugues) and variations for the piano and a brief opera entitled *Das Waldmädchen*. This last work, through his father's influence, was produced in Freiberg and Chemnitz (as well as other towns) in 1800.

Weber's education, owing to the circumstances of his life, was irregular, but, perhaps because he was not bound by curriculum, wide in range. For instance, he became deeply interested in literature and aspired to be a writer. Indeed, in addition to much musical criticism and essays on general matters, he undertook a semi-autobiographical novel – *Tonkünstlers Leben* – which he never completed. The reason for this interest was personal (Weber recognized his own talent for expression through words), but it was stimulated by the great revival of German literature taking place during his impressionable years.

Through a combination of German literature, especially lyric and dramatic poetry, and music, Germany asserted national independence and national pride during the Romantic era, and one of their chief architects was Carl Maria von Weber, who saw how the fusion of words and music could be brought about in opera. Altogether Weber composed eight operas, of which the best-known are *Der Freischütz*, *Euryanthe* and *Oberon*. In his operas, Weber based his vocal style on German models – remembering especially the popular plays-with-music (*Singspiele*) that had maintained themselves in provincial towns against the fashionable Italian opera.

With so much experience of the theatre, Weber understood how to make his vocal parts dramatic, and an instinct for harmonic colouring and a fine sense of orchestration brought to the German audiences of his day a new experience. Since the libretti reflected the ideas that inspired Romantic artists in general, and since the intention of Weber's operas was to advance an enthusiasm for German ideals, the composer was in tune with the aspirations of his fellow-countrymen. The fact was realized by many in Weber's lifetime, but by more after his death, and his example was one of the principal sources of inspiration for Richard Wagner.

It is one thing to compose works, it is another to hear them performed. When Weber's father first entered the profession of music, as a servant of the Elector of Mannheim, composers could look forward to their commissions and to the regular performance of what they wrote. When Carl Maria came to artistic maturity the case was different. The composer must make his own way in the world. Thus Carl Maria was a concert pianist, a freelance teacher, a private secretary to the Duke Ludwig of Stuttgart, and a music critic, before he obtained a musical post in the theatre – at Prague. Although it was apparent at Prague that Weber had great gifts of organization, it was not until his appointment to the Royal Opera in Dresden that his talents were fully employed in this sphere. At Dresden, despite opposition, Weber so laboured to build up a German company to take priority over the long-established Italian company that he won the respect of all patriots. Weber's greatest triumph, however, was in Berlin on 18 June 1821, when *Der Freischütz* was chosen as the first opera to be performed in Karl Schinkel's new Schauspielhaus. Political feeling was running high in Berlin at that time, particularly against the French. It happened that the chief opera director in Berlin, and a favourite of the King, was Gasparo Spontini, half Italian and half French. The Berliners were prepared to applaud new German opera because it enabled them to show their feelings, but when they heard *Der Freischütz*, which Weber conducted, they were carried away by the beauty and freshness of the music, and their demonstration of enthusiasm was as much for the quality of the opera as for what they wished it otherwise to represent. Nevertheless, during the nineteenth century political issues and opera came close together on many occasions, and composers such as Verdi in Italy, Smetana in Bohemia, and Glinka in Russia became figures of importance – not necessarily through their own wish – in other fields than that of music.

The ecclesiastical style in general use until the Renaissance was highly specialized. It was designed for a minority. From the Renaissance until the classical period of the later eighteenth century, music was set in an aristocratic environment, and also for a minority. In the nineteenth century a composer such as Weber aimed at appealing to a wider circle. For the most part, however, newly composed music then was a preserve of the middle classes, in that the composer set himself the task of coming to terms with middle-class taste and opinion.

The problem of the twentieth-century composer is to extend the range of musical creation still further. A notable attempt to do this was made by the American composer George Gershwin (1898–1937).

As we have seen, in earlier times the composer was educated thoroughly in the craft of composition. Of the great nineteenth-century composers, some – like Schubert, Berlioz, Schumann, Wagner and Weber – learned composition in a more casual way. None of them – although each was a great craftsman in that he could subdue the musical material on which he worked – was trained in the old 'academic' manner, and because of this each was able to expand the language of music because he felt less obliged to study the conventions.

Now George Gershwin came from a modest home in Brooklyn where there was no musical background. As a boy he had spasmodic piano lessons and drifted into a hack job – demonstrating popular numbers – in a publishing house. A few harmony lessons provided him with enough technical equipment to discipline his fertile musical ideas and to attempt composition. By one of those freaks that distinguish the commercial and the artistic worlds he very soon produced a 'hit' number in 'Swannee'. Thereafter he continued to compose in the same idiom and achieved further successes. His distinction was that he could use a popular idiom sometimes with grace and often with originality.

Most composers, if they are honest, try to take into account what people say they like, and in composing 'popular' music Gershwin was doing no more than follow the general principle that inspires composers to search out opportunity. Gershwin was speaking in terms that were acceptable to the broad masses of the under-privileged, whom, because of his own origins, he felt himself in some way to represent. At the same time he took a higher and not a lower view of human character, and from the basic, commonplace, vulgar vocabulary of music he aimed at reaching some sort of agreement with the conventions of art-music. Thus he composed jazz-symphonic works such as the *Rhapsody in Blue* and the Piano Concerto in F. But his outstanding achievement was the opera *Porgy and Bess*.

Porgy and Bess was based on real-life issues of the time in which Gershwin was living: indeed the theme is still topical and seems likely to remain so. The story of the opera reveals the life of a Negro community in squalid urban society. Gershwin tried to make his music true to life by making a special study of Negro music. The result was an opera distinguished by so many beautiful and moving melodies – for Gershwin was an original melodist – which so carried the narrative forward that the whole work appeared as a passionate call to humanity. *Porgy and Bess* achieved the rank of a classic in America, was the first American opera ever to be staged at La Scala in Milan, and in recent years has toured triumphantly in the Middle East, in Latin America, and in the Soviet Union.

From the study of the lives and works of composers, these points emerge. A composer is made and not born. He has certain developed skills which often show themselves early in life (this is so in other spheres of activity). He learns the grammar of music, and how to use it: this he does by listening to and looking at a variety of works in different mediums. He selects details of technique and turns of phrase from others and adapts them to his own purposes. The result of this selection combined with tendencies to behave in particular ways and to canalize musical ideas into some departments rather than others (e.g. Schubert wrote more songs than anything else, Chopin more piano pieces, Verdi more operas) eventually produces what is recognized as a distinctive style.

Music, however, is not generally composed in a vacuum. It is composed to be performed by some people in the presence of others. It communicates. This being so, the composer tries to clarify his musical intention. This he does by following certain precedents, as of symphony, or string quartet, or theme and variations, or else by appealing to external aids, such as words, or movement, or scene. To a greater or lesser degree he may bring music into line with other forms of expression – thus we may speak of Christian music, or pagan music, or national music, understanding that the composer is trying to underline a particular message. However, the composer's main concern is that his music shall be performed. How it is performed, where it is performed – those are matters that more often than not lie outside his immediate control. This is where the community governs the artist, who may only use what is available to use.

Emotion, feeling, beauty? These are matters which cannot be dissociated from the whole of what has gone before. Emotion and feeling are read into composition by those who look from without, they are not shovelled into works like sugar into tea. As for beauty, this is dependent on the point of view. Fortunately what is beautiful to some is not so to others, and vice versa. The composer, in composing, is making. He makes according to the best of his ability. Any further observations must come from his audiences.

from MUSIC *1963*

Dunstable, Okeghem and Josquin

WALLACE BROCKWAY and HERBERT WEINSTOCK

From a strictly pragmatic point of view, music blossoms at that moment in the fourth century when Ambrose, Bishop of Milan, decided to regulate the singing for the services in his diocese. The Ambrosian chant – the first recognizable ancestor of music as we hear it – is the leanest and most solemn adaptation of the Greek modes, the ancestor of our modern scales. This sombre singing can still be heard in certain Milanese churches, but today we are more familiar with the elaboration of St Ambrose's system known as the Gregorian chant, which largely superseded the older musical service at about the beginning of the seventh century. Some think that St Gregory, the greatest Pope of the early Middle Ages, sponsored, or even devised the innovation; less romantic historians believe that he was too busy with barbarians, heretics, and the plague to bother with ideas about music.

For a thousand years the music of the Church was rigidly melodic: that is, it attained its ends without the use of harmony as we conceive it today. The troubadours and minnesingers accepted unquestionably this purely horizontal tradition of music, and lavished their imagination on the melody and words. But neither these gay itinerant musicians nor the formulators of primitive counterpoint (whoever they were) can be called real composers.

The Renaissance, which exploited the individual ego, gave birth to the composer with a name. Until then men had been content to submerge their names in anonymous giving of their talents: the musician was as nameless as the altar-boy swinging his censer. In the Middle Ages music had no separate identity: it was as much an accessory of the sacred rite as Greek music was of the drama. Definitely, purposely, a part of some greater whole, it was designed to recede. It is no coincidence that the first pieces of self-sufficient music are (with few exceptions) not anonymous: they were still written for the Church, but the composer had begun to think of his music as a living thing he had created.

Considering the exalted and ancient lineage of the other arts, it comes as a shock to find that the first composer, in the modern sense of the word, was an Englishman who died in 1453. This man, John Dunstable, is an almost mythical figure, a sort of English Orpheus who was even credited with the invention of counterpoint – a feat obviously beyond the abilities of a single individual. Also, for no apparent reason, he has been confused with St Dunstan, an Archbishop of Canterbury, who had died more than four centuries before. Add that he was even confused with another English composer of his time, and was reputedly astrologer and mathematician, and this sums up what is known of the man who was probably Geoffrey Chaucer's most gifted artistic contemporary. Little of Dunstable's music survives, and he might have vanished from history altogether if it had not been for his long and fruitful association with Continental musicians of his age, whose successors – especially the Flemish masters – evidently studied his methods to great advantage.

Dunstable's suave and euphonious style tended temporarily to soften the harsh contours of the music of the Flemings. But Jean de Okeghem reverted to the austerity of earlier Flemish music, while vastly increasing its technical resources. Okeghem has been called the greatest teacher of all time, and in his relentless pursuit of a new methodology has been likened to the modern experimentalist, Arnold Schoenberg. This is by no means a forced comparison, for the purely aesthetic results of their efforts are, in both cases, open to question.

Like many another outstanding theoretician, Okeghem was fulfilled in the work of his pupils, the greatest of whom was Josquin des Prés. Coming upon Josquin after mingling with his still shadowy predecessors is like emerging suddenly into the light of day: he is a recognizably modern man, an erratic genius whose chequered career extended well into the sixteenth century. He was born in the dawn of a new age, when the Turks swarming into Constantinople and Gutenberg devising the printing press helped to liberate forces that would destroy the Middle Ages. Josquin emerges from the mists as a singer at Milan in 1474. He was then about thirty years old, and it seems probable that his sophistication was already such that even the excessive splendour of the court of the Sforzas could not overawe him. For he was no stranger to court life, as he himself testifies: he had studied under Okeghem at the Royal Chapel of Louis XI. As he left the then cheerless city of Paris with a whole skin, we may be sure that he did not make the sour French monarch the butt of those practical jokes for which he later became notorious.

Within the next decade or so, Josquin made a leisurely progress through the burgeoning duchies of northern Italy, where beauty-loving and neurasthenic princes welcomed good musicians with the extravagant warmth of those lush and expansive times. He finally arrived at Rome, which was for two hundred years to be the centre of the musical world, and became a singer in the papal chapel, thus choosing a road to fame that became stereotyped with his successors. Perhaps the choristers in the Pope's service lived aloof from the dissolute life of Renaissance Rome, but if they came much into contact with that grand old rake, Innocent VIII, or his even more riotous successor, Alexander VI, they must have witnessed some of the most colourful and improper scenes in the history of even the Eternal City. Here, despite the obvious distractions of Borgian Rome, Josquin worked on his first book of Masses – probably some of them were sung in the Sistine Chapel with the composer himself taking part.

Louis XI had died, Charles VIII had climaxed a humiliating career by mortally bumping his head, and that brilliant match-maker, Louis XII, was firmly seated on the French throne before Josquin wandered back to Paris to seek preferment. At first he had to live on glory and promises: his first book of Masses, published in 1502, was received with great acclaim, and though Louis XII began to hint cheerfully about church benefices, these failed to materialize. Josquin was no respecter of the person of the most Christian King, and dared to jog his memory. Being commissioned to compose a motet for performance in the King's presence, he chose two telling phrases from the Psalm CXIX – 'Let Thy words to Thy servant be remembered' and 'My portion is not in the land of the living' – for his contrapuntal embroidery. He received a benefice.

Josquin died in 1521.

from MEN OF MUSIC *1959*

Weelkes

GUSTAV HOLST

Thomas Weelkes is my favourite Tudor composer because I get more enjoyment and less disappointment from his music than I do from that of any of his contemporaries.

'Less disappointment' is important when we compare him – as we can hardly avoid doing – with William Byrd. No artist is always at his very best. Byrd's misfortune is that when he is not first-rate he is so rarely second-rate – he drops to third or fourth-rate and gives us music that might have been written by anyone.

Weelkes, on the other hand, rarely descends below his second rate. All his music is Weelkes and Weelkes is in all his music. This is probably due to the variety of his work. No one in any age or country has expressed so many different ideas and moods in pure choral music; and – being like Byrd, a master of choral writing – he always expresses them beautifully and well.

It is characteristic of Weelkes that a volume of his shorter choral works should be entitled *Airs or Fantastic Spirits*. The spirit of fantasy, which was to disappear from choral music less than a hundred years after his death, runs through all his work and is only absent when the subject forbids its presence. Weelkes shows this fantastic spirit in his choice of words. Take some of the titles of his madrigals: 'Mars in a Fury'; 'Thule, the period of Cosmography'; 'The Ape, the Monkey and Baboon'; 'Come Sirrah Jack Ho! fill some Tobacco'; 'Four Arms, Two Necks, One Wreathing'; 'As Deadly Serpents'; 'Like two Proud Armies marching in the Field'. You will not find the like among Byrd's and Palestrina's works. Nothing is so certain with Weelkes as the unexpected. . . .

To find Weelkes in his most fantastic mood one must go to such things as 'Thule, the period of Cosmography' and 'The Andalusian Merchant' who returns home 'laden with cochineal and china dishes'. But the spirit of fantasy was so strong in him that it is seen and felt equally well when Weelkes treats more conventional subjects, such as his contribution to *The Triumphs of Oriana* ('As Vesta was from Latmos Hill descending'); or 'As wanton Birds' and 'Sweetheart, Arise'. One feels its influence even in his sad music. In the latter he brings a fresh element into his work – that of chromatic harmony. . . .

Until recently we have always looked upon Weelkes as a secular composer, and even now we know very little of his sacred music, but that is as characteristic and as beautiful as his madrigals. Take the six-part motet 'Hosanna to the Son of David'. One remembers the well-known setting of the same words by Orlando Gibbons, with its joyous brilliancy, its elaborate inter-weaving of parts. How has it been set by Weelkes, the 'fantastic spirit', the master of counterpoint, of chromatic harmony, of complicated rhythms? As usual, Weelkes gives us the unexpected. His motet is *stern*! Coming to it after that of Gibbons is like entering St Bartholomew's, Smithfield, after leaving King's College Chapel, Cambridge. And while Gibbons, Bach, and all other contrapuntal composers seize on the word 'Hosanna' to display all possible wealth of brilliant intricacy of part-writing, Weelkes stays the flow of his counterpoint and blends his voices in one tremendous Shout!

Weelkes is the true English artist. He is an individualist as opposed to the Latin artist who tends to be a member of a school, and as opposed to the inartistic Englishman whose thinking and feeling are arranged for him by convention. There is nothing to suggest that Weelkes hated conventionality. It simply did not exist for him. When his treatment of a subject happened to coincide with the convention of the day, it just coincided, and there is only the superb craftsmanship to show us which is his work. In everything he wrote, this craftsmanship enabled him to express all he felt in his own inimitable manner, whether simply or with elaboration, whether in a style that was to vanish from the earth after his day, or in a style similar to that which most people regard as belonging to the twentieth century.

Such is Weelkes. It is good to know him, and better still, to hear his music. To sing it is best of all.

originally from The Midland Musician *1926,*
reprinted in HEIRS AND REBELS *1959*

Some Aspects of Handel's Genius

J. A. WESTRUP

Handel's bulk impressed his contemporaries. "He was in his person," says Sir John Hawkins, "a large made and very portly man." Posterity cares nothing for his physique, but his music suggests a giant. It touches the heavens and bestrides mountains. "Handel," said Beethoven, "was the greatest composer who ever lived" – and meant it. The hundred volumes of Chrysostom's edition are a challenge to mediocrity and sloth. They are also the proper tribute that scholarship pays to a great man. Other tributes have been paid in the past – not least public approbation. In the old days Handel was not merely a giant, he was also an idol. The foundations were laid in the last years of his life, and when he was dead the passion for commemoration solidified into a tradition of regular performance. In his lifetime *Messiah* had been given annually at the Foundling Hospital. The practice of repetition grew. The oratorios became firmly embedded in the main stream of English music, they were constantly sung, and they were horribly imitated by puny men. As Georgian license receded before Victorian morality the cult grew stronger. Handel became a priest. The oratorios dealt with Biblical subjects; they must be listened to devoutly. If they had Bible words, as in *Messiah*, all the better; if not, no matter. Occasional frivolity or pagan gusto could be discreetly ignored. Here music offered a solid pillar for religion. Another was needed, and Mendelssohn obligingly supplied it.

This was not Mendelssohn's only service to music. He also disinterred the corpse of J. S. Bach. Since then the grain of mustard-seed has grown into a tremendous tree. Bach, once the preserve of a few earnest scholars and enterprising organists, has become a composer for the multitude. "Good old J. S. B.", says the ordinary listener after a good soaking of the Brandenburg Concertos. Wednesday night at the 'Proms' is like a mass meeting of good fellows. Handel has suffered in consequence. Public appreciation cannot distribute equal favours. The scales must drop one way or the other. Up Bach, down Handel. In thirty years' time it may be the other way about. This does not seriously matter, since good music does not rust through neglect. Nor for that matter is Handel actually neglected today. But only a fraction of his music is heard and it is commonly presented in a way that fogs his merits. The Victorians may have made the mistake of supposing that Handel was a 'sacred' composer; but having set the oratorios on pedestals they were faithful in performing them, and a quantity of splendid music was regularly heard. Nowadays *Messiah* is turned on like an intermittent fountain, but the other oratorios have to wait their turn. *Samson* and *Israel in Egypt* pop up occasionally; the rest are performed in semi-secrecy by private societies who value faith above convention.

The Victorians not only performed the oratorios. As was natural in an age that believed in universal progress, they also were convinced that music is grander in direct proportion to the number of people performing it. Massive forces had been employed as early as the first Handel commemoration in Westminster Abbey. The Victorians went further. They invoked battalions. Handel was a giant; let the choir be a giant too. So hundreds, even thousands, of voices united to drown the orchestra. A new problem was raised. Handel's instrumentation could not hold its own against such a hubbub. Mozart's additional accompaniments had merely been designed for use when an organ was not available; they could not be considered a suitable adaptation for Festival conditions. Hence the theory, now widely accepted, that wholesale rescoring was essential. Batteries of drums, trumpets, horns and trombones hurl slabs of sound at the attentive audience; and though the chorus is still too big for the orchestra, the total effect is at least deafening.

We are assured that Handel would revel in these orgies. There is no ground for supposing so at all. His gianthood is in the scope and vastness of his invention, not in the forces it is presumed to require for its interpretation. It is true that he had several instruments to each part when his *Music for the Royal Fireworks* was first performed in 1749. There were to be nine trumpets, three sets of timpani, twenty-four oboes, nine horns and twelve bassoons. But this was simply because the performance took place in the open air. The Green Park is not a concert hall, and in any case the total forces on this occasion numbered less than sixty. Handel was sometimes credited by his contemporaries with a love of noise. His music hardly supports the charge; and there is nothing in it to suggest that he would have revelled in coarseness and vulgarity.

The oratorio tradition laid stress on Handel's vocal writing. Festival performances emphasized the choruses; soloists were midgets in the Crystal Palace desert. There was good justification for this. Handel was a master of choral writing. He achieved, as Hawkins said, sublimity, and often by the simplest means. This presentation of tremendous sentiments in monumental homophony was something new, something that has never been successfully imitated or surpassed. But these grand enunciations are only one aspect of Handel's art of choral writing. The other is the masterly weaving of parts into a fabric that makes rhetoric of counterpoint. That Handel displays this skill is a proof of his universal genius. No one could have foreseen from the earlier part of his career this wealth of choral writing. In opera, to which he devoted so many years of his life, the chorus's function was negligible. There the soloist was king – or queen. The whole resources of the Italian operatic style – the vehemence of dramatic recitative, the brilliance and suavity of the *da capo* aria – were employed to beautify and ennoble the most conventional situations. Lay figures strutted and languished on the stage; and from their lips flowed golden streams of melody.

The fountain seems to have been inexhaustible. Handel was always himself, but he was too much of a personality to be content with the repetition of tags. If we apply the label 'Handelian' to period cadences or conventional melodic progressions we miss altogether the signposts of a great mind. Cadences and fragments of melody do not make a composer. Style is something vaster than textbook indexing: with Handel, as with other great artists, it is the man. 'It is difficult,' says Romain Rolland, 'to speak of *the* opera or *the* oratorio of Handel. One must say operas or oratorios. It is impossible to reduce them to a single type.' He speaks too, of the various styles on which Handel drew freely in order to create his own. Handel was always open to influences. Like a clever linguist who insensibly imitates the accents of the foreigners among whom he lives, so Handel in England absorbed the English idiom. How Purcellian in rhythm and melody is the bourré in the *Fireworks* music! And he was not afraid to make experiments. In all his oratorios the chorus has an important function; it comments, it participates, it gives thanks. But in *Israel in Egypt* the chorus is the work; it represents the soul of a people. Even recitative is made communal.

Handel the instrumental composer we still know imperfectly. A harpsichord suite is heard occasionally at recitals, sometimes a violin sonata. But the *concerti grossi* are still unknown to hundreds of people who can sing the Brandenburg Concertos in their baths.

from The Listener *1939*

"If Income Tax collectors ever indulge in community singing, I have no doubt that they sing the choruses from the *Messiah*, for the *Messiah* is the first great anthem of man's enslavement by materialism." *Compton Mackenzie.*

Bach

ALBERT SCHWEITZER

The immediate impression Bach's works make upon us is of a dual kind. Their message is quite modern; but at the same time we feel that they have no kinship whatever with post-Beethovenian art. Bach's music seems to us modern in so far as it makes a strong effort to get beyond the natural indefiniteness of musical sound, and aims at the most thorough musical expression possible of the poem with which it is associated. Its object is pictorial, represent-ative. It differs from modern art, however, in its manner of reproducing the poem, and the means by which it does so. There lies between Bach and Wagner not only a century and a half of time, but a whole world. The former represents a wholly different species of representative music from that of his Bayreuth champion. . . .

In the Capriccio on the departure of his brother, Bach entered upon the path that leads to programme music. It was not, however, the naïve programme music of a Johann Kuhnau, who

undertook to tell whole histories in music, but an art fully conscious of the limits of what can be intelligibly expressed in tone,
and confining itself to a sequence of a few plastic scenes, admirably
characterized in the music. Bach's experience in this youthful
experiment led him afterwards to aim at expresssion on other lines.
His artistic greatness is shown in the fact that in an epoch of
confident programme music he rises superior to it from the beginning, and never aims at trying to express in music what music is
incapable of expressing.

The naïve programme musicians of the past and the present are
like the Biblical painters who, relying on the fact that every detail
of certain of the sacred stories is known, deluded themselves that
they had really represented these scenes when they had accumulated the various objects and persons concerned on the canvas,
while all the time they had failed to make the real thing, the event
itself, comprehensible. A man with a knife; a boy bound to a pile
of wood; a ram's head in a bush; a bearded face looking down
from the clouds – this, they thought, was the sacrifice of Isaac. A
man and a woman at a well; in the background a town; on the
road leading to it twelve men scattered about here and there in
pairs – this was supposed to tell the story of Jesus and the woman
of Samaria. The real action is added by the spectator, out of the
convention that resolves the simultaneous grouping of the figures
on the canvas into a succession in time. As a rule very few of the
Biblical stories are really 'paintable', in the true sense of the word,
for the event does not present a single pregnant situation which
contains and elucidates the whole action. Thus the majority of
Biblical painters, by having to presuppose so much knowledge
of the subject on the spectator's part, have given us not pictures,
but illustrations, that exceed the limits of true painting to the same
extent that descriptive programme music exceeds those of true
music.

Bach, however, did not let the general knowledge of the
chorales and Biblical texts mislead him into an attempt to depict
in his music all the details and salient episodes of his text. He
keeps within the real possibilities of musical expression, even in
cases where another man would think it safe to rely on the general
knowledge of the words to carry off his strokes of pictorialism.

He thus makes no effort to represent all the episodes and evolutions of the text. He expresses the essential elements in the idea, not its vicissitudes. He underlines, indeed, any characteristic detail, brings out contrasts, employs the most powerful nuances; but the vicissitudes of the idea, its struggles, its combats, its despair, its entry into peace, all that Beethoven's music and that of the post-Beethoven epoch try to express – of this there is nothing in Bach. Nevertheless his emotional expression is not less perfect than Beethoven's. It is simply another kind of perfection. His emotional utterance has a power and an impressiveness such as we rarely meet with in other music. His capacity for characterizing the various nuances of an emotion is quite unique.

Thus, Bach's music is also emotional music in the truest and deepest sense, though he pursues a path far remote from that of Wagner. Both composers aim at realizing poetic ideas in music; both avoid programme music, i.e. a naïve translation of the poem into sound; both remain strictly within the real possibilities of musical expression. But they are different in this respect, that Bach depicts the idea in its static, Wagner in its dynamic life. There is no art to which Wagner's definition of the nature of music is less applicable than that of Bach. According to Wagner, the harmonic changes must be inevitable in the sense that they are motivated by the poetry, and express an emotion that demands the intensifying power of music. This is not the case with Bach's modulations. Generally speaking they are of a purely musical nature. They too are 'inevitable', but in the sense that they are a logical unfolding of what was latent in the theme from its beginning. So far those are right who meet all modernizations of Bach, good and bad, with the objection that his art is 'pure music'. In this way they express, even if obscurely, the truth that, unlike Beethoven and Wagner, he does not represent an emotion as a series of dramatic incidents. The perception of this distinction is of the first importance for the performance of Bach's music. It makes us realize the error of imposing upon Bach the Beethovenian and Wagnerian dynamics, the purpose of which is to heighten the harmonic expression of the various poetic incidents. Bach's music is of a different order.

Beethoven and Wagner poetize in music, Bach paints. And Bach is a dramatist, but just in the sense that the painter is. He does not paint successive events, but seizes upon the pregnant moment that contains the whole event for him, and depicts this in music. That is why the opera had so little attraction for him. He knew the Hamburg stage from his youth; he was intimate with the leading people at the Dresden Theatre. If nevertheless he never wrote an opera, it was not because the external circumstances were unfavourable, but because, unlike Wagner, he did not conceive action and music in one. The musical drama is for him a succession of dramatic pictures; he realizes it in his Passions and cantatas.

In Bach the poetic idea is embedded in the theme. This is not, as in Wagner, a melodic determination of a certain harmony welling up out of the depths of the ocean of tone; it is more akin in origin to the thematic invention of Berlioz. It resembles the latter's themes in its emotional vehemence and a certain pictorial tendency, for it is the product of the same kind of plastic imagination. Bach's view of tone-painting is different from Wagner's. For the latter, self-existent tone-painting is only a makeshift. His ideal is that music shall address itself, as in drama, to feeling rather than imagination. Bach, on the other hand, appeals to the conceptual imagination. Tone-painting is an end in itself with him. The ideal before him is not the self-expression of this pictorialism, but the carrying of it to the extremist limits of realism.

The first thing he looks for in a text is the image or idea that gives an opportunity for a definitely plastic musical expression. This image may lie at the very root of the thought, or it may be a mere incident in the text; in either case it is for Bach the essential element in the words, and he works it out without troubling whether, by so doing, he is really expressing or not the emotional content of the poem.

His idea of a good poet is one who gives the maximum of images that are translatable into sound. We sometimes wonder that he did not weary of the doggerel of Picander, his chief librettist. When, however, we consider the plastic variety of these libretti, we can see at once what attracted Bach to them time after time. Nor does he object to his librettist giving him the same pictures again and again; on the contrary, he reproduces them in tone with ever new delight. We really get the impression that he demanded pictorial opportunities of this kind. He even forgives his librettist when he adds extraneous pictures of his own to the classical text of a chorale-strophe. In the *St John Passion* he cannot dispense with the rending of the curtain and the earthquake at the death of Jesus; he inserts these events in his text, although they do not occur in the fourth Gospel.

The difference between Wagner and Bach becomes more evident in their conceptions of natural events. Wagner conceives nature through his emotions; Bach – in this respect like Berlioz – through his imagination. Bach is not satisfied until he is sure that the hearer actually sees the dust of the whirlwind, the clouds scudding across the sky, the falling leaves, the raging waves. When his poets came to the end of their tether, all they had to do was to bring nature on the scene; they could be sure of satisfying him in this way. This is the explanation of the fact that the secular cantatas are veritable nature-poems.

The great thing, however, is that this nature-painting is always musical. Abt Vogler, the other great master whom Weber placed by the side of Bach, also aimed at tone-painting, but found that though it was very successful with the people, the musicians looked askance at him for it. 'They complained,' he says, 'that I tried to represent on the all-powerful instrument, the organ, natural phenonema such as thunder, earthquakes, collapsing walls, etc.' – and he tells how he succeeded, in the village church of Upsala, not only with crying children and howling dogs, but in making a deaf mute 'feel' the thunder. Bach certainly could not cite such testimonies for *his* painting. However realistic it is, it always keeps within the limits of musical symbolism. Here again the whole expression lies in the theme; it is this that stimulates the conceptual imagination of the hearer.

His tone-painting is never obtrusive. It lasts as long as the occasion that called it forth, but not a moment longer. This perfect moderation, in spite of the great vivacity of the tone-painting, becomes all the more astonishing when we examine his recitative accompaniments. In the *St Matthew Passion*, he gives the most drastic musical expression to every characteristic word in the account of the Passion. But it never delays the story for a moment. The tone-painting merely heightens the plastic impression of the words. . . .

The establishment of a musical language in Bach is not a mere pastime for the aesthetician, but a necessity for the practical musician. It is often impossible to play a work of his in the right tempo, and with the right phrasing and right accent, unless we know the meaning of the motive. The simple 'feeling' does not always suffice. The serious errors that even judicious commentators can commit when, without taking into consideration Bach's musical language as a whole, they try to explain pieces that call for elucidation, may be seen from [Philip] Spitta's remarks upon [two of] the cantatas. There is only one way to avoid falling into the fantastic – a comparative study of all the cantatas. They explain each other. No one can conduct one cantata properly unless he knows them all.

Short explanations may be given to an audience if they are confined to simple hints as to Bach's method of musical characterization. They are objectionable when they are meant to induce the audience to regard the cantata in question as 'modern music'. Unintelligent modernization of Bach is the greatest hindrance to the true understanding of his works.

To the plain man, indeed, many explanations will seem fantastic that are not really so. This, however, is due to Bach himself, whose music is often extraordinarily audacious. Apart from that, there are certain movements in his works the riddle of which will never be fully solved, and the elucidation of which will always be somewhat arbitrary. Very often, however, a musical picture that has been regarded as undecipherable is suddenly explained by an analogous picture that we have come across by hazard in another cantata.

The understanding of Bach's musical language is also valuable for the interpretation of the purely instrumental works. Many pieces in the *Well-tempered Clavichord*, in the violin sonatas, or in the Brandenburg Concertos speak quite definitely to us, as it were, when the meaning of their themes is explained by the text that accompanies similar themes in the cantatas.

Two objections may be raised to the assumption of a complete musical language in Bach – that he occasionally parodied his own works in a really thoughtless way, and that so far as we know he never said anything, either to his pupils or to his sons, with reference to his pictorial purposes. Both objections are unanswerable from the historical standpoint. On the other hand they cannot invalidate the facts as revealed to us by his scores. They only make us ask to what degree Bach was conscious of his musical language being a means of expression peculiar to himself, and the result of profound artistic reflection. But to this question, again, no definite answer is possible, for it is even more difficult to fix upon the border-line between the conscious and the unconscious in the case of Bach than in that of any other genius. His musical language is so clear, and makes so deep an impression, that we cannot but regard it as deliberate. Unlike Wagner, Bach never felt the necessity of explaining his own mental processes either to himself or to others. A psychological common denominator between the two cases will probably never be found.

from J. S. BACH *1908*

Domenico Scarlatti

SACHEVERELL SITWELL

Music can mean anything to anybody (this is the greatest of its prerogatives): but to one person, at least, the music of Scarlatti differs in essentials from all other music of the keyboard. If this, perhaps solitary, opinion may be allowed a hearing the difference lies in that it is inhabited music. The piano sonatas of Beethoven portray the conflicts of the soul; and, on occasion, it may be thought, of a soul more simple than that of Beethoven. By contrast, Chopin is inhabited, but only by himself and his various shades, in poses of gallantry or disillusionment. Perhaps it is the music of his personality more than inhabited music! Delacroix was only right in saying that no person like Chopin had ever existed before, and that everything about him, his music, his appearance, his playing were an integral part of this abnormal presentation. Schumann seems (still to this same solitary opinion) as the artist of the whole romantic age who most nearly achieved reality – reality, in that classical sense of true counterfeit. Poetry is all but transmuted by the heat of the crucible, so that music

becomes an experience in terms of poetry. If the Arabesque of
Schumann is not a walk by the edge of a cornfield, then imagery
is not an art of the senses. The music of Schumann is most essentially inhabited by beings, but seldom by more than one, and never
by more than two. Do we not know enough of Schumann's
character to be certain that this is true?

Mozart, in contrast to this, and in order to return nearer to
Scarlatti, seems to be a composer whose purpose is always mis-
interpreted in his piano music. His works for the piano (for the
piano concertos are a world in themselves which may be preferred
in their entirety to his symphonies) must not be searched for
Tartarean landscapes, or deep resolutions of the will. Apart from
the four great Fantasias, and a few kindred works, it is surely
right to look upon Mozart's piano compositions as his wanderings
into an ideal world. This would, of necessity, be a world of deeper
sensibility than that of Beethoven, lit by a more poetical imagination, and portrayed by his extraordinary faculty for extempore
poetry into distances which lead along new directions upon the
breath of inspiration. The beauty of his second subjects is, surely,
only to be explained by the assumption that they are in the nature
of a poetical extemporization. To take one of the loveliest of all
Mozart's works, the exquisite air which appears in the middle of
the clarinet quintet (first movement), cannot have been, to the
mind at least of a humble poet, anything else except the sudden
afflatus, the inexplicable accession of poetry. If this is proved in
one of the most important of his instrumental works, it is all the
more to be expected in his solitary imaginings, in works in which
we are alone with Mozart and the direct prey, therefore, to his
imagination. But, to tell the truth, the endless beauty of these
apparently simple works is one of the miracles of art. What their
inspiration may have been it is impossible to conceive; and Mozart,
himself, admits this. 'When I am, as it were, completely myself,
entirely alone and of good cheer – say, travelling in a carriage, or
walking after a good meal, or during the night when I cannot
sleep; it is on such occasions that my ideas flow best and most
abundantly. Whence and how they come I know not; nor can I
force them.' It is hopeless to attempt any explanation of these
things. Their purpose, of enchantment, is more easily understood; and surely this was never so well achieved as when Keats

describes himself as 'Kept awake, as if by a tune of Mozart's'. Such should be the haunting effect of these experiences of loveliness, though seldom have they had such a breast to cling to.

Even when Mozart does not touch the sublime heights in the more slight of his piano works, his sense of shape and the filigree delicacy of his ornamentation raise the work on to a level of enchantment. At such moments it is, perhaps, not inappropriate to compare the effects to those of the most graceful stucco decoration. In these, he is the most accomplished of all the workers in rococo, and those who know the achievements of this delicate art in Austria and Southern Germany will admit that to say this is no derogation of Mozart in his lesser works. These arabesques impel admiration by the nice adjustment of their angle. Their trills and flourishes are inimitable – but the music is uninhabited.

If we return, now, to Scarlatti the difference dawns on us immediately. His music is, in comparison, as inhabited as a drawing by George Cruikshank. Perhaps we can define the difference still further by another illustration in poetry. The poetry of Keats and Shelley is unpeopled. The poetry of Alexander Pope, by contrast, is alive with figures. *The Rape of the Lock* is the instant breath of contemporary time. The incredible delicacy of its texture is not torn by the admission of figures into that gossamer world. Nor have those inhabitants any shame of the moment in which they are living: they appear perfectly contented and at ease in their environment. There is nothing of nostalgia or discontentment in them. In Keats and Shelley the age of complaint has already begun. Even in *The Dunciad*, Pope is not so much grumbling at the stupidity of his fellow men as upbraiding them for their ignorance in what he considered, obviously, to be an age of knowledge. It is not, perhaps, invidious to see a similarity between Alexander Pope and Scarlatti. The bustle and stir of their subjects, but, above all, their possession of a caustic and sinister wit, puts them into a division of mind in which we must not expect to find Mozart, or Bach, or Handel, as their companions. Both Alexander Pope and Scarlatti, we may feel sure, preferred the company of those who lived in towns. Pope was, most particularly, the product of London: Scarlatti was, more than all else, the Neapolitan. He had, even, the alert nerves of someone who is used to traffic. No one who has passed his life in the country could have written the music of Scarlatti. He has no time to waste, and makes his points as sharply and as rapidly as a jazz composer. The character of each separate piece is discernible from the start, even if it is the certainty that a surprise is coming. Speaking in terms of the nerves, of the sensibilities, Scarlatti is thinner and more rapid than Haydn; not broad-shouldered, with no peasant blood, honest more from education than from instinct, more dry and caustic in his wit. Haydn, we are told, and we may easily believe it, used to construct little contrivances of fire-irons, of books, of little pieces of furniture, making little houses and scenes out of such imaginary bricks and mortar in order to inspire and amuse himself. But the mind of Scarlatti will have been already stored with incident; he was under no necessity to invent, for his mental processes consisted in the transference of his direct observations into terms of music.

Haydn, in the andante of the *Clock* symphony, provides us with a perfect illustration of his own system. This is a construction as complete in itself as a fairy story. And it takes much less time in the telling than *Cinderella* or *The Sleeping Beauty*. The atmosphere of this piece of music is so finished, or, by extending the word, so furnished, that we might even say the cupboards are full. The cupboards are full, and, as well as the chiming of the different clocks, there is a cage of birds, and a saucer of milk for the cat. But, then, the kitchen is just as likely to drop its domestic tidiness and change into a high, empty room full of nothing but clocks, with tall doors in pairs along the walls, and no notion who may open them and come into the room. But nothing is sinister: it is only that everyone is asleep, leaving the mice to play and the clocks to tick. And so this extraordinary piece comes to an end, and we are left with the sensation of having travelled into the past, but found everyone asleep. The clocks are ticking and the inhabitants may wake again. The illusion of life is given by the very fact of its omission. It is just because the clocks are still ticking that their hearts must be beating and their bodies breathing. The purpose, then, of this visit to deserted rooms is to make a safe departure without waking the inmates, and the accomplishment of this leaves the riddle unanswered. The terrible question has not even been broached. It is, therefore, somewhat in the nature of a dream about dead friends. One is sorry for the dream to end, but glad that it finished without the posing of any awkward questions; and, all the time, that comforting voice which is ever by one's side in a pleasant dream and which is personified in the tone of this music, tells one not to worry and to enjoy it while it lasts.

The *Clock* symphony is the best example of Haydn in that vein in which Dr Burney so admired him. In fact, the nearer he comes to Beethoven, but Dr Burney could not know this, the less strongly does his own character emerge. It is Haydn, who is Haydn, whom we admire: not the Haydn who was the precursor to Beethoven. Of all the composers of his lifetime Dr Burney seems to have most admired Scarlatti and Haydn: it is when they approached each other that he was most content with either. The *Clock* symphony is certainly an instance in which Scarlatti and Haydn are not far removed from each other; but their attack, we have tried to suggest, was of an entirely different nature. We may put further stress upon this by the insistence that their habits of work must have been diametrically opposed. Haydn was in the habit of working for five or six hours of every day of his life. His habits were regular in the extreme, as is proved by the vast mass of his accomplishment. It is certain that he was a person of intensely punctual disposition, sitting down to work every day, at exactly the same hour. We may imagine that his hours of rest were regulated in exactly the same way. No one who appreciates Haydn can think of him finishing a work in the heat and fury of inspiration. His was not the method of Berlioz, who would write nothing for months and then complete everything in a few days. Haydn was a slow worker, a person of steady inspiration, accomplishing his projects at his own deliberate pace. Scarlatti, with his essentially Latin temperament, will have worked more upon the system of Berlioz. But the neat conciseness of his shape, compared with the Babylonian schemes of that unruly genius, did not call for such strenuous exertions on his part. It seems probable that his sonatas were written with extreme rapidity and worked over with meticulous care. And from what we know of other artists with the same disposition of nerves, one may think that he must have written them in batches of several at a time. Many of them represent different aspects, or different solutions, of the same problem, attacked from different angles.

Let us try, then, to build up his temperament in the light of what we know of his music and his surroundings. He was a Latin, a Neapolitan, and more probably a Sicilian. He was a native of the largest town in Italy, and, until he was forty-five years old, if he was not living in Naples he was residing in Rome, which was the capital of the arts. His father [Alessandro Scarlatti] was the most famous musician in Italy; while, at Naples, he was in the midst of the most numerous school of musicians known to history. German music, even in its height of fame, is a mere handful of names compared to the school of Naples. He inherited his talent and brought it to early perfection. Before he was twenty-five years of age he was the finest virtuoso in Italy. We have tried to prove that in Rome and at Naples there was a large society of amateurs and of other artists who were interested in music. Vienna, in the time of Mozart or of Beethoven, was much smaller a town than Naples. It had no tradition of the arts. It was not Italian. Music was to Naples what painting was to Venice: it was the renown and fame of the Southern city.

For twenty years, after this, Scarlatti had the leisure to compose an extraordinary number of pieces for his instrument. A space of twenty years is sufficient time for any artist with energy to accumulate an imposing mass of material. It is as long by itself as the entire working life of Chopin. But, more than that he was an Italian, we must emphasize the point that Scarlatti was a Neapolitan. He portrays for us the animation of a great city; and this is the town where gesture almost takes the place of language. These are not the burghers of Halle or Eisenach: they are inhabitants of a town of classical origin with an active volcano outside their doors. There is seldom a fall of snow, while the heats of summer necessitate the siesta. This, in itself, is an interruption to regular hours. His music represents the workings of the quickest race of brains. And by the very limitations of his art Scarlatti was absolved from wasting his energies on religious themes. This had been the bane of Italian art of all and every description, throughout its history. Its absence, in his music, is one of its delights.

We, then, see him, at forty-five years of age, accepting an appointment which withdrew him altogether from popular fame. The circumstances of this, while they gave him every opportunity of continuing his work, are unrivalled in picturesque improbability. We have endeavoured to show that music, far from being isolated at the Court of Spain, and only represented by his person, was, in actual fact, of daily incidence, and the best thing of its kind procurable by money. During the twenty-five years that he passed in Spain, it is not to be wondered at if he became tinged, to some extent, with the Iberian character. No one can spend a quarter of a century in a foreign land and not be affected by the transplantation. In dealing with a person of Scarlatti's lively intelligence, it would be still more peculiar were Spain to pass over him and leave no marks of its strong and bitter blood. Even today it has more individuality than any land in Europe: in the early part of the eighteenth century it was a world apart and content with itself. That book of fabulous intent, Mme D'Aulnoy's *Voyage en Espagne*, gives us a picture of Spain that we know is not exaggerated, even if it is strange. For Spain will not have changed much between 1660 and 1729; and even if it is true that Mme d'Aulnoy never went there and only compiled her book from the accounts of her daughter and sister, it only doubles the evidence and does not alter the facts. If it be a masterpiece of imagination, let it stand and do not contradict it! But all the circumstances point to its veracity. In any case the authoress of those famous fairy stories can have thought of nothing more fantastic and improbable than the true state of affairs, sixty years later, at the Spanish Court. The names of Farinelli and Egizziello are a perpetual reminder of this, while the addition of Domenico Scarlatti to their company steadies that strangeness with its certainty of touch. The poor, mad Kings and Queens lose something of their pathos by these proofs of their extreme normality and their exquisite taste. João V is shown as more sensible than a dictator who prepares for war, and money given to music is better spent then money gone on battleships. Golden coaches, or silver plate, or palaces built for a single night, all these extravagances have both an argument, and a modern counterpart more easily confuted.

The brief aftermath to Scarlatti's life, when he returned to Naples to die, must have seemed like a return to reason, with the enchantment gone. It is to be hoped, and may be surmised, that he was in circumstances of affluence after so considerable an absence. In all probability he was given a generous pension, for his patrons, Fernando and Barbara, did not die, we must remember, until five years after Scarlatti's return to Naples. In fact they outlived their musician. On the other hand, we are told that Scarlatti was a gambler, that his family was reduced to destitution, and they had to be rescued by the generosity of his old friend Farinelli.

Naples was, by now, a kingdom ruled over by Carlos III, the half-brother of Fernando. His reign may be described as the golden age of Naples. The city flourished, as never before, and great works such as the building of Caserta were undertaken. This project of Roman magnificence, the last work of slaves, was begun, in fact, in 1752, just before the return of Scarlatti to Naples. Carlos III was heir to the Spanish throne, so that the political illusion in which Scarlatti's last years were spent was one of Spanish dominion – historically, the greatest power in Europe. Most of Scarlatti's life had been passed in Spanish service; and, once and for all, there is this last opportunity to emphasize Spain and the two Sicilies as his background. He was the subject of this double-kingdom, just as much as Goya was the subject of Carlos IV or Fernando VII, his contemporary Kings of Spain. It is a vanished kingdom, but it had its existence as surely as the lost lands of Poland or Burgundy.

For the last moment let us listen to those neat and rapid hands. No music, before or since, has been so inhabited by character. And this peculiar talent is only magnified in scope by its seclusion in the haunted precincts of that palace. All normal life, and all the stir and excitement of ordinary mortals, passed into the possession of this ghostly King and his dwarf Queen. The flowering of daily life in that noisy city of the South filled the stillness. For the melancholic silence must be broken, if only by the chiming of musical clocks. When we listen to the music of Domenico Scarlatti we must imagine it interrupted by those exotic tones, and followed by the warblings of Farinelli and Egizziello. The patrons of Scarlatti were more extraordinary phantoms of over-breeding than have ever disturbed naturalist or botanist. This race of ghostly monsters lived in an isolation comparable to the survival of a race of dinosaurs. And they were the gluttons of music. It was their only defence against melancholia.

Such, in short, was the life of this great composer and executant, as we have painted him in his different phases. For all the smallness of his compass he remains one of the most important figures in musical art. There are but few things, in all the arts, done to such perfection and worked to so bewildering a variety out of such simple material. In this respect, it is only possible to compare Domenico Scarlatti with Chopin; and if we long for a less troubled existence we prefer Scarlatti, and find him living in a world, not occupied exclusively by himself and his aspirations and disappointments, but crowded with figures, enlivened with living architecture, lit with tradition, and enlarged, finally, into a land of magical opportunity, where his own skill and poetry were matched as they have seldom been in the annals of chance. It was only a step, or a short sea-voyage, from the magic of his own music to the enchanted palace.

from A BACKGROUND FOR DOMENICO SCARLATTI *1935*

Haydn

H. C. ROBBINS LANDON

At the end of the eighteenth century, shortly before Haydn's seventieth birthday in March 1802, it must have seemed to Europe's music-loving public that never had any composer been so completely popular among all levels of society, so thoroughly understood by his contemporaries and so certain of a place in the history of music. If they could have seen Haydn's position 100 years later, they simply would have refused to believe their eyes and ears. The spectacular rise in Haydn's popularity was only matched by his spectacular eclipse. Schumann, that perspicacious critic, could listen to a Gewandhaus Concert in Leipzig including Haydn's Symphony No 102, and write afterwards that Haydn's music 'has nothing to say to us any more'.

Even accounting for the rise of the Romantic movement, this almost incredible lack of comprehension of Haydn's music thirty or forty years after his death is a phenomenon almost unique in music history. The curious fact is that the message that Haydn had for his contemporaries quite literally did not mean the same thing only a generation later. For instance, the famous F-sharp-major Largo from the late (1796–7) Quartet in D, op. 76, No 5, which for *fin-de-siècle* continental listeners was poetic, rhapsodic and profoundly melancholic, thirty years later was hardly anything more than a pleasant slow movement for the musically inclined, and we find Mendelssohn remarking with some surprise on this very fact. For him it was quite incomprehensible that the older generation could have found this music in any way sad. By the beginning of the twentieth century, Haydn's popularity had reached an all-time low, so that a new biography, by J. C. Hadden, published in 1902, could write of Haydn's quartets that many 'were bald and uninteresting' but that 'at least he wrote in four-part harmony'.

This rejection of Haydn may, in part, be traced directly to Beethoven, whose relationship to Haydn is shown, from many new documents which are coming to light, to have been ambivalent in the extreme, bordering occasionally on the pathological. Beethoven was at great pains to show that he 'never learned anything' from Haydn. And Beethoven's larger-than-life continuation of Haydn's style soon rendered it impossible even for thinking people to see Haydn as anything but a dwarfed and undeveloped version of Beethoven. Haydn, and not as is often supposed Mozart, is Beethoven's musical (if perhaps not spiritual) father; and thus it was that Mozart managed, at least in part, to escape the total lack of comprehension with which Haydn's music was soon greeted. Not that Mozart, during the later part of the nineteenth century, was ever allowed to be spoken of in the same breath as Beethoven. Felix Weingartner, the great German conductor, writing in 1907 about Beethoven, said: 'Much of Haydn, Mozart and Schubert, most of Weber, enjoy an artistic existence only in the light of the imperishable works of this master, but already belong to past history; not true of Beethoven, if we perhaps except some youthful works and *pièces d'occasion.*' It is characteristically ironic that, as Weingartner was writing these lines, he was seeing through the press his critical edition of the first forty Haydn symphonies in Breitkopf and Härtel's new *Gesamtausgabe*.

In the twentieth century various attempts at a Haydn renaissance have been launched – first in conjunction with the new

collected edition just mentioned, then in connection with the
bicentenary in 1932 and then again after the last war. None of
these efforts has been more than temporarily successful: the
Breitkopf and Härtel *Gesamtausgabe* never progressed beyond a
dozen volumes out of a projected 120; the impetus of 1932 was
soon spent; and such an admirable undertaking as Walter Legge's
Haydn Quartet Society, set up to make recordings for H.M.V.,
nearly floundered three times, so that the *Gramophone* was constantly chiding readers not to let down such a worthy project.
The latest attempt at a Haydn renaissance, with which the present
writer has not been unconcerned, cannot be said to have achieved
anything more than a temporary, or local success. Haydn is still
unsatisfactory as a box-office attraction, and we are told that a
recording of even such a major work as the *Nelson Mass* by a
well-known British company has not been successful as far as
sales are concerned. Haydn has now become the one thing which
neither he nor we Haydn scholars could have imagined: a musician's musician. Recent statistics in France and America (we have
no others at our disposal) show that Vivaldi is a far more popular
composer than Haydn. In a sense, there is nothing anyone can do
about this situation: you can lead a horse to water but you cannot
make him drink. Possibly when the complete works of Haydn are
known in their entirety, which will be at the end of this century,
a new phase in the appreciation for, and understanding of, his
music will occur. Until then, the ups and downs of public reaction
to Haydn's music since his death in 1809 must remain one of the
most inexplicable and baffling phenomena in the history of our
musical taste.

from The Listener *1968*[1]

---

[1] Since the original publication of this article the BBC has done fuller
justice than hitherto to Haydn's compositions. *Ed.*

The Nature of Mozart's Genius

A. HYATT KING

If we would understand more of the spirit that gives the finest of
Mozart's compositions their peculiar beauty, we shall find a close
analogy in the spirit of the ancient Greeks, with whose art and life
Mozart has greater affinities than any other composer. Now this
does not mean that to appreciate these things one must be a
learned Hellenist; for on them are based many of the most precious
moral and artistic values of that European civilization in which
everyone can share, whatever his educational background. It is
curious that this analogy has been appreciated only by very few
writers – Warde Fowler, for example, H. F. Amiel, and Schumann.
The last, however, was right only in a limited sense when he
remarked how Greek was the G minor Symphony, and it is not
really helpful to restrict the parallel to this and similar compositions. For there are many other works written by Mozart (particularly his chamber music) in which we meet a far wider range
of emotions corresponding more nearly than this symphony to
those expressed in the art and literature of Athens in the fifth
century B.C. Their two chief qualities were restraint and proportion, which dominate all branches of Greek art, whether a tragedy
of Sophocles, the designs of Ictinus for the Parthenon, an epigram
of Simonides, or vases by masters such as Epictetus or Sotades.
All have the same purity of line and thought. Greek art at its
flowering was the product of a people fully conscious of their own
genius, yet until the time of their decline quite free from over-
bearing egoism; of a people constantly searching after the true
values of human life, with a happy serenity born of self-knowledge, and tempered by a just sense of the sadness and
inscrutability of man's brief destiny. Are not these qualities
prominent in Mozart's personality, as revealed in his letters and
his music, as they are in no other composer?

"You Greeks," said the Egyptian priest in Plato's *Timaeus*,
"are always children: no Greek is ever old." By which he meant
that they were instinct with the generous frankness, the simple
yet ardent seriousness, the sense of wonder and pleasure in experi-

ment which mark the child. Such were certain aspects of Mozart's character. To the end of his life, moreover, he retained a childlike freshness of vision, unclouded by disappointment and worry, which imbues many of his works – for instance, the finale of the String Trio in E flat, K. 563, and the three songs, K. 596, 597, 598, composed for a children's album in January 1791 – with a simplicity quite free from affectation. At the same time Mozart developed as a man who, in the phrase of Simonides, stood 'foursquare without a flaw', which does not, however, imply that his character was faultless, for even genius is human. Rather should those words be referred to the balance of mind and to the perfect control of emotion that find expression in his music, the embodiment of the 'golden mean' to which the Greeks attached so much importance. Far from being passionless, untroubled creatures, they craved an artistic expression that quivered with controlled excitement. It was because they were susceptible to extremes of emotion that they valued the mean so highly, and strove incessantly for restraint and balance. So with Mozart.

Of these qualities there is no finer example than his Quintet for clavier and wind instruments (K. 452). It is significant that he himself expressed a high opinion of it, one of the few pieces of self-criticism that have come down to us. All through it he achieved a triumphant solution of one of the hardest problems in musical construction, that of giving full scope to elements of contrast without sacrificing the essential unity of the work. This profound quintet is serene, unrhetorical music, full of confidence, with spacious but not grandiose melodies, and the ornamentations are a marvellous blend of grace and dignity. But behind its strength and continuity lies a transcendental quality, which never fails to arouse in us emotions that may vary greatly each time we hear it, but are always equally satisfying. This is so with many of his best works. The more limpid and simple they seem, the more subtle and charged with meaning do they reveal themselves on close study. Yet revelation in any complete sense is impossible, for this music, though profoundly lovable, remains utterly impersonal and aloof.

Perhaps it is in Mozart's blending of passion with purity that we may find one of the sources of this paradoxical quality – a blending which, as Warde Fowler pointed out, is so truly Greek.

It is most interesting that Brahms, a romantic composer if ever
there was one, should have highly praised this purity of Mozart
in a letter to Dvořák. It seems to come partly from the formal
precision and economy of the music, and from the ingeniously
varied spacing of the parts, but even more from the absence of
false or exaggerated sentiment. This is connected with the restraint described above, but different elements enter into this question. Naturally it is most readily to be discerned in the operas. A
song like Susanna's 'Deh vieni, non tardar' in *Figaro* is the incarnation of this purity, with its buoyancy, its tenderness, and delicate
truth.

   Another aspect of Mozart's genius, and one that lifts him above
all other musicians, lies in the universality of his music. It was
Plato who first enunciated the truth of the matter in that passage
of his *Symposium* where Socrates maintains that it is the essence of
a truly great poet to be able to write both tragedy and comedy,
types which, for the Greeks, included a wide variety of lyrical
verse. To whom, beside Mozart and Shakespeare, can this canon
be applied? The intensity and style of their dramatic power may
differ, but they are at one in their unique ability to move us profoundly over the whole gamut of human emotions. In Mozart,
the dividing line between tragedy and comedy is unusually fine.
It must also be remembered that all his life he cherished a passionate enthusiasm for *opera seria* (in which he achieved his greatest
success at the age of twenty-three with *Idomeneo*, despite an almost
impossible libretto), and when writing *opera buffa* or *dramma
giososo* he was often carried away by the momentarily tragic aspects
of a character or situation. There are scenes in which we feel Don
Giovanni to be a truly tragic figure, despite their proximity to
the buffoonery of Leporello. So, too, in *Die Zauberflöte* the intense
pity aroused by Pamina's despairing attempt at suicide is not made
incongruous by the antics, just past or to come, of Papageno or
Monostatos. Mozart sweeps us along on a flood of emotion which
derives much of its strength from implied contrast, just as the fool
in *King Lear* makes his master's sufferings all the more poignant
by his ironical jesting.

   In instrumental music Mozart is one of the few spontaneous
humorists who also wrote works of tragic intensity. The wit and
charm of the divertimenti of his twentieth year are coeval with the

sombre power of his Violin Sonata in E minor. In the gay Divertimento in D (K. 334) the element of contrast consists of a profound and gloomy set of variations in the tonic minor. The tragic vein of the String Quintet in G minor is followed very shortly by the riotous parody of contemporary clichés in his *Musikalischer Spass* for horns and string quartet. We feel that Mozart plays with notes quizzically, weaving them into patterns of fantastic grace and elegance, just as in his letters he revels in the swift play of words. Yet it must be emphasized that with Mozart laughter is never far removed from tears and the most moving pathos; it is impossible to foretell exactly what the whole mood of a movement is going to be, though there is rarely any feeling of incongruity.

In this he resembles the Greek dramatist Aristophanes, whose comedies combine a unique blend of airy, ribald wit with moments of affecting sadness, when the grotesque figures suddenly become human, and excite our pity by identifying themselves with the dark fate and suffering of mankind. In his *Lysistrata* there is no feeling of false sentiment when the heroine suddenly turns from scenes of unrestrained license to deliver a great speech on the agony of women in time of war. Mozart was gifted with this power to raise fantasy to the plane of great poetry, increasing his effect by means of that swiftness of thought which has all the elusive qualities to be expected in such impersonal music as his. Shakespeare, too, often contrives the same kind of transition from the ridiculous to the sublime. It would, of course, be absurd to maintain that no artists besides Mozart and Shakespeare have possessed this range of qualities. Many have had two or three of them, but no others have had them all together, or combined deep insight into the emotions of the human heart with the ability to interpret them with truth and conviction in so many forms.

Mozart is sometimes denied a place among the very greatest composers on the ground that he is inferior to Beethoven and others in his capacity for the expression of suffering. It has been maintained that in his G minor Quintet, where the poignant intensity of the earlier movements finds release in a light-hearted finale, he should rather have transformed his emotion into something more noble. But we cannot say dogmatically that this movement was an error or a makeshift. He had no difficulty in solving the problem most successfully in the finale of his Clavier Concerto in C minor, written just before, and in that of the G minor Symphony, written not long after this Quintet. Until 1787, in his thirty-second year, he had not drained the cup of sorrow to the full; only in the next two years did he plumb the depths of suffering and disappointment, and his emotions found their transcendental expression in *Die Zauberflöte*. Here and in some of his late chamber works we meet much of the same tranquility and spirituality that Beethoven expressed in his last quartets and sonatas, but with the difference that Mozart achieved his end without passing through any stage of exaggerated heroics.

Mozart's artistic instinct was never led astray by his emotions. The truest capacity for suffering is not that which flaunts it before the world, or that which represses all sorrow. Rather does a really great man avail himself of the natural right of humanity to obtain some alleviation of his sorrow through his art, but without obtruding it on the world with exaggerated or egotistical sentiment. He will rise superior in the end; he will not make capital out of his emotions or debase them, but will bequeath to posterity a legacy of beauty and inspiration born of his own adversity. Bigness in music is far from being synonymous with greatness, but universality, the power to create both comic and tragic opera, to write religious works whose deep sincerity still moves us, and to enrich in form and feeling the whole range of chamber and orchestral music, is the hallmark of one type of the greatest genius. Mozart achieved all this without ever allowing bitterness to betray his sense of artistic proportion.

Perhaps we may now attempt to define the way in which his manifold qualities gave him his unique place among musicians. The focusing point of them all is his personality, about which his letters and the trustworthy evidence of contemporaries leave us in no doubt. Besides being endowed with exceptional powers of detachment and concentration, in his self-confidence and self-knowledge Mozart must have been an extraordinarily lovable person. Fully conscious of his genius, yet wholly free from arrogance and from condescension towards his friends, he was generous and always ready to help others, though desperately poor himself. He hated humbug and was outspoken, sometimes to the point of truculence, but was free from any touch of boorishness and thoroughly enjoyed the good things of life. The wit and grace of his music and his letters are not incompatible with the brand of coarse schoolboy humour that we find in the latter, for it was common to many people of his time, and probably represented a reaction to the ban placed on most forms of sexual humour by the strong moral influence of the Church. He retained the mind of a poet, never stultified by his brilliant technical gifts or fecundity of invention, and with it a marvellous insight into the human heart, which is the source of the idealization in his music of such fundamentally ordinary people as Susanna, Zerlina and Cherubino. How he detested mere prettiness, and how he reacted to the morally ugly and terrifying things of life, we can tell from the grandeur and ferocity of much of his music in minor keys, such as the Clavier Concertos in D minor and C minor, and from the savage utterances of Figaro.

Mozart's range of emotional sympathies did not preclude him from remaining a normal man in his daily life and behaviour. For many, the satisfying excellence of his music lies in its essential humanity, because we can feel that 'the matter of which the work is made has been, as it were, penetrated and impregnated by an idea with which we associate ourselves. We see something akin to ourselves penetrating and moulding the matter.' As a complement to Roger Fry's words, we may quote a sentence which Gounod wrote about Mozart: 'In very truth, he touches and moves us, we all recognize ourselves in him, and we proclaim that in this he knows human nature well and truly, not only in its different passions, but in the variety of form and character which they may affect."

from MOZART IN RETROSPECT *1955*

E

Beethoven

ERNEST WALKER

'The greatest genius,' Emerson has said, 'is the most indebted man'; and though the aphorism is not one that can be altogether blindly accepted, it emphasizes a great truth that is too often forgotten by those who confuse real originality with mere newness. The sources of Beethoven's style are, owing to purely historical circumstances, less complex than the sources of the styles of most later composers: but nevertheless it is absurd to consider him as independent of his great predecessors. His chief and almost his only definite debts were due to Haydn and Mozart, more especially the latter, as Haydn's greatest works date from years when Beethoven was rapidly shaking off his influence: both of them had given him lessons, and indeed their spirit was in the air to the practical exclusion of all other at the time when the younger genius was assimilating his material. All through Beethoven's life he looked at instrumental music in the light of the general structural principles which Haydn and Mozart had developed, and however much he broadened and bent them, the thread of connection is always there: and, quite apart from form, we see on every page of the early work the influence of their technical methods. Of other composers the traces are much slighter: the influence of Handel and Gluck is practically non-existent, though there are passing glimpses of the models of second-rate people like Hummel in some of the piano pieces. *Fidelio* owes, however, a good deal to Cherubini, for whose operas Beethoven had an especial admiration, often praising their librettos for their high ethical tone as contrasted with the subjects of most stage works: and the general style of the music is certainly more akin to *Les deux journées* than to any opera of Mozart – of the less important parts of the music, that is to say, as the great parts are well above Cherubini's head. As regards Bach, Beethoven no doubt knew familiarly all the comparatively small portion of Bach's music that was available before the days of the Bach-Gesellschaft edition: but the direct influences are very slight. Purely contrapuntal texture was not Beethoven's natural medium of expression: and the few fugues

that he did write owe very little to Bach's methods. But nevertheless the extreme closeness of texture and organic subtlety of most
of Beethoven's writing, though paralleled to some extent in
Haydn and still more in Mozart, is yet more akin in essence to
Bach than to either of the later models: and whether consciously
or not, the great works of Beethoven represent in a very definite
and important sense a return to Bach in their entire disregard of
any considerations of immediate popularity. Bach, from year to
year, poured out in the course of his regular duties an enormous
mass of masterpieces in apparently quite comfortable acquiescence
in the fact that there was no obvious chance of their being ever
known beyond the most limited circle: and Beethoven, if not so
calmly self-centred, certainly never troubled (in his serious
work) to satisfy anybody but himself, and when told that his new
quartets did not please, could simply remark 'they will please some
day' – a sentence that it is rather difficult to imagine on the lips of
Haydn or Mozart. Not, of course, that Haydn or Mozart were, as
it is foolish in the fashion of today to imagine, in any sense 'superseded' by Beethoven: they were colossal geniuses living, through
no fault of their own, under conditions somewhat more artificial
than those under which Bach and Beethoven worked. And we
should not forget that these conditions, though they produced an
enormous mass of mere stilted 'Conversations-musik' produced
also in the masterpieces of Haydn and Mozart a sort of wonderful,
great, happy childlikeness that music has known neither before
nor since: the *Creation* and *Don Giovanni* contain something which,
after all, Beethoven, with the whole of his immense range, could
not carry on. . . .

No doubt the many thick volumes of Beethoven's complete
works contain a considerable mass of material which the music
lover can well afford to disregard: indeed, compared with many
of the great composers, and especially with Bach and Brahms, the
other two chief landmarks in the music of the last two centuries,
his output is distinctly unequal. There are a good many things of
various shapes and sizes – all quite unknown to the concert-goer
of today – which he seems to have turned out unconcernedly in
odd moments without any sort of really artistic impulse: in a sense,
indeed, enormously self-critical as he usually was, his self criticism
took occasional holidays. No musician who ever lived had a more

supreme feeling for organic structure, yet he could pen, and publish separately, for his own concertos, cadenzas which are mere incoherent meanderings, that no modern pianist with a real reverence for the rest of the works would venture to perform. But, after all, this comes to very little: no one thinks, let us say, Milton superior to Shakespeare merely because the latter left a larger refuse heap behind him. It is the business of the historical critic to set down everything without favour: but a great man must be judged by his greatness.

And before the greatness of the great works of Beethoven criticism is dumb. Like all products of supreme genius in every age and style, they are independent of historical limitations: other things change and grow old, but they endure. All kinds of performers, from the rigid dullard to the incoherent sentimentalist, can do their worst on them: but they remain with all their strength and beauty undiminished and inexhaustible, and the man who has been probably the noblest personal influence ever known among executants can modestly say, in his seventieth year, that he thinks he is just beginning to understand them. And the more we study the great music of Beethoven or anyone else, the more do we recognize the impossibility of 'describing' anything but the mere shell. It has no 'meaning', it is simply itself: and great art is something in connection with which language, which after all is only one of the media for the expression of thought, is both inadequate and irrelevant. We may throw out vague adjectives: but the essence is far too deep and subtle to fix in this clumsy way. Still, beyond our attempts at analysis of externals, it is all we can do: but our last word must be to send readers to the music itself. To talk about what we do not know is a singularly futile proceeding: our business, if we wish to try to go ever so little on the way to understand Beethoven, is to read or perform or hear his works, remembering always that, for everyone who claims to be a musician, to reverence the great composers and to keep oneself artistically alive are the first and last commandments.

from BEETHOVEN *1905*

"Beethoven was lacking in aesthetic cultivation and feeling for beauty." *Louis Spohr.*

"The extravagances of Beethoven's genius have reached the *ne plus ultra* in the Seventh Symphony, and he is quite ripe for the madhouse." *Carl Maria von Weber.*

Schubert

MAURICE J. E. BROWN

To appreciate Schubert's achievement as an artist, that is, to view his work as a whole and estimate his originality, his workmanship and his range, and do so with a fresh and uninfluenced mind, is today difficult to the point of impossibility. So powerfully original a genius as his produced an ardent and adoring following, impatient of criticism; but it also provoked misunderstanding, misguided interpretation, and even hostility. The years following his posthumous fame abounded in these mixed emotions and very able spokesmen voiced them. Today, the judgements of the middle and late nineteenth-century critics on Schubert are accepted by the majority of music lovers, for, preserved in books and periodicals, these judgements have determined the twentieth century's approach to his music. To reach a portrait of the essential artist behind this firmly entrenched mass of mixed commentary is therefore impossible, for no one can rid his mind completely of it. But some of it must go – it genuinely obstructs a vision of the true Schubert.

It is difficult to keep out of one's words a note of protest in the clearing away of obstructions; but while, it is hoped, the protest will not grow shrill, one has to risk the accusation that a defensive note is unnecessary for Schubert's greatness, that he needs no protest. This is hardly true. No Schubert lover wishes his composer acclaimed for doubtful virtues or from dubious standpoints. Nor, on the other hand, can he leave ill-considered detractions unchallenged. Only from those who view his work steadily, and view it whole, can informed judgements be expected or acceptable. Otherwise distortions of the man and his music will continue to be repeated without challenge.

There is, first, the question of Schubert's 'education' or 'culture'. The point interested Vincent d'Indy and he wrote:

> Schubert must be considered as the type of genius without culture. In forms where a plan is indispensable his works are very unequal, not to say utterly defective.

And to this judgement of a minor French composer may be added that of a similar English one, Hubert Parry:

> Schubert is conspicuous among great composers for the insufficiency of his musical education. His extraordinary gifts and his passion for composing were from the first allowed to luxuriate untrained. He had no great talent for self-criticism, and the least possible feeling for abstract design, and balance and order.

One tries to read these passages patiently and avoid brushing them aside with a word, but they are too widely heeded to be so peremptorily dismissed. But what do d'Indy and Parry mean by 'culture', 'education' and 'training'? They were actually, whether aware of it or not, taking over the critical outlook of the previous generation, which had dubbed Schubert a 'natural' musician, 'untaught, unschool'd', who sang 'as the birds sing', and so forth, because his phenomenal genius and fertility were incomprehensible. But to believe that Schubert had no musical training, and to base arguments upon it, is simply false: it ignores the facts. His education, both general and musical, was as thorough, as prolonged and as practical as that of any of the composers whom Parry had in mind. For five years he attended the chief boarding-school in Vienna, one, if not under the direct patronage of the court, at least very closely attached to it. His music teachers were accomplished musicians and one of them, Antonio Salieri, internationally renowned. His friends were poets, painters and composers. Schubert, it is true, knew only Vienna: but what rival, in the world of music, had his city amongst the cities of Europe?

Both Parry and d'Indy in their remarks on balance and form are voicing the views of their day, a day in which any departure from Beethoven's and Mendelssohn's methods with sonata-form were looked upon almost as a heresy: a viewpoint which to us is no longer tenable. It is Schubert's chief glory that he could be con

temporary with a dominating figure like Beethoven, without
slavishly imitating him. To be fair to Schubert, and these detractors, it is easy to name many of his mature works in all of which a
'plan is indispensable' and which display that plan, and which are
neither unequal, nor in any way defective: the 'Unfinished' Symphony, the String Quartet in A minor, the last Sonata, in B flat
major.

But quite apart from these tentative answers to such judgements
on Schubert's 'culture', there is a third, devastating one. Genius
is so powerful a factor in these matters, that other factors are, by
comparison, negligible. Even if it were true that Schubert is a
type of 'genius-without-culture', then that state is all-conquering,
and 'talent-with-culture', even if the culture be gathered from the
finest flower of the world's scholarship, droops and fails. If
musical genius, without plan, or the least feeling for abstract
order, can produce the D minor String Quartet, or the String
Quintet in C major, then d'Indy's criteria are false ones, and we,
and our judgements, are wrong.

The reason why Schubert is criticized on the grounds that his
movements lack an organically planned structure, lies possibly in
his approach to the composing of music. He wished to feel
intensely, and to express to the utmost of his powers, the present
moment in his music: not for its significance as a link with what
has gone and what is to come, but for its momentary effect as
sound, as pleasure for the listener. This is not to say for one
moment that he was indifferent to the structural necessities of
sonata-form, in fact the contrary has been urged where his purely
transitional passages are concerned; but drive and cohesion – the
achievement of which was second nature with Mozart and Beethoven – are not Schubert's first consideration. His invention flows
strongly; his themes and episodes and figuration are unified by it,
they are not a succession of poetic notions, nor does he simply
graft a series of intensely felt miniatures cleverly on to each
other. . . .

His methods of work were not understood, and certainly not
correctly presented by early biographers; as a result not very
serious consideration has been given to Schubert as a craftsman.
In those early biographies, Kreissle's, Grove's, Reissmann's,
emphasis was laid on the more sensational aspect – his speed of

working: a string quartet in a week, a symphony in less than a
month, seven songs in one day, and so forth; and these are facts,
of course, except that they give the extent of his fair copies of the
particular compositions, and we do not know any of the preliminary work on them. But the reader is only too prone to assume
that such *speed* of production must be attended by *carelessness* of
production. In this connection Parry can be quoted again:

> As a rule this speed of production was almost a necessary
> condition of Schubert's work in all branches of art. He had no
> taste for the patient balancing, considering and re-writing again
> and again, which was characteristic of Beethoven.

More will be said later on about Schubert's re-writing again and
again; here, it is enough to say that, when discussing genius, no
hard and fast rules can apply. We know today very much more
about Schubert's procedures, and his work, than did the biographers of the nineteenth century. The new attitude began with
Eusebius Mandyczewski in the 1890s, when every available song-
manuscript of the composer's was scrutinized and correlated and
edited for the ten-song volumes of the 'Gesamtausgabe'. Mandyczewski was staggered to find how many manuscripts often went
to the making of one song: two, three, even four versions were
made by Schubert in his search for the ideal setting. We know of
yet more of these manuscript preparations than Mandyczewski
did, and it is a fairly sound surmise that Schubert sketched all his
major works, and most of his minor ones, too, and did so throughout his life. Sometimes, in a burst of inspired writing, the sketch
needed no radical revision, and so we have those hastily written
songs like 'Waldesnacht' of December 1820. But it is also obvious
that other song manuscripts, for instance, 'Der Leiermann' at the
close of the *Winterreise*, are beautifully copied from a sketch no
longer extant. For a number of Schubert's compositions we
possess the finished work and the preparatory sketch, or sketches;
those for the Piano Trio in E flat and the 'Unfinished' Symphony
provide inexhaustible interest to a student. The sketches for the
Symphony in D, of 1818, enable us to generalize a little on Schubert's methods with instrumental composition. As with his songs,
he starts with a melody: ideas of accompaniment are sketched
here and there, sometimes quite fully. Occasionally he will go

back and insert the introductory bars. If he decides that, for the sake of balance or amplitude, a few bars must be inserted into music already written down, connecting signs are clearly marked over the insertion and its ultimate place in the sketch. These are 'aides-memoires' for his own benefit.

'His sketches,' writes Gerald Abraham, 'are generally short-hand memoranda on a large scale, not germinal ideas to be watered with blood and tears like Beethoven's'; and while this is in the main true it must be pointed out that Beethoven's sketches do not, like Schubert's, tell the whole story; themes and transitions caused Beethoven to shed his blood and tears, but it is obvious that when these difficulties were overcome, he found large tracts of his movements rising as spontaneously and easily to his pen as ever Schubert did. Parry does not mention this fact.

When Schubert's melodic phrases begin to germinate, and ideas grow rapidly in his mind, his writing degenerates to a scribble – but never to illegibility. His mental excitement is obvious in the shaky handwriting. The difficulty which rises, when this kind of composition reaches its perfect expression in his finished work, is that of our intellectual apprehension. When he is intellectually on fire, so much arises in his mind and goes down on to paper at once, that it is impossible to apprehend the creative process: one gratefully accepts the result, but is left with a feeling that the process has elements almost of the supernatural in it. This explains why his friends attributed 'clairvoyance' to his methods, which is an explanation untenable today. In the last resort genius evades analysis, and one is thankful that it is so.

With later instrumental work Schubert's facility is astonishing and the pros and cons of what he intended to set down must have been debated and settled in his mind with hardly any delay. Even then afterthoughts refined and improved his initial ideas. In the manuscript of the Sonata in A minor of 1823 the episode immediately following the announcement of the main theme was revised and altered after its re-appearance in the recapitulation had shown Schubert a better way with it. The change he made in the subject of the 'Allegro ma non troppo' of the C major Symphony of 1828 is well known, but, for all that it is so familiar it is an extraordinary modification; being made after the whole movement was written, it entailed literally hundreds of revisions to the score. . . .

Schubert's utter self-devotion to his genius made him abandon all regular methods of earning a living; it was not to spend his days in Bohemian idleness or conviviality, but to devote himself solely to the hard work of learning his craft as a composer. His decision makes the charge of 'dilettante', sometimes levelled at him, a preposterous accusation. This is how such an accusation was worded in the *Edinburgh Review* of October 1883:

> His attitude towards the art was throughout his life that of a very gifted amateur, who wants art just as far as he can get enjoyment out of it, and turns away at the point where hard work begins.

It is hard to refute this with patience. Josef Hüttenbrenner was probably telling the truth when he reported that the easy way of earning money by giving lessons was refused by Schubert who said that he would rather eat dry bread than do so, for lessons would interrupt the tireless application to his musical work, and deflect his energies. He never swerved from his high ideals; even though he was not entirely aware of the greatness and force of his own genius, he never, in order to earn a living, descended to the easy production of inferior, catch-penny work, nor to the undertaking of regular hack-work, for that would have prevented the total dedication to his art. Anything less like the amateur, the dilettante, or the idling Bohemian of the arts can hardly be imagined. He was, and made himself so by hard work, the professional composer *par excellence*.

It might perhaps be a fitting conclusion to this chapter on Schubert's art, to consider in a brief paragraph what not to look for in Schubert. The very elements which many music lovers find most congenial are either absent altogether in his music, or only briefly encountered: wit, understatement, sophistication, picturesqueness, delicacy, bravura. These attractive qualities must be sought elsewhere, in the songs and piano pieces and orchestra suites of other men. Schubert's song-texts are neither erotic nor cynical. His expression is full-blooded, personal, extravagant, and the nearest he gets to humour, as Richard Capell has said, is good humour; but it is not an urbane expression, nor an introverted one, and it is the power already spoken of, by which his music achieves sublimity, and radiates a 'light that never was on sea or land', that raises him above the level of lesser composers who are otherwise almost his equals in melodic charm and the affectionate spirit.

from SCHUBERT: A CRITICAL BIOGRAPHY *1958*

Chopin

J. CUTHBERT HADDEN

There is no style of music that is better known to the musician and amateur than that of Chopin. Yet when one sits down to write of it, to try to analyse it, to say exactly what are its essential characteristics, to what it owes its peculiar fascination, it is then that one feels the inadequacy of the language. True, the grammarian might go through it, classify all its progressions, and label all its chords. There is no more reason why this analytical process should not be possible with Chopin's music than with Bach's or Mendelssohn's. But the result of such a process would be mainly a negative one. It would show that Chopin was not a great master of form in the larger sense, not a skilled contrapuntist, not a deep thinker with a 'message'. It would show, indeed, that he was a master of melody and an innovator in harmony, but it would help us not a whit to understand the qualities which make him unique. His spirit is 'too volatile for our clumsy alembics, too intangible for our concrete methods of investigation. It eludes our glance, it vanishes at our touch, it mocks with a foregone failure all our efforts at description or analysis.'

To some who know it only superficially it may seem easy enough to characterize the music of Chopin in general terms. Its extraordinary beauty and finish are perhaps the leading qualities. One thinks instinctively of Tennyson – the Tennyson of *The Princess*, in which we have the best words best placed and that curious felicity of style which strikes us instantly and without cavil as the perfection of art. 'Load every rift with ore' was the advice which Keats gave to Shelley. In Chopin it is as if every rift had been consciously loaded with ore. Not a single bar seems to be wanting, not a single bar seems to be redundant. There is no commonplace, nothing stale, nothing hackneyed, nothing vulgar. The perfection of form, the complexity of figure, the delicate elaboration of ornament, the rich harmonic colouring, the fine polish of phrase, the winning melody, the keen vital quality of passion, the grace and the tenderness – these at least can be pointed out in terms of everyday vocabulary. I have mentioned Keats and Shelley. In the music of Chopin there is something of the spirit of both. Chopin's world, like Shelley's, is a region 'where music and moonlight and feeling are one' – a fairy realm where nothing seems familiar. Both look upon a night of 'cloudness climes and starry skies'. The warmth, the spirituality, the colour of the romance spirit is in the one as in the other. We note the ethereal grace of both, the beautiful images, the exquisite, if sometimes far-drawn fancies. Like Keats, too, Chopin often sees:

Charmed magic casements, opening on the foam
Of perilous seas, in faëry lands forlorn.

His philosophy is of the beautiful, as is Keats'; and while he 'lingers by the river's edge to catch the song of reeds, his gaze is oftener fixed on the quiring planets'. He is nature's 'most exquisite sounding-board, and vibrates to her with intensity, colour and vivacity that have no parallel'. A whole volume might be written about Chopin the composer. The essence of the matter is here. Chopin is pure emotion. 'Make me the lyre,' he might have prayed the spirit of Poesy. His music is all expressive of moods, of phases of feeling, now strenuous, now morbid, now tender, now simply tricksy. There is nothing of Bach's calm dignity or Beethoven's titanic energy; you find no traces of intellectual wrestling, of thoughts too deep for tears; you find instead tears that are, perhaps, a little too facile, like the tears of women, the cause not always commensurate with their copiousness. There is gaiety, yearning, pathos, but nothing that even touches sublimity, little that stirs one to the healthful activity that is the true life of man. Chopin's music is, first and last, emotion surcharged, not intellectualized, not finding its legitimate development in action. As with Chopin the player, so with Chopin the composer: he stands alone. He is the one master *sui generis*, a genius for whom the musical critic and historian has no pigeon-hole in his bureau of 'classified' composers. His art ended with him. As he sprang from no existing 'school', so he founded no school. It is this absolutely unique quality of his music which has preserved him so effectively against the flattery of imitation. His work is entirely beyond the reach of the imitator. Its charm is so wholly personal to himself that only another Chopin, like in all things – in temperament, in bias, in environment, in emotion, in experience – could hope to reproduce it. 'None but himself could be his parallel.' Followers he no doubt has had. But the follower can at best copy only the method, and Chopin had practically no method. What he had was a manner. . . .

It is a subject of remark with all writers on Chopin that he never once attempted the choral composition and such of the larger forms of his art as the Symphony, the Overture, and the Opera. With some this is regarded as a reproach. It is really no reproach. Chopin knew his own *métier* and he stuck to it. Shelley once said that is was as vain to ask for human interest in his poems as to seek to buy a leg of mutton in a gin-shop. It is all but certain that as a composer of opera, Chopin would have been a total failure; it is entirely certain that if he had attempted the Symphony he would have altogether overstepped the bounds of his genius. He was no 'mighty-mouthed inventor of harmonies'. His genius was essentially lyric – elegiac, not epic, nor even truly dramatic. As his character was deficient in virility, so his muse must have broken down on a big undertaking. Technique aside, he lacked that power of concentrated effort, that sustaining quality, which must be the possession of the composer who would successfully work our primary ideas to their logical and inevitable ending on a large scale. His thoughts were excellent, and his original ideas in the way of themes were excellent, but they depended greatly upon the clothing given them on the keyboard and on the peculiar genius of the instrument. They could never have been heard to advantage in an orchestral dress. The delicate embroideries, the broken arpeggios and scale passages, are all quite unsuited to orchestral work and totally unfitted for orchestral treatment. . . . He was a composer for the piano and for the piano alone. His style is suited to it and to no other instrument whatever. He cannot be 'arranged', as most of the great masters, from Handel to

Wagner, have been 'arranged'. Divorce him from the keyboard and you rob him of his native tongue. It is as if Paganini had been set to play the oboe or the French horn. [Anton] Rubinstein said finely: 'The piano bard, the piano rhapsodist, the piano mind, the piano soul is Chopin. Tragic, romantic, lyric, heroic, dramatic, fantastic, soulful, sweet, dreamy, brilliant, grand, simple: all possible expressions are found in his compositions, and all are sung by him upon his instrument.' In a lesser man this oneness of theme would have led to monotony: in him it led to concentration of the very highest order. He scaled no Alpine heights of art. He worked in a small field, as Edvard Grieg has worked. As we see in Grieg, so we see in him – a personality graceful without strength, romantic without the sense of tragedy, highly dowered with all gentle qualities of nature, but lacking in the more virile powers, in breadth of vision, in epic magnanimity, in massive force. We may not call him a 'great' composer: we cannot deny his claim to genius. The great composers went their way; Chopin went his. He lived his life, gave what was in him, and died with a name destined, like the name of Mary Stuart, to exert over unborn generations a witchery and a charm unique in the history of his art.

from CHOPIN *1903*

"The entire works of Chopin present a motley surface of ranting hyperbole and excruciating cacophony." *The Musical World*.

Berlioz

AARON COPLAND

Berlioz is the archetype of artist who needs periodic re-appraisal by each epoch. His own period couldn't possibly have seen him as we do. To his own time Berlioz was an intransigent radical; to us he seems, at times, almost quaint. Wystan Auden once wrote: 'Whoever wants to know the nineteenth century must know Berlioz.' True enough, he was an embodiment of his time, and because of that I can't think of another composer of the past century I should have more wanted to meet. And yet, enmeshed in his personality are throwbacks to an earlier time; these tend to temper and equivocate the impression he makes of the typical nineteenth-century artist.

His biographer, Jacques Barzun, claims that one rarely finds a discussion of Berlioz 'which does not very quickly lose itself in biographical detail'. Berlioz is himself partly responsible for this because he wrote so engagingly about his life. Moreover, there is the fabulous life itself: the tireless activity as composer, critic and conductor; the success story of the country doctor's son who arrives unknown in the big city (Paris) to study music and ends up, after several tries, with the Prix de Rome; the distracted and distracting love affairs; the indebtedness due to the hiring of large orchestras to introduce his works; the fights, the friends (Chopin, Liszt, De Vigny, Hugo), the triumphal trips abroad, the articles in the *Journal du Débat,* the *Mémoires,* and the bitter experience of his last years. No wonder that in the midst of all this the music itself is sometimes lost sight of.

Admirers and detractors alike recognize that we are living in a period of Berlioz revival. Formerly his reputation rested upon a few works that remained in the orchestral repertoire: principally the *Symphonie fantastique* and some of the overtures. Then came repeated hearings of *Harold in Italy, Romeo and Juliet,* and the *Damnation of Faust.* Recordings have made *L'Enfance du Christ* and *The Trojans* familiar; even the *Nuits d'Été* are now sung. Perhaps before long we may hope to hear unknown works like the *Song of the Railroads* (1846) or *Sara the Bather* (1834).

What explains this recent concern with the Berlioz *oeuvre?* My own theory is that something about his music strikes us as curiously right for our own time. There is something about the quality of emotion in his music – the feeling of romanticism classically controlled – that reflects one aspect of present-day sensibility. This is allied with another startling quality: his ability to appear at one and the same time both remote in time and then suddenly amazingly contemporary. Berlioz possessed a Stendhalian capacity for projecting himself into the future, as if he had premonitions of the path music would take. By comparison, Wagner, in spite of all the hoopla surrounding his 'music of the future', was really occupied with the task of creating the music of his own period. And yet, by the irony of musical history, Berlioz must have seemed old-fashioned to Wagner in the 1860s.

By the end of the century, however, it was clear that the French composer had left a strong imprint on the composers who followed after him. A study of *Harold in Italy* will uncover reminders of the work of at least a dozen late-nineteenth-century composers – Strauss, Mahler, Mussorgsky, Rimsky-Korsakov, Grieg, Smetana, Verdi, Tchaikovsky, Saint-Saëns, Franck, Fauré. (Nor should we forget the impact he had on his own contemporaries, Liszt and Wagner.) How original it was in 1834 to give the role of protagonist to a solo instrument – in this case the viola – and create, not a concerto for the instrument, but a kind of obbligato role for which I can think of no precedent. The line from *Harold* to *Don Quixote* as Strauss drew him is unmistakable. The second movement of *Harold in Italy* has striking similarities to the monastic cell music in *Boris Godunov*, with all of Mussorgsky's power of suggestibility. Indeed, the history of nineteenth-century Russian music is unthinkable without Berlioz. Stravinsky says that he was brought up on his music, that it was played in the St Petersburg of his student years as much as it has ever been played anywhere. Even the Berlioz songs, now comparatively neglected, were models for Massenet and Fauré to imitate. Nor is it fanciful to imagine a suggestion of the later Schoenberg in the eight-note chromatic theme that introduces the 'Evocation' scene from the *Damnation of Faust*.

When I was a student, Berlioz was spoken of as if he were a kind of Beethoven *manqué*. This attempted analogy missed the point: Beethoven's nature was profoundly dramatic, of course, but the essence of Berlioz is that of the *theatrical* personality. I once tried to define this difference in relation to Mahler – who, by the way, bears a distinct resemblance to Berlioz in more than one respect – by saying that 'the difference between Beethoven and Mahler is the difference between watching a great man walk down the street and watching a great actor act the part of a great man walking down the street'. Berlioz himself touched on this difference in a letter to Wagner when he wrote: 'I can only paint the moon when I see her at the bottom of a well.' Robert Schumann must have had a similar idea when he said: 'Berlioz, although he often conducts himself as madly as an Indian fakir, is quite as sincere as Haydn, when, with his modest air, he offers us a cherry blossom.' This inborn theatricality is a matter of temperament, not a matter of insincerity. It is allied with a love for the grand gesture, the naïve-heroic, the theatric-religious. (In recent years Honegger and Messiaen have continued this tradition in French music.) With Berlioz we seem to be watching the artist watching himself create rather than the creator in the act, pure and simple. This is different in kind from the picturesqueness of Beethoven's 'storm' in the 'Pastoral' Symphony. Berlioz was undoubtedly influenced by Beethoven's evocation of nature, but his special genius led to the introduction of what amounted to a new genre -- the theatric-symphonic, and there was nothing tentative about the introduction.

The fact that Berlioz was French rather than German makes much of the difference. Debussy said that Berlioz had no luck, that he was beyond the musical intelligence of his contemporaries and beyond the technical capacities of the performing musicians of his time. But think of the colossal bad luck to have been born in a century when music itself belonged, so to speak, to the Germans. There was something inherently tragic in his situation – the solitariness and uniqueness of his appearance in France. Even the French themselves, as Robert Collet makes clear, had considerable trouble in fitting Berlioz into their ideas of what a French composer should be. In a sense he belonged everywhere and nowhere, which may or may not explain the universality of his appeal. In spite of Berlioz's passionate regard for the music of Beethoven and Weber and Gluck, it is the non-German concept of his music that gives it much of its originality.

This can perhaps be most clearly observed in his writing for orchestra. Even his earliest critics admitted his brilliance as orchestrator. But they would hardly have guessed that a century later we would continue to be impressed by Berlioz's virtuoso handling of an orchestra. It is no exaggeration to say that Berlioz invented the modern orchestra. Up to his time most composers wrote for the orchestra as if it were an enlarged string quintet –

none before him had envisaged the blending of orchestral instruments in such a way as to produce new combinations of sonorities. In Bach and Mozart a flute or a bassoon always sounds like a flute or a bassoon; with Berlioz they are given, along with their own special quality, a certain ambiguity of timbre that introduces an element of orchestral magic as a contemporary composer would understand it. The brilliance of his orchestration comes partly by way of his instinctual writing for the instruments in their most grateful registers and partly by way of his blending of instruments rather than merely keeping them out of each other's way. Add to this an incredible daring in forcing instrumentalists to play better than they knew they could play. He paid the price of his daring, no doubt, in hearing his music inadequately performed. But imagine the excitement of hearing in one's inner ear sonorities that had never before been set down on paper. It is the sheen and sparkle, the subtle calculation of these masterly scores that convince me that Berlioz was more, much more, than the starry-eyed romantic of the history books. . . .

Apart from his orchestral know-how there is hardly a phase of his music that has not been subjected to criticism. His harmonic sense is said to be faulty – that's the reproach most frequently heard – his structure too dependent on extra-musical connotations, his melodic line disappointedly old-fashioned. These oft-repeated strictures are now due for revision. Any clumsiness in the handling of the harmonic progressions should be viewed in the light of our extended notions of right and wrong in harmonic procedures. The Berlioz harmony admittedly is sometimes stiff and plain, but is it so awkward as to disturb one's overall enjoyment? That always has seemed an exaggerated claim to me. His formal sense is unconventional – refreshingly so, I would say, for even when he lacks the inevitability of a Beethoven, one senses that he is finding his own solutions arrived at from his own premises. More often than not these are unexpected and surprising. The reproach concerning his melodic writing has some basis in fact, especially for the present-day listener. Berlioz depends upon the long-breathed line and the unconventional phrase length to sustain interest, rather than the striking interval or pregnant motive. His loveliest melodies give off a certain daguerrotype charm, redolent of another day. This must have been true even at the time he penned them. Looked at from this angle they lend his music a quite special *ambiance*, as if they came from a country not to be found on any map.

Let us concede, for the sake of argument, that the weaknesses are there. The fact remains that, whenever a composer is adjudged worthy to stand with the masters, a remarkable willingness to overlook what were formerly considered to be serious weaknesses is apparent. The weaknesses remain, but public opinion tacitly agrees to accept them for the sake of the good qualities – and I consider that public opinion does right. My prognostication is that we shall, in future, be hearing less and less of Berlioz's weaknesses and more and more of his strengths.

For I repeat that there is something strangely right about Berlioz for our time. The French historian Paul Landormy put my meaning well when he wrote: "His art has an objective character by comparison with the subjectivity of a Beethoven or a Wagner. All the creatures that he created in his imagination detach themselves from him, take on independent life, even if they are only an image of himself. The Germans, on the contrary, have a tendency to fuse the entire universe with their interior life. Berlioz is essentially a Latin artist." It is the objective handling of romantic elements that makes Berlioz an especially sympathetic figure in our own time. That and our clear perception of his musical audacity. For he is clearly one of the boldest creators that ever practised the art of musical composition.

An aura of something larger than life-size hangs about his name. After hearing a Berlioz concert Heinrich Heine wrote: 'Here is a wing-beat that reveals no ordinary song-bird, it is a colossal nightingale, a lark as big as an eagle, such as must have existed in the primeval world.'

from COPLAND ON MUSIC *1961*

"M. Berlioz is bizarre and ill-ordered, because he lacks inspiration and knowledge; he is violent, because he has no good reasons to offer; he wishes to stun us, because he does not know how to charm us. . . . There is nothing in these strange compositions but noise, disorder, a sickly and sterile exaltation. He gasps, he prances, he fidgets, he behaves like a demon disinherited from divine grace who wants to scale the heavens by force of pride and will." *P. Scudo.*

Mendelssohn's Engrossing Pursuits

GEORGE GROVE

No musician – unless perhaps it were Leonardo da Vinci – and he was only a musician in a limited sense – certainly no great composer, ever had so many pursuits as Mendelssohn. Mozart drew, and wrote capital letters, Berlioz and Weber also wrote good letters, Beethoven was a great walker and intense lover of nature, Cherubini was a botanist and a passionate card-player, but none of them approached Mendelssohn in the number and variety of his occupations. Both billiards and chess he played with ardour to the end of his life, and in both he excelled. When a lad he was devoted to gymnastics; later on he rode much, swam more, and danced whenever he had the opportunity. Cards and skating were almost the only diversions he did not care for. But then these were diversions. There were two pursuits which almost do rank as work – drawing and letter-writing. Drawing with him was more like a professional avocation than an amusement. The quantity of his sketches and drawings preserved is very large. They begin with the Swiss journey of 1822, on which he took twenty-seven large ones, all very carefully finished, and all dated, sometimes two in one day. The Scotch and Italian tours are both fully illustrated, and so they go on year by year till his last journey into Switzerland in 1847, of which fourteen large highly-finished watercolour drawings remain, besides slighter sketches. At first they are rude and childish, though with each successive set the improvement is perceptible. But even with the earliest ones there is no mistaking that the drawing was a serious business. The subjects are not what are called 'bits', but are usually large comprehensive views, and it is impossible to doubt that the child threw his whole mind into it, did his very best, and shirked nothing. He already felt the force of the motto which fronted his conductor's chair in the [Leipzig] Gewandhaus – *Res severa est verum gaudium*. Every little cottage or gate is put in with as much care as the main features. Everything stands well on its legs, and the whole has that architectonic style which is so characteristic of his music.

Next to his drawing should be placed his correspondence, and this is even more remarkable. During the last years of his life there can have been few eminent men in Europe who wrote more letters than he did. Many even who take no interest in music are familiar with the nature of his letters – the happy mixture of seriousness, fun and affection, the life-like descriptions, the happy hits, the naïveté which no baldness of translation can extinguish, the wise counsel, the practical views, the delight in the successes of his friends, the self-abnegation, the bursts of wrath at anything mean or nasty. We all remember, too, the length to which they run. Taking the printed volumes, and comparing the letters with those of [Walter] Scott or [Matthew] Arnold, they are on the average very considerably longer than either. But the published letters bear only a small proportion to those still in manuscript. In fact the abundance of material for the biographer of Mendelssohn is quite bewildering. That, however, is not the point. The remarkable fact is that so many letters of such length and such intrinsic excellence should have been written by a man who was all the time engaged on an engrossing occupation, producing great quantities of music, conducting, arranging, and otherwise occupied in a profession which more than any other demands the surrender of the entire man. For these letters are no hurried productions, but are distinguished, like the drawings, for the neatness and finish which pervade them. An autograph letter of Mendelssohn's is a work of art; the lines are all straight and close, the letters perfectly and elegantly formed, with a peculiar luxuriance of tails, and an illegible word can hardly be found. To the folding and sealing, everything is perfect. It seems impossible that this can have been done quickly. It must have absorbed an enormous deal of time. While speaking of his correspondence, we may mention the neatness and order with which he registered and kept everything. [There were, for instance,] the forty-four volumes of manuscript music, in which he did for himself what Mozart's father so carefully did for his son. But it is not generally known that he preserved all the letters he received, and stuck them with his own hands into books. Twenty-seven large thick green volumes exist, containing apparently all the letters and memorandums, business and private, which he received from 29 October 1821 to 29 October 1847, together with the drafts of his oratorio books, and of the long official communications which, during his latter life, cost him so many unprofitable hours. He seems to have found time for everything. [Ferdinand] Hiller tells how during a very busy season he revised and copied out the libretto of his oratorio for him. One of his dearest Leipzig friends has a complete copy of the full score of *Antigone*, including the whole of the words of the melodrama, written for her with his own hand; a perfect piece of calligraphy, without spot or erasure! And the family archives contain a long minute list of the contents in all the cupboards of the house, filling several pages of foolscap, in his usual neat writing, and made about the year 1842. We read of Mr [Charles] Dickens that 'no matter was considered too trivial to claim his care and attention. He would take as much pains about the hanging of a picture, the superintending of any little improvement in the house, as he would about the more serious business of life; thus carrying out to the very letter his favourite motto that What is worth doing at all is worth doing well.' No words could better describe the side of Mendelssohn's character to which we are alluding, nor could any motto more emphatically express the principle on which he acted throughout life in all his work.

His taste and efficiency in such minor matters are well shown in the albums which he made for his wife, beautiful specimens of arrangement, the most charming things in which are the drawings and pieces of music from his own hands. His private account books and diaries are kept with the same quaint neatness. If he had a word to alter in a letter, it was done with a grace that turned the blemish into a beauty. The same care came out in everything – in making out the programmes for the Gewandhaus concerts, where he would arrange and re-arrange the pieces to suit some inner idea of symmetry or order; or in settling his sets of songs for publication as to the succession of keys, connection or contrast of words, etc. In fact he had a passion for neatness, and a repugnance to anything clumsy. Possibly this may have been one reason why he appears so rarely to have sketched his music. He made it in his head, and had settled the minutest points there before he put it on paper, thus avoiding the litter and disorder of a sketch. Connected with this neatness is a certain quaintness in his proceedings which perhaps strikes an Englishman more forcibly than it would a German. He used the old-fashioned C clef for the treble voices in his scores to the last; the long flourish with which he ornaments the double bar at the end of a piece never varied. A score of Haydn's 'Military' Symphony which he wrote [out] for his wife bears the words 'Possessor Cecile'. In writing to Mrs Moscheles of her little girls, whose singing had pleased him, he begs to be remembered to the *drei kleine Diskantisten*. A note to [Ferdinand] David, sent by a child, is inscribed *Kinderpost*, and so on. Certain French words occur over and over again, and are evidently favourites. Such as *plaisir* and *trouble*, *à propos*, *en gros*, and others. The world *hübsch*, answering to our 'nice', was a special favourite, and *nett* was one of his highest commendations.

But to return for a moment to his engrossing pursuits. Add to those just mentioned the many concerts, to be arranged, rehearsed, conducted; the frequent negotiations attending on Berlin; the long official protocols; the hospitality and genial intercourse, where he was equally excellent as host or as guest; the claims of his family; the long holidays, real holidays, spent in travelling, and not, like Beethoven's, devoted to composition – and we may almost be pardoned for wondering how he can have found time to write any music at all. But on the contrary, with him all this business does not appear to have militated against composition in the slightest degree. It often drove him almost to distraction; it probably shortened his life; but it never seems to have prevented his doing whatever music came before him, either spontaneously or at the call of his two posts at Berlin and Leipzig. He composed *Antigone* in a fortnight, he resisted writing the music for *Ruy Blas*, he grumbled over the long chorale for the thousandth anniversary of the German Empire, and over the overture to *Athalie*, in the midst of his London pleasures; but still he did them, and in the cases of *Antigone* and the two overtures it is difficult to see how he could have done them better. He was never driven into a corner.

The power by which he got through all this labour, so much

of it self-imposed, was the power of order and concentration, the practical business habit of doing one thing at a time, and doing it well. This no doubt was the talent which his father recognized in him so strongly as to make him doubt whether business was not his real vocation. It was this which made him sympathize with Schiller in his power of 'supplying' great tragedies as they were wanted. In one way his will was weak, for he always found it hard to say no; but having accepted the task it became a duty, and towards duty his will was the iron will of a man of business. Such a gift is vouchsafed to very few artists. Handel possessed it in some degree; but with that exception Mendelssohn seems to stand alone.

from GROVE'S DICTIONARY OF MUSIC
AND MUSICIANS *1883*

Classic and Romantic in Schumann

ALFRED EINSTEIN

Quite differently divided [from in Mendelssohn] are the proportions of inheritance and conquest, the relationship of the Classic and Romantic, in Robert Schumann. Schumann had begun his career as a revolutionary Romantic, or Romantic revolutionary of the first water: no other Romantic, not even Chopin, is comparable to him in youthfulness and in originality. In common with Chopin, he used the piano exclusively as the medium for the expression of his 'storm and stress' up to his Opus 23. Like Chopin, he was able to say at the piano all that he had in his heart. At the same time, he was able to use his new, virtuoso – and much more than merely virtuoso – piano style as a protest against the empty, shallow, brilliant, drawing-room virtuosity which, after Hummel and Weber, was making a great show in his period, along with the activity of the really great virtuosi like Liszt or Henselt. This new, bold, original piano music adopted the titles and forms of *études*, toccatas, intermezzi, variations, and dances; but the true title for them all would be the one that was given only to a few: *fantasies* for the piano – Kreisleriana, Jean Pauliana, Eichendorffiana in music. It is only logical that, after twenty-three 'opuses' for the piano, the twenty-fourth should blossom forth into a song cycle.

Among these twenty-three works there had already appeared three sonatas, the *Grandes Sonates* in F sharp minor, Op. 11, and in F minor, Op. 14, and the G minor Sonata, Op. 22 – an apparent compromise of the revolutionary with the classical form. It is apparent only, however, for even these three sonatas filled the outlines of the classical four-movement scheme with very new content. But it is true that Schumann, after the first stormy out-bursts of his creative urge which had been so long repressed, felt the need of an agreement, of an act of communication with a less subjective form. The many-sidedness, the strife within him, the fact that 'two souls' (and more than two) 'dwelt within his breast', he symbolized as a writer by his personification of the fictitious members of his 'David's League', the fiery Florestan, the dreamy Eusebius, the wise, meditative, and even-tempered Raro. He was everyone in turn and at the same time – Florestan, Eusebius, Raro. And Raro made it necessary that he express himself in more general, more objective form than he had hitherto used. So, after piano works, songs, and other vocal compositions, Schumann wrote in 1841 his first symphony, Op. 38, and in the following year his three string quartets, Op. 41. These latter remained his only ones.

To begin with the three quartets: they have not become 'classics' of quartet literature. They are written after Beethoven, as is shown by the slow movement in each. That in the first is a direct echo of the Adagio of the Ninth Symphony. That in the second – Andante, quasi Variazione – is like a variation of the Adagio ma non troppo of Beethoven's String Quartet Op. 127; even the key corresponds. Similarly the Adagio molto of the third quartet is also a fully developed slow movement – though more passionate, more excited, more agitated than any in Haydn, Mozart, or even Beethoven.

But this lyrical centre in each of the three quartets did not cause Schumann to invest the other movements with a similar fullness and depth. In Beethoven's quartets there prevails a complete equilibrium of the movements, from first to last; the structure is always completely stable. In Schumann the first movements (that of Quartet No. 1 in A minor is in F major!) have the qualities of a lyric or ballad; the Scherzo of this quartet is a galloping piece, as if taken over from the *Scenes of Childhood* and arranged, with intermezzi such as might have been taken over and arranged from his songs. The Classical structure falls to pieces, despite the fact that the compositions are reminiscent of Beethoven – particularly, of course, of late Beethoven, who was considered a destroyer of form. The finest and most original of the three quartets is the last, with marvellous variations (*assai agitato*) in place of the Scherzo, with 'Hommage à J. S. Bach' – the imitation of the Gavotte from the French Suite in E – as a 'Quasi Trio' in the Finale. This is not the place for a critique of the admirable work; we are here concerned not so much with criticizing as with understanding the movement that is referred to as musical Romanticism. The Romantic era *had* to break up the Classical form, if it did not wish to remain academic imitation; for there is no development above and beyond that which is perfect – in this instance, the Beethovenian string quartet.

The same thing applies to the Schumann type of symphony. It becomes more lively, youthful, 'Romantic' than Mendelssohn's as it departs further from the Classical pattern. Like Mendelssohn's two great symphonies, Schumann's First Symphony, in B flat major, is descended from Beethoven's *Pastoral*. Schumann called this composition of his the *Springtime* symphony and originally gave the movements the following headings: 1. The Beginning of Spring (Andante); 2. Evening (Larghetto); 3. Merry Play (Scherzo); and 4. Spring in Bloom (Allegro animato e grazioso). The impulse to compose this work had come from a poem by Adolf Böttger. But it is significant that Schumann finally suppressed those headings, and that only a rhythmic suggestion of the poem was left, namely of its last line: 'Now spring is blooming in the vale' ('*Im Tale blüht der Frühling auf*') in the principal motif of the first movement. This *Springtime* Symphony has much less programme, much less 'painting', than does Beethoven's Sixth Symphony, if one does not take the use of the triangle in the first movement as a symbol of that 'Awakening of Spring', or interpret the horn call and the flute cadenza in the Finale naturalistically.

Everything has become an 'expression of feeling'; the poetic stimulus has been transfigured and subjected to the laws of symphonic form.

We need not go into the other three symphonies of Schumann's in great detail. The one counted as No. 2, Op. 61, completed in 1846, follows a programme similar to that of the First. It was explained by Schumann with only a few words when he called it 'a regular Jupiter' (it is in C major) and 'somewhat in armour' (*etwas geharnischt*). The Third, in E flat, Op. 97, written in 1850, bears the cryptic title 'Rhenish', and is actually supposed to reflect – according to Schumann's remark – 'a bit of life on the Rhine'. But it is hard to understand how it is to do that; even the second of the two slow middle sections, which at the *première* still bore the inscription 'In the nature of the accompaniment to a solemn ceremony' points only quite generally to something mystical, ancient, Catholic, and not to the specific locality of the Cologne or any other of the Rhenish cathedrals.

The most characteristic symphonic work of Schumann's is his Fourth Symphony, Op. 120, in D minor, which, although re-worked and re-orchestrated in 1851, actually originated a few months after the First, in the summer of 1841, and really must be counted as the Second. It joins together five movements – Intro-duction, Allegro, Romanze, Scherzo, and Finale – into an unin-terrupted whole; and, quite logically, in its original form of 1841 it bore the title *Symphonic Fantasy*. This unity is not merely an external feature, for all the movements are developed from melodic seeds that are given in the Introduction; they are blossoms of various colours springing from the same bush. Here again Schumann, after his usual manner, concealed the poetic incentive for this work, and gave only a possible hint in the guitar accom-paniment of the Romanze. He did not wish to be more clear than that: the music buries the 'programme' in mysterious depths. We here stand before a new form of the symphony – one possessed of a thematic homogeneity which Beethoven had felt no need of, although this feature perhaps goes back to the 'reminiscences' in the Finale of the Ninth Symphony.

Alongside this achievement of homogeneity, there stands something truly Romantic – disintegration. This trend appears clearly in Schumann's *Overture, Scherzo and Finale* in E major, Op.

52, which had its origin between the B flat major and D minor symphonies, a work that Schumann in all seriousness wanted to bring out as his Second Symphony, or at least a 'Symphonette'. But does not the lack of a slow movement make even a sinfonietta into a suite, a more or less disconnected succession of movements?

Romantic disintegration of Classical structure is found also in the most beautiful and most compellingly lovable of all Schumann's works, his Piano Concerto in A minor, Op. 54, the first movement written in May 1841, the last two in the summer of 1845. We are here not dealing with Schumann's relationship to the problem of virtuosity; instead, we are here concerned with the co-operation of two forces – piano and orchestra – which no longer displays the pure equilibrium that it did with Mozart, nor the dramatic give-and-take that it did with Beethoven. The soloist now is carried, supported and caressed by the orchestra. In the relative importance of the three movements there prevails a new subjectivity; for the Intermezzo, to which Beethoven's slow movement had shrunk, breathes an intimacy which the heroic Beethoven would never have permitted himself.

Within the Florestan-Eusebius-Raro union in Schumann's creative faculties, Raro achieved more and more the predominance – so much so that one must speak of a dissolution or disruption of this union. In no branch of Schumann's creative activity, except in his songs, does this dissolution admit of such exact observation as in that of his chamber music with piano. The transition from his youthfully free, 'unclassical' piano music to these works is afforded by a trio entitled *Phantasiestück* (Op. 88, 1842), consisting of Romance, Duet, and Alla Marcia – a whole, marked by freshness precisely because it seems to be disconnected. Alongside this, Schumann set up a model of Classic-Romantic chamber music in his Piano Quintet, Op. 44 (1842), the piano setting the pace, brilliant, never virtuoso, a work of high spirits in all the rapid movements, and in the slow or marchlike movement full of mysterious sorrow and indignation. At first slowly, then faster and faster, the descent ensues – in a Quartet Op. 47 (1842), in three Trios Op. 63 (1847), Op. 80 (1847), and Op. 110 (1851), in two Violin Sonatas Op. 105 (1851) and 121 (1851) – to repetitiousness, to mannerism.

Mannerism is a part of the diagnosis of the pathological aspect of the Romantic movement. In earlier centuries copying – even the weaker sort of copying – was a part of the craft; in the new century the heightened conception of the artist demanded ever new creative effort. Fortunate was the man who, like Wagner, Verdi, or Brahms, was equal to this effort, and in his own work increased in stature. Schumann was not such a person. One may say that his real tragedy lay in the fact that he disintegrated in the attempt to do as the 'great ones' had done – to become universal. The attacks of insanity are but an outward symbol of this tragedy, a typically Romantic fate. Schumann is a representative of eternal adolescence, of enthusiastic intimacy; the task of becoming a man, in the creative sense, weighed too heavily upon him. Liszt, in a letter to Heinrich Heine on 15 April, 1838, understood very well the split in his generation when he said that the artists of his time were 'very badly situated' between the past and the future. 'The century is ill.' Schumann began as a champion of the future; in establishing a connection with the past he collapsed. But Schumann as a young man did not as yet know anything of the end in store for him. Had Schumann never passed his thirty-fifth birthday, he would have been the Shelley of music, the star of youth most resplendently gleaming.

from MUSIC IN THE ROMANTIC ERA *1947*

Liszt's Personality and his Art

ERNEST NEWMAN

There are some composers whose lives, so far as we can see, have had practically no bearing on their work. Even if we knew, for instance, that the Aria of the D major Suite had been written by Bach immediately after the death of a favourite child, it would be fatuous to suppose that that event had anything to do with either the genesis of the work or the nature of the music; Bach's impulses to compose came out of a general fund of musical feeling that was independent of external incitements of the moment. In other composers some emotional shock or upheaval, the chance impact of some blinding experience or other, may have been the primal germ from which the impulse to create the work arose; but between the germ and the full-grown organism there has intervened a psychological something that makes the provenance of the germ of virtually no account at the finish. Wagner explained this process very lucidly. The composer, he said in effect, must not sit down immediately after the moving experience and straightway project a tonal equivalent of it; he must leave it to germinate for some time within him according to its own unconscious inner law and according to the peculiar nature of music; in this way a particular mood is in time generated that constitutes the composer's starting-point; but from that point he will proceed purely and simply as a *composer*, without reference to the external event that had moved him in the first place – he will allow his ideas to evolve purely and simply in terms of *music*. In its way, the statement is just a variant of Wordsworth's well-known dictum as to poetry being emotion remembered in tranquillity.

Another type of composer does not wait for this remembering in tranquillity, for the slow metamorphosis of the first outer stimulus into an inner spiritual substance out of which the work of art will grow organically according to its own laws and those of the special artistic medium, but hastens to record the stimulus while it is still diffusing its first heat within him. To this type Liszt may be said to have belonged; many a work of his was not merely embarked upon but finished while he was still under the shock of the experience. There are composers, in fact, whose life is mirrored in their art, and their art elucidated by their life; and Liszt was one of them. Our perception of this fact, however, has nothing to do with 'criticism'; we are content, for the time being, to put on one side the question of whether the resultant work is 'good' or 'bad': we simply note the mirroring, the parallelism, as an interesting phenomenon.

In Liszt's case the parallelism between his life, his character and his work is often obvious; few composers have painted themselves so accurately in their music. Peter Raabe is not being in the least fanciful when he points out that 'Liszt's whole nature' is reproduced in the great piano sonata; of the *Faust Symphony* [he] writes thus:

The first movement is a self-confession the analogue of which is to be found only in the sonata. The brooding protagonist whom he has drawn with such uncanny certainty in the first movement, the ardent lover, the aspirant towards the ideal, who again and again sinks back into darkness when victory seems at hand, is Liszt himself. If anyone wishes to know Liszt's inmost thoughts about the soul of woman he needs to read no books about his relations with women; he has only to listen to the Gretchen movement.

(This, of course, is an exaggeration. The Gretchen movement may tell us Liszt's inmost thoughts about the soul of a virgin, but it tells us nothing of his inmost thoughts, which must have been no less interesting, about that of a Lola Montez; and it was of the Montez type, not the Gretchen type, that Liszt had by far the more experience. He may have 'respected chastity', as he told Adelheid von Schorn; but in the matter of female companionship he generally preferred the other thing.)

This correlation of the moods, the sequences of moods, and the outcome of the conflict of them in a given piece of music with what we know of the nature and the life of its composer would in most cases be illegitimate. But in the case of Liszt it is not only legitimate but actually forced upon us by the most obvious features of the man's life and those of his music. The two are here interrelated in a way that is without parallel anywhere else in musical history. Perception of this fact has within recent years set musicologists at work at the task, not of 'criticizing' Liszt, but of trying to understand him. 'Criticism' of him, in the ordinary sense of that word, will never take us much further with regard to Liszt than we are at present. His music will always appeal strongly to some temperaments and as strongly repel others, and the opposing camps may be left to fight out their tiresome quarrel in their own way; neither will ever convince the other, or make the least impression on spectators who are not of their particular way of thinking. Apart from the futility of this wrangling about what is at bottom merely a temperamental difference between the disputants, there is the curious fact to be faced that, as Raabe points out, Liszt and rational criticism have come together rather too late. In his own lifetime, for one reason

and another, intelligent discussion of him, intelligent appraise-
ment of what was really significant in his music, in spite of its
many faults, was comparatively scarce; while the present generation, that is willing to do justice to him, has lost the key to many
chambers of his soul. . . .

Recognizing, then, that in Liszt's case our ordinary 'critical'
apparatus is somewhat flawed at base, thoughtful students of him
are tending more and more to leave questions of 'values' in his
work to be settled by individual tastes, and to concentrate on the
effort simply to understand the man's mind. And once we begin to
do that, we realize how closely the man is paralleled in his music.
An admirable commencement in this understanding of him was
made by Arnold Schering a few years ago in an article in the
Jahrbuch der Musikbibliothek Peters on *Liszt's Personality and His
Art*; and Peter Raabe has carried the investigation a few points
further. Liszt's music invariably reflects his nature and his life.
He had no real nationality, a fact that has undoubtedly stood in
the way of his full appreciation by any country. Though there was
something of the Zigeuner in him, his music is not specifically
Hungarian. His early romanticism was of the French, not the
German, variety, a fact that made him seem alien to the ordinary
German mind of the mid-nineteenth century. In his middle period
he took up certain lines of musical development that were specifically German; but he never projected himself with complete success
into the purely German mentality of which these lines of development had been, and still were, the natural inevitable expression.
He had as little fixed a spiritual home, his long life through, as
he had a fixed physical home. It was probably this feeling that
Liszt was fundamentally non-German that accounted for much of
the German opposition to him in his own day: Germans sensitive
to their own poetry must have turned with wry face from some of
his mishandlings of German verse-rhythm and accentuation in
his songs and from his tendency, as shown, for example, in his setting of Goethe's 'Ueber allen Gipfeln ist Ruh', to load the pithiest
of poems with repetitions that destroy the very breath of their
being. The psychical essence of a work like the *Faust Symphony*
was too French for the nineteenth-century Germans and too
German for the French. No approach to an understanding and an
appreciation of Liszt can be made until we have learned to avoid

trying to categorize him under any of the usual national heads, and to see him just as he was.

Raabe calls this non-national quality of Liszt by the name of universalism. It was universal, however, only in the negative sense that it was not local. It can hardly be called universal in the sense that it corresponds to a basic something in his music in which humanity in general, regardless of its geographical and cultural divisions, can find itself with full conviction, as it can, for instance, in the music of Bach, Mozart, Beethoven, Schubert or Wagner. It seems truer to say that Liszt was not universal, but simply himself – a personality of a peculiarly self-centred kind, which, while it reaches out now to the French, now to the Italian, now to the German, now to the Hungarian spirit, is not sufficiently French, Italian, German or Hungarian to allow either of those nations to claim him positively and wholly for its own, or to find its own historic culture faithfully mirrored in him. Schering, for example, has pointed out that while the ethical element in Liszt's nature attracted him to German ethical subjects, his treatment of them was not German enough for the Germans.

Schering [also] speaks of 'the religious', 'the idyllic', 'the heroic', and 'the erotic' as 'the four powers of Liszt's soul'. His music is, indeed, as his life was, a perpetual oscillation between these; frequently within the same short work we pass from the idyllic or religious aspiration to a stormy outburst that reminds us of those episodes in Liszt's life in which the suppressed fury of his being had to clear the air for itself with a Donner-stroke at the black clouds around and within him. His mournful sense of his general inability to master himself and shape his life as he would have wished to shape it is curiously reflected in his choice of certain poems for his songs and as epigraphs to his piano works – a feature of his work that cannot be dwelt upon in detail here, but that will well repay the student's investigation. In work after work, and in the different sections of each long work, we come upon the musical equivalent of the traits that can be seen to make up the zigzag pattern of his life – religious aspiration, perfumed eroticism, the heroic gesture, the theatrical attitude, the over-elaboration of manner, the studied effect, the alternation of the noble and the flashy, the prayer, the malediction, peace succeeded by tempest and tempest by peace, the eternal combat between a higher and a lower element, and so on. There is no musician whose music so closely resembles his life, and whose life is so manifestly his music made flesh, as Liszt. The more clearly, then, we see the man as he really was, the more thoroughly we may hope to understand the many contradictions of which he was constituted, and so with all the more interest shall we renew our study of his music.

from THE MAN LISZT *1934*

Bruckner

ERWIN DOERNBERG

There are certain composers who have rightly been recognized by posterity as being representative of the period in which they lived and worked. Even if we knew very little about the social changes in the European world during the last fifteen years of the eighteenth century, a comparison between the music of Mozart and Beethoven might bring us close to a real understanding of some essential points of that transitional period. Certainly we should be able to draw significant conclusions from the contrast between Mozart's graceful style with its frequent undercurrent of darkness and Beethoven's unfettered self-expression. In the case of Mozart and Beethoven, this observation is so patently clear as to be almost a truism. It is mentioned here to demonstrate a contrast; for no such comparison between music and period can be applied to Anton Bruckner.

Bruckner's symphonies were written during the last third of the nineteenth century. In their external form they follow some precepts of Beethoven's last symphony and Schubert's great Symphony in C major. In this respect, Bruckner's chronological position corresponds with his place in the history of music: Beethoven and Schubert before him and Gustav Mahler after him. Mendelssohn, Spohr and Schumann remain unmentioned in this connection; Bruckner was the first composer to accept the great challenge of Beethoven's Ninth: the expanded first movement, the

highly significant Scherzo, the spacious and transcendent Adagio
and the supremely important Finale. By combining this classical
inheritance with something of the monumental means and
proportions demanded by Wagner and Mahler as the most
representative figures of the later nineteenth century, Bruckner
stands in line with the musical development of his time. Besides
the external, formal appearance of his symphonies, there are other
links with his contemporary world: his orchestration and his
harmony.

Important as all this is, the significance of Bruckner does not
lie in the mere fact that he was a man of his time. This he shared
with many other musicians who never became a problem for
posterity, because posterity forgot, in charity, all about them. The
greatness of Bruckner lies in the fact that a spirit speaks in his
music which is strikingly individual and which is not dictated by
or acquired through influences. Not only did Bruckner possess
musical 'originality', that prime factor of works of lasting value,
the spirit of his music is quite outstandingly, peculiarly his own,
and it is this which makes his place in the history of music so
difficult to determine. It has been labelled with the word 'mysticism'. Since Bruckner certainly had that religious awareness which
by its very nature demands self-expression, it is possible to talk
of similarity with more familiar instances of mysticism. On the
other hand, Bruckner's most important works are secular composition, absolute music, and it is therefore advisable to use the
word 'mysticism' with great caution – it is probably impossible
to speak of him without introducing it at all – lest one overburdens
with unnecessary elaborations what is fundamentally a very
simple phenomenon. What is important is to realize that the term
is not necessarily restricted to the Church. Bruckner's symphonies
are not at all Church music; they are not 'Masses without words' or
'liturgical symphonies' – slogans coined by writers who make the
distinction between the spiritual and the secular realm which in
true mysticism is characteristically ill-defined or ceases to exist.
Bruckner's symphonies are simply symphonies. Spiritual experience was neither consciously imposed on these works nor is it
continuously evident, but spiritual experience was obviously the
very root of Bruckner's being.

It may be strange to begin the discussion of a composer with the clarification of religious terminology, but here it is necessary for two reasons. Firstly, the 'mystical' element in this composer's music is unique in so far as there is nothing comparable to it in the work of any other secular, modern musician. Secondly, whenever 'mysticism' crops up – the term or the thing itself – confusion almost invariably follows, a danger to which musicologists are no less exposed than theological writers. After all, most of us know the world of mysticism only from the outside; furthermore, it is a concept which seems to lend itself all too readily to the attention of idle talkers whose verbosity reveals little distinction between substance and mere words. In the case of Bruckner, a number of bombastic books have been written in which the man and his work are artificially 'spiritualized' beyond all recognition. The most formidable work of Bruckner-mystification even subjects the music to the introduction of semi-mystical concepts such as 'symphonic waves' as Bruckner's formal element.

The era in which Bruckner lived was marked by a fashionable shallow and optimistic rationalism which – in conjunction with the equally shallow doctrine of progress – most people apparently found satisfying. Those who were too intelligent to accept simplifications or had a more acute sensibility were driven to a personal search for salvation. The ever-recurring theme of 'salvation' on the Wagner stage, the soul-searching conflicts of Gustav Mahler and also the sweet, small and non-committal pious sentimentality in, for instance, Gounod's Church music are typical musical results.

Bruckner was not in contact with these tendencies of his time. He was one of the exceedingly rare people of whom one can say that they live perpetually in a state of grace. There is little to be said on it. There was nothing extraordinary in his religious observance. There was neither a spectacular conversion nor, at any time of his life, a religious crisis. His whole being shows a personality quietly in contact with God. His faith was an entirely unsentimental, firm and masculine belief. As a Catholic musician Bruckner was the very opposite of the Abbé Liszt, whose biographers can supply a date list of religious paroxisms which occasionally added spiritual drama to the otherwise exceedingly worldly drama of his life. For Bruckner, 'religion' was as elemental as the atmosphere in which we breathe. At a tender age, he was called out from among the village boys for a personal blessing by a dying priest. As an old man he dedicated his last symphony *dem lieben Gott* 'if he wants to accept it'. When he spoke of 'the demon of his life' he referred not to God or to Satan but to the leading music critic of the Viennese press.[1]

When the soul and mind of Bruckner became eloquent, he chose absolute music – symphonies – as his main medium and we are therefore prevented from too close an interpretation in words of what we are convinced is the utterance of a God-inflamed soul. And, would it even be desirable here to destroy a mystery by discoursing on it? The fact that there is a 'mystery' in these symphonies in no way affects their value as musical compositions. So far Brahms was right when he said that Bruckner's piety was his private affair. What Brahms, as so many others, was unable to realize is that the fundamental trait of a personality such as Bruckner's would not allow of separate departments for private 'piety' and the artistic impetus of the composer. Bruckner's whole achievement is firmly rooted in his essential spirituality even in such profoundly disturbed experiences as those which speak to us in his last two symphonies. . . .

Bruckner's life and personality stand in surprising contrast to those of almost all great composers of the recent past. Like most of the others, he began composing in his early childhood, but unlike any of them (with the one exception of César Franck) he reached the age of forty before writing a great work. His name became widely known only when he was over sixty. He composed all through the early part of his life, but even the best of those numerous works written before 1863 [when he was thirty-nine] cannot be said to foreshadow what he produced in later years. At a time when he had already outlived the span of Mozart's or Schubert's life, Bruckner was still writing exercises and taking courses of tuition.

Apart from his unusually slow development, Bruckner shows a striking difference in comparison with most other composers by reason of his astonishing simplicity as a man. No intelligent reader of Mozart's letters, even if he were quite unmusical, could possibly fail to enjoy them; his correspondence might have qualified him for lasting fame even had he been an ordinary court musician and

Eduard Hanslick. *Ed.*

nothing more. Beethoven's life and his extraordinary 'entirely untamed personality' (as Goethe saw it) show a peculiar intensity which make him highly interesting even apart from his compositions. Bruckner's life and personality appear almost barren in comparison with those of Beethoven, Wagner, Brahms, Tchaikovsky – men whose life and character reflect in one way or another something of their status as composers. His is the career of the poor village boy who, step by step, made a successful career as cathedral organist and professor of theory without at all widening his horizon. The one and only really surprising thing about him was that after completing his career as an organist he suddenly began to compose music with a range of vision which in such a man would appear quite incongruous.

The biography of an artist depends usually for its momentum on the relationship of his life and personality with his works; the life at once explaining and failing to explain the greatness of the artistic achievement. The spacious world of Bruckner's symphonies would certainly lead one to expect the composer to be a man of considerable mental span. But what was visible in Bruckner to those who have known him? A simple, devout countryman with an immense knowledge of musical theory and the ability to teach it. That was all. Because most people's judgement depends on immediate impressions, Bruckner's rural inflexion, his frequent use of the upper-Austrian dialect, his servility and also, of course, his piety offered opportunity for jest to the 'intellectuals' of Vienna. An interminable number of Bruckner stories is the result, not all of them *ben trovato*. And there can be no doubt that Bruckner's friends, particularly among the circle of his young students, were not fully aware of Bruckner's significance; their enthusiasm rarely revealed deeper insight than the attacks of the derisive critics. . . .

The story of Bruckner's life is the account of the struggles and trials of an awkward man who seemed ill-fitted for contest with those lesser beings on whose attitude his happiness depended. Humiliation and disappointments fill many pages while little can be said about the one fact that far outweighs them: that nothing could usually prevent the composer, sensitive as he was to the reaction of the world, from continuing his work as though undisturbed. The fundamental enigma of Bruckner has always been the unaccountable capacity of this timid and apparently limited man to write music with an assurance and resourcefulness which were totally absent from his daily life.

from THE LIFE AND SYMPHONIES
OF ANTON BRUCKNER *1960*

"Bruckner writes only for effect; his symphonies are a colossal swindle." *Johannes Brahms*

Impressions of Brahms

ETHEL SMYTH

Some people, I believe, have youthful enthusiasms, even in their own branch of art, that wane as years go on, but I can remember no musical recantations. A favourable judgement seems to me to imply a satisfied need; you may have many needs, but why should one interfere with the other? Why, when you come to know and admire, say, Anatole France, should you delight less in someone at the opposite pole, for instance, Dickens? From the very first I had worshipped Brahms' music, as I do some of it now; hence was predisposed to admire the man. But without exactly disliking him, his personality neither impressed nor attracted, and I never could understand why the faithful had such an exalted opinion of his intellect. Rather taciturn and jerky as a rule, and notoriously difficult to carry on a conversation with, after meals his mind and tongue unstiffened; and then, under the stimulus of countless cups of very strong black coffee, he was ready to discuss literature, art, politics, morals, or anything under the sun. On such occasions, though he never said anything stupid, I cannot recall hearing him say anything very striking, and when his latest pronouncement on Bismarck, poetry, or even music was ecstatically handed round, it generally seemed to me what anyone might have said. Once only do I remember his taking an exceptional line. A portrait of the old

Kaiser by Lenbach, recently exhibited at the Museum, had aroused such a storm of indignation that it was withdrawn, and I believe ended by being 'verboten' as far as public galleries were concerned. The reason was that whereas all other portraits of Wilhelm I, represented a martial-looking veteran of about sixty, of whom the Press stated that he swung himself on to his horse without the aid of a mounting block, Lenbach had painted a very tired old man of eighty-four, with pale, flabby cheeks, and sunken, lacklustre eyes – in short the fine old wreck he was, of whom it was whispered that, as a matter of fact, he had to be lifted on to his horse in the recesses of the stable yard in order to make his daily appearance in the Thiergarten. This picture was infinitely pathetic and even beautiful; so, it seemed to me, was the idea of the old warrior determined to sally forth as long as he could sit on a horse's back, no matter how he got there. But the people who manufacture public opinion in Germany saw in this record of human decay something detrimental to monarchical prestige, some going so far as to declare the picture should be publicly destroyed and the painter arraigned for *lèse-majesté* – in short the incident opened one's eyes to the gulf that lies between German and Anglo-Saxon mentality. There was a minority of another way of thinking, but these kept pretty quiet, and I was delighted to find that Brahms, who always had the courage of his opinions and truckled to no one, thought the whole outcry preposterous, and said so.

I think what chiefly angered me was his views on women, which after all were the views prevalent in Germany, only I had not realized the fact, having imagined 'mein Mann sagt' was a local peculiarity. Relics of this form of barbarism still linger in England, but as voiced by a people gone mad on logic, worshippers of brute force, and who visualize certain facts with the hard stare of eyes devoid of eyelashes, these theories would, I fancy, repel even our own reactionaries. George III, himself a German, might have subscribed 150 years ago to William II's famous axiom about women being out of place anywhere except in the kitchen, nursery, and church, but you often heard it quoted with complete assent by German women themselves in my day.

Brahms, as artist and bachelor, was free to adopt what may be called the poetical variant of the 'Kinder, Kirche, Küche' axiom namely that women are playthings. He made one or two exceptions, such as men will, and chief among these was Lisl [Herzogenberg], to whom his attitude was perfect . . . reverential, admiring, and affectionate, without a tinge of amorousness. Being, like most artists, greedy, it specially melted him that she was such a splendid Hausfrau; indeed as often as not, from love of the best, she would do her own marketing. During Brahms' visits she was never happier than when concocting some exquisite dish to set before the king; like a glorified Frau Röntgen she would come in, flushed with stooping over the range, her golden hair wavier than ever from the heat, and cry: "Begin that movement again; that much you owe me!" and Brahms's worship would flame up in unison with the blaze in the kitchen. In short he was adorable with Lisl.

In his relations with her husband, who completely effaced himself as musician in the master's presence, he took pains to be appreciative, but could not disguise the fact that Herzogenberg's compositions did not greatly interest him. Once when he had been in a bad temper and rather cruel about them, Lisl rated him and wept, and Brahms kissed her hand and nearly wept too, and it appears there was a most touching scene; but the thing rankled in her bosom for a long time.

To see him with Lili Wach, Frau Schumann and her daughters, or other links with his great predecessors was to see him at his best, so gentle and respectful was his bearing; in fact to Frau Schumann he behaved as might a particularly delightful old-world son. I remember a most funny conversation between them as to why the theme of his D major Piano Variations had what she called 'an unnecessary bar tacked on', this being one of the supreme touches in that wonderful, soaring tune. She argued the point lovingly, but as ever with some heat, and I thought him divinely patient.

His ways with other women-folk – or to use the detestable word for ever on his lips 'Weibsbilder' – were less admirable. If they did not appeal to him he was incredibly awkward and ungracious; if they were pretty he had an unpleasant way of leaning back in his chair, pouting out his lips, stroking his moustache, and staring at them as a greedy boy stares at jam-tarts. People used to think this rather delightful, specially hailing it, too, as a sign that the great man was in high good-humour, but it angered me, as did also his jokes about women, and his everlasting gibes at any excepting Lisl, of course, who possessed brains or indeed ideas of any kind. I used to complain fiercely to her about this, but her secret feeling was, I expect, that of many anti-Suffragist women I have known, who, for some reason or other on the pinnacle of man's favour themselves, had no objection to the rest of woman-kind being held in contempt – the attitude of Fatima, the Pride of the Harem. To be fair to Lisl I never heard her express definite sentiments on the subject, about which I had never thought my-self, but as she was of her epoch and intensely German, her instinct was probably that of Fatima.

A delightful trait in Brahms was his horror of being lionized. He had a strong prejudice against England which he would jocularly insist on for my benefit, but what chiefly prevented his going there was dread of our hero-worshipping faculties: "I know how you went on with Mendelssohn," he said. What with their own embarrassment and his total lack of ease – or, as the Italians put it, lack of education – ordinary mortals who humbly tried to convey to him their admiration for his music had rather a bad time. The only person who sailed gaily through such troubled waters was Consul Limburger, but this again did not please Brahms and outraged the elect. After some performance, Lim-burger once remarked in his airy way: "Really, Herr Doctor, I don't know where you mean to take us in the slow movement, whether to Heaven or Hell," and Brahms remarked with a mock bow: "Whichever you please, Herr Consul," which was quoted as a brilliant piece of repartee that ought to have crushed the audacious Limburger. But one retort of his was really rather good. The first subject in one of his chamber works is almost identical with a theme of Mendelssohn's, and when some would-be con-noisseur eagerly pointed out the fact, Brahms remarked "Ganz richtig – und jeder Schafskopf merkt's leider sofort!" ("Quite so – and the worst of it is every blockhead notices it directly.")

I am bound to say his taste in jokes left much to be desired, and can give an instance on the subject of my own name, which all foreigners find difficult, and which, as I innocently told him, my washerwoman pronounced 'Schmeiss'. Now the verb 'schmeissen', to throw violently, is vulgar but quite harmless; there is however an antique noun, 'Schmeiss', which means something unmentionable, and a certain horrible fly which frequents horrible places is called 'Schmeiss-Fliege'. As Brahms was for ever commenting on the extreme rapidity of my movements he found the play upon words irresistible and nicknamed me 'die Schmeiss-Fliege', but Lisl was so scandalized at this joke that he had to drop it.

Among his admirers it was the fashion to despise Wagner, but to this he demurred, and a remark he often made "His imitators are monkeys (*Affen*) but the man himself has something to say" was cited as proof of his noble, generous disposition. People like Joachim and Herzogenberg considered Wagner a colossal joke, and I remember their relating how as a sort of penance they sat through a whole act of *Siegfried* keeping up each other's spirits by exchanging a 'good morning' whenever a certain chord, let us say a diminished ninth, occurred in the score – a very provoking pleasantry even to hear about.

I like best to think of Brahms at the piano, playing his own compositions or Bach's mighty organ fugues, sometimes accompanying himself with a sort of muffled roar, as of Titans stirred to sympathy in the bowels of the earth. The veins in his forehead stood out, his wonderful bright blue eyes became veiled, and he seemed the incarnation of the restrained power in which his own work is forged. For his playing was never noisy, and when lifting a submerged theme out of a tangle of music he used jokingly to ask us to admire the gentle sonority of his 'tenor thumb'.

One of his finest characteristics was his attitude towards the great dead in his own art. He knew his own worth – what creator does not? – but in his heart he was one of the most profoundly modest men I ever met, and to hear himself classed with such as Beethoven and Bach, to hear his C minor Symphony called 'The Tenth Symphony',[1] jarred and outraged him. Once, when he turned up to rehearse some work of his, Reinecke had not yet finished rehearsing one of Mozart's symphonies – I forget which – and after the slow movement he murmured something to Lisl that I did not catch. She afterwards told me he had said: "I'd give all my stuff (*Kram*) to have written that one Andante!"

[1] The implication was that it equalled, or surpassed, Beethoven's Ninth Symphony.

Among desultory remarks of his which remained in my mind, I remember his saying that he had given up predicting what a young composer's development would be, having so often found that those he thought talented came to nothing and *vice versa*; and in this connection he pointed out that all the work of Gluck that still lives was written after he was fifty. I have never looked up Gluck in a Lexicon to see if this opinion would still hold good.

To me personally he was very kind and fatherly in his awkward way, chiefly, no doubt, because of the place I held in his friend's heart; but after a very slight acquaintance I guessed he would never take a woman-writer seriously, and had no desire, though kindly urged by him to do so, to show him my work. At last one day, without asking my leave Lisl showed him a little fugue of mine, and when I came in and found them looking at it he began analysing it, simply, gravely, and appreciatively, saying this development was good, that modulation curious, and so on. Carried away by surprise and delight I lost my head, and pointing out a constructive detail that had greatly fussed Herzogenberg – the sort of thing that made him call me a bad pupil – asked eagerly: "Don't you think if I feel it that way I have a right to end on the dominant?" Suddenly the scene changed, back came the ironic smile, and stroking his moustache he said in a voice charged with kindly contempt: "I am quite sure, dear child, you may end when and where you please!" . . . There it was! he had suddenly remembered I was a girl, to take whom seriously was beneath a man's dignity, and the quality of the work, which had I been an obscure male he would have upheld against anyone, simply passed from his mind.

Now let us suppose a publisher had been present – and they swarmed at the Herzogenbergs – what would have been the effect of this little scene on a budding inclination to print for me later on? And does the public realize that unless it is published music cannot possibly get known? . . . .

I have no intention of alluding to my own work in these memoirs, unless to make passing mention of such early performances as happen to come within its scope; but there is one incident that happened some years later which, for women at least, has general application, and of which the fugue story reminds me. I once showed a big choral work to Levi, the great

Wagner conductor – an open-minded man and one not afraid to look truth in the face. After hearing it he said: "I could never have believed that a woman wrote that!" I replied, "No, and what's more, in a week's time you won't believe it!" He looked at me a moment, and said slowly: "I believe you are right!" Prejudice was bound to prevail over the evidence of his senses and intellect – in the end he would surely feel there must have been a mistake somewhere! . . . It is this back-wash that hampers even more than material obstacles. . . .

One day I had a small triumph over Brahms. Among my exercises for Herzogenberg were two-part 'Inventions' in the Bach manner, and Lisl played him one of these as a new find unearthed by the Bach Society. In it was a certain harmonic turn not of Bach's time, but which he, who anticipated most things, might quite well have used, and Brahms's remark, which I must quote in the original, was "Dem Kerl fällt doch immer wieder was Neues ein!" ("That fellow is always hitting on something new.") When the truth came out, the composer was warmly commended – and this time did not deserve it. It was just a bit of successful mimicry that any fairly clever musician might pull off.

But my greatest success with Brahms – who, by the by, held that everyone resembles some orchestral instrument and called me 'the Oboe' – had nothing to do with music. Piqued by his low estimate of my sex, I wrote a little sarcastic poem the last verse of which ran:

Der grosse Brahms hat's neulich ausgeprochen:
   "Ein g' scheidtes Weib, das hat doch keinen Sinn!"
D'rum lasst uns emsig uns're Dummheit pflegen,
Denn nur auf diesen Punkst ist Werth zu legen
   Als Weib und gute Brahmsianerin!

Translation

As the great Brahms recently proclaimed,
   "A clever woman is a thing of naught!"
So let us diligently cultivate stupidity,
That being the only quality demanded
   Of a female Brahms admirer!

That night he was at a supper given in his honour, and the

mouth of everyone who approached him to talk about his music was stopped by his taking the poem out of his breast pocket and insisting on the unfortunate person reading it. This characteristic proceeding went on, I was told, throughout the evening and must have maddened the admirers.

In post-Leipzig days I saw little of him, but once when I was passing through Vienna and called on him, he was more than kind and cordial and begged me to fix up a meal at his house on my way back. Alas, when the time came he was away.

In jotting down these various impressions I am quite aware they do not do him justice. Even then I knew all about his wonderful generosity to poor musicians and old friends fallen on evil days. I noticed, too, that even the cynicism about women was belied by the extreme delicacy and tenderness of his work, and more especially by his choice of words to set to music. But all I can say is that this poetical insight did not determine his working theory (ascribed by some foolish persons to an early disappointment in love); and the point of memoirs – so it seems to me – is to relate what you saw yourself, not what other people, books, or subsequent reflections tell you. I saw integrity, sincerity, kindness of heart, generosity to opponents, and a certain nobility of soul that stamps all his music; but on the other hand I saw coarseness, uncivilizedness, a defective perception of subtle shades in people and things, lack of humour and of course the inevitable and righteous selfishness of people who have a message of their own to deliver and can't run errands for others. When Wagner died he sent a wreath and was bitterly hurt at receiving no acknowledgement. A friend of the Wagners told me gloatingly that Cosima had said: "Why should the wreath be acknowledged? I understand the man was no friend to Our Art" – and my informant added: "It was a mistake to send it at all." Of such was the Kingdom of Wagner.

The accounts that reached the world of his cruel illness and death were infinitely tragic, for he fought against his doom, they say, and like a child when bedtime comes, wept and protested he did not want to go. The only consolation is to believe, as I for one do, that his best work was behind him, and that perhaps Nature did well to ring down the curtain.

from IMPRESSIONS THAT REMAINED *1919*

"He is Brahms – my profound respect. But I am Bruckner and I prefer my own stuff." *Anton Bruckner.*

Mussorgsky

GERALD ABRAHAM

Mussorgsky's art is essentially that of 'a man of the 'sixties'. The phrase conveys little, perhaps, to the average Western reader. But to a Russian it is as familiar and as precise in meaning as the words 'Elizabethan' or 'Victorian' to an Englishman. 'The 'sixties' mark an epoch in Russian history; and 'the men of the 'sixties', alternately worshipped as heroes and derided as back-numbers, seem a race apart. Coming after the appalling despotism of Nicholas I, the reign of Alexander II (at least, in its first half) appeared almost millennial. With the freeing of the serfs, which altered so much and seemed to have altered so vastly much more, Russia took one of the greatest of all her clumsy strides from feudalism towards the modern Western state. The freed *mujik* was suddenly elevated to a pedestal and sentimentally worshipped – particularly by aristocrats like Tolstoy and Mussorgsky who saw that he was free from the vices of their class and were wilfully, happily blind to those of his own. To all that was young and generous and intelligent in Russia it was a dawn as blissful as that which intoxicated young Wordsworth.

But the expression of this exuberant emotion took a surprising form. Just as the business-like Western, in such moments of spiritual intoxication, turns his back on harsh reality and kicks up his heels in the most fanciful antics, the enthusiasm of the dreamy Slav takes the form of fiery determination to be practical. (The 1860s help us to understand the 1920s.) He works himself up to the facing of facts and the grappling with them, enthusiastically resolves to put behind him the seductions of mere sensuous beauty to which he is generally so susceptible. Mussorgsky's art is a manifestation of both the spiritual and intellectual exuberance, the intense aspirations of the period (towards the brotherhood of man, and so on), and a relentless determination to be truthful at all costs, a contempt for that which is merely beautiful. And at its best, when these two elements are in perfect equilibrium as in *Boris*, Mussorgsky transcends 'the 1860s' and rises to universality as completely as Shakespeare transcends the Elizabethan age. If Mussorgsky is in every fibre a Russian 'of the 1860s', he is so only as Shakespeare is, through and through, an Elizabethan Englishman.

Leaving aside all technical, purely musical considerations, the head and front of Rimsky-Korsakof's offending against *Boris* is that he completely altered its values. It is as if Rubens had repainted a Pieter Breughel. The 'truth' is carefully toned down, the beauty made correspondingly more luscious. It is all very splendid – but it is the negation of that which is Mussorgsky's special, and still unique, contribution to music in general and to opera in particular. It parallels Dryden's *Tempest*, Cibber's *Richard III*, *Othello*-with-a-happy-ending; and Korsakof's justification is precisely that of the 'practical men of the theatre' who made the crudities of Shakespeare tolerable to polite English audiences of the Augustan age. But if Rimsky-Korsakof is to be indicted for his well-intentioned crime, practically the whole of musical Russia must go into the dock with him for aiding, abetting and approving. For not only the rank and file of professional musicians and cultured amateurs, but critics of the high standing of Findeisen and Karatygin long agreed in preferring the Korsakof version to the original. The resuscitation and revaluation of the genuine *Boris* is principally due to the efforts of a few critics in France, Russia only following suit after the Revolution. Professor Lamm of Moscow must be given the highest praise for his recent admirable edition of the authentic texts of Mussorgsky's complete works.

Apart from his harmonic forthrightness and his consistent refusal to 'manufacture' music by conventional technical processes, the most striking of Mussorgsky's musical innovations are in the field of naturalism – truth to the spoken word, truth to plastic movement (the 'writing' themes in *Boris* and *Khovanshchina*, the 'Promenade', the two Jews and so on in the *Exhibition Pictures*) – a naturalism equally effective in comedy and tragedy. In all this, particularly as regards the musical opportunities offered by humour, Mussorgsky was indebted to Dargomyjsky. Yet his actual musical style owes little to the older man, even in *The Marriage* or the most naturalistic of the songs. (And neither Dargomyjsky nor anyone else had possessed anything like Mussorgsky's ability to get inside the minds of children.)

Even if we object, on general aesthetic grounds, to Mussorgsky's musical prose in his less inspired moments, when he is content to give a mere literal translation of word and gesture into tone, we are left with an extraordinary wealth not only of inspired 'translation', of sheer lyrical loveliness and of racy, vital melody, but – the seal of Mussorgsky's genius – of dramatic points produced by non-naturalistic means: the moving innocence of the 'Tsarevitch' motif at its first appearance in *Boris* (cut even from Mussorgsky's own version of 1874) where it accompanies Pimen's words, "All steeped in blood and lifeless lay Dimitri"; the brass chords in the second scene of the Prologue, just before Boris's words "Now let us pay a solemn tribute to the tombs of Russia's rulers", chords (particularly the unexpected D major) almost as thrilling as those of Mozart's trombones in *Don Giovanni*; the music which accompanies Golitsyn's departure into exile in *Khovanshchina* (based on that of Marfa's divination), so simple and beautiful, yet loaded with such an intolerable weight of tragic destiny; the irony of the lovely snatch of folk-song sung by Shaklovity over the body of the murdered Khovansky; the equally effective, but more brutal irony of the banal march of the Preobrajensky Guards in the last act of the same opera. There is no end to these strokes of dramatic genius, astounding in their simplicity, each as definite and final as an overwhelming line of Shakespeare's.

What Mussorgsky's operas do on the large scale is done in miniature by his songs. They cover an even wider field of emotion and experience, and explore each corner with even greater daring. Things like 'Savishna', 'The Magpie', 'The Peep-Show' and the *Nursery* cycle are unique in song-literature; and each is an adventure along a different line from the others. A man who had written nothing but the *Songs and Dances of Death* and *Sunless* would have to be given an important place among the world's song-composers. Nor have even twentieth-century musicians given us anything quite like the *Pictures from an Exhibition* for piano.

And we owe all this to a poor, drink-sodden, inefficient little Government clerk, more than half a child to the end of his life, a naughty child, vain, affectionate, lovable – a pitiable creature who happened also to be a genius.

from MASTERS OF RUSSIAN MUSIC *1936*

Dvořák

ALEC ROBERTSON

Dvořák knew where he wanted to go quite soon in his creative career, but he was not certain of the means of getting there. Smetana, on the other hand, was single-minded. He submitted himself, in the event, to a martyrdom to give his people, in the form that most appealed to them, the opera, music which would reflect their highest thoughts and aspirations, as well as their lighter moments and national customs. It would be impertinent and untrue to suggest that Dvořák loved his country less; but fair, I think, to say that the order of his artistic ambitions was different. He had not, therefore, Smetana's single-mindedness; he wanted to give the world music that would be recognized as cosmopolitan first and Czech second. Politics and propaganda of any sort were alien to him. How much personal ambition was included in his vision none can say. The enormous success he had in England might have ruined a man of less integrity. And *Saint Ludmila* stands as a warning sign to a downward path. The huge success of the *Slavonic Dances* might, again, have tempted him to exploit the national vein, but this too he resisted and, instead, in his use of it he enriched all music. And it must not be forgotten that when Vienna offered him thirty pieces of silver for a German opera he did not hesitate to refuse. Nevertheless the ambition remained and was with him until the end of his life. One notes his frequent use of the term 'Slav'. He would not be hemmed in behind the frontiers. He was more race- than nation-conscious. Of the works of the greatest period of his creative career only one, the *Hussite Overture*, is distinctly national: the others are personal documents.

The problem that faced Dvořák, therefore, was that of finding a style through which he could fulfil his ambition of conquering the frontiers and showing the world that a Brahms could be found in Bohemia. If the *Slavonic Dances* can be taken as the types of his national style there is the fact, which has defeated so many composers, that the folk-tune is not susceptible to development, being self-contained, lacking generative power, and therefore unsuitable for large-scale works. But the music he had grown up with 'moved in his veins like blood', it was his own dialect, his natural method of speech. He did not imitate folk-tunes as, for example, Rimsky-Korsakov confessedly did, he created in the spirit of them. He thus showed that he understood the difference between nationalism and the national spirit. We see him, then, as a sort of Eliza Doolittle, rich and racy as his own self – and an infinitely poetical Eliza too – learning painfully how to speak with the voice of the musical *haut monde* and apt, sometimes almost as disconcertingly as Eliza, to relapse at any moment into his native speech.

I do not, therefore, recognize different periods in Dvořák's development so much as these reckless changes of direction, aimed at solving a complete problem. We cannot know just how far he was actually conscious of all this; but I do suggest that the impurity of style which is bound to strike unfavourably anyone who looks over the whole corpus of Dvořák's work arises from the fact that he never wholly succeeded, in his larger works, in forging a style which completely satisfied him.

The casual listener, to whom Dvořák means the 'New World' symphony, one of his most 'impure' works, will find all this an unnecessary pother. But, others may reflect, which of the early nationalist composers, Chopin, Borodin and Smetana apart, ever succeeded in the larger instrumental forms without writing highly repetitive works, such as *Scheherazade*, or compromising as Dvořák does? He was not, as was Rimsky-Korsakov, essentially a writer for the stage: he was a composer of absolute music, and yet he was too much of a Czech and too different a man to adopt, and continue in, the cosmopolitan but yet very personal style that we find in Tchaikovsky. He was, in my opinion, always seeking and often coming very near to finding a wholly integrated style, a harmonious marriage of two opposed worlds. If great success had not robbed him of the severe critical faculty of his youth he might have found and kept it. . . .

In the old days of the music-hall a familiar turn was the quick-change artist. He was now Napoleon, now Gladstone, but always unmistakably himself behind the disguises. Dvořák is never convincingly disguised, and one is therefore bothered by the assumed personalities. This process continues up to the end of his life; and it does not seem to me possible that it can be written down by the serious student of Dvořák's music, however great his sympathy with its causes, as other than a severe limitation. . . .

But let us look at one of the greatest gifts bestowed on Dvořák, one that has the power to float his music even when it is dead weight: the gift of movement. His music never sags as sometimes does the music of a composer in whom so many of his faults of style and construction are found in an unpleasantly over-ripe form – I mean Mahler – for whatever is moving, whether it be a finely shaped tune, a soggy stream of sixths and triplets, a formula of dotted quavers, continues to move. With this gift, as has been well said, he vitalizes the entire mass of his tone and gives rhythmic individualization to under parts. His never-failing store of counter-melodies are no better, and no worse, as counterpoint, than Wagner's in, say, the *Mastersingers* overture or the 'Dance of the Apprentices', but they both fulfil their purpose effectively and give plenty of jam to those who have to play them. He has, indeed, an endearing habit of distributing good things to all and sundry A second oboe or second violin is made to feel that he is of importance in the scheme of things. The sum of this rhythmic genius plus a wide and often sharply contrasted range of dynamics, give Dvořák's music the vitality that is one of its most delightful qualities. . . .

Now that the writing of this book is done, and, with it the long period of examination of [Dvořák's] whole output, I rise from i with the feeling that I have been in the company of a good, san and healthy man whom one has grown to love for his faults as we as for his virtues: for indeed, his weaknesses are a condition of hi strength.

from DVOŘÁK *194*

Elgar

FRANK HOWES

Elgar was the first composer of full stature to be thrown up by English music since Purcell. He was not a direct product of the renaissance movement initiated by Parry, nor like Vaughan Williams had he dug in English soil to thrust his roots to the life-giving waters of nationalism. He is a curious figure, enigmatic from whatever aspect he is regarded, and his place in European music is still the subject of debate. The Continent has never wholly accepted him as a front-rank composer – it likens him to Strauss but holds him in lighter esteem. Yet it was the Continent – Germany in fact in the person of Richard Strauss – who hailed him as a 'Master' after the famous performance of *The Dream of Gerontius* at Düsseldorf in 1902, which was the chief factor in reversing English judgement of the work upon its disastrous first performance at Birmingham in 1900. Strauss's toast of Elgar on this famous occasion was in these terms: "I raise my glass to the welfare and success of the first English progressivist (Vorwärts-mann), Master Edward Elgar of the young progressive school of English composers." Strauss recognized in Elgar a kindred spirit, striving for a larger expressiveness against the then hardening arteries of the German romanticism which had dominated European music for three-quarters of a century. Such a toast was certainly unusual, but the performance of English works abroad was not. Stanford had had operas performed on German stages – so had Ethel Smyth. Elgar, however, went farther than any previous English composer since the Elizabethans in penetrating the European mainland, by writing one of the few really great violin concertos and getting it played first by the Austrian, Kreisler. Menuhin in more recent times has carried it round the world, and the Violoncello Concerto has also engaged the interest of international artists like Feuermann and Casals, Fournier and Tortellier. The *Enigma Variations* has a world-wide vogue as far as Japan and the *Introduction and Allegro for Strings* has found a place in the repertory of the great continental (including Russian) and American orchestras. Five works, and those his greatest, have, then, won a place in the international repertory, and foreign opinion may therefore be said to endorse the highest claims made for Elgar by his compatriots, though the two symphonies have so far failed to convince foreign opinion that they are music of the same calibre and importance.

We are not, however, bound to defer to foreign opinion and should have the courage of our own judgement. But here at home opinion, or rather perhaps taste, is quite sharply divided. Professor Dent raised a hornet's nest about his ears when in a contribution in 1931 to Adler's *Handbuch der Musikgeschichte* he enumerated, with the bluntness required by the compression of a handbook, four features of Elgar's style which gave offence to a section of English opinion (which incidentally Dent described by implication as the academic and conservative): 'too emotional', 'not quite free from vulgarity', 'pompous', and 'too deliberately noble in expression'. This criticism offers a parallel to the literary criticism of Kipling, his contemporary who similarly reflects the Edwardian age of English social life. Indeed it is tempting to regard Elgar's music as representative not so much of his country as of his period, and it is significant that European music critics, invited to London in 1935 by the British Council, sooner or later fell back on the name of Richard Strauss to describe to their readers the kind o' music Elgar's was (independently of the judgement they may have passed on it). Elgar reflects the last blaze of opulence, expansiveness and full-blooded life, before they perished in the twentiet' century, qualities which take one somewhere near to that abun dance of vitality which we call vulgarity. We may well envy th Edwardians the liberty, wealth and well-being which was to b swept away by world-wide wars, but we need not be deterre from saying that it was after all just a little vulgar. . . .

All musicians used to serve their day and their generation an be content that that should be their work in life. But under th influence of the romantic movement, with Beethoven glowerin at them from immortal masterpieces, they, their critics and eve their public began to demand nothing but masterpieces. Tl dichotomy of serious and light music became equated with tl struggle between good and evil. English musicians, while n exempt from the requirements of the code of perpetual sublimit were still required by institutions, festivals, coronations and pub' occasions to produce music of temporary validity. Elgar began as a musician serving local needs and present times and only entered the serious category in middle life and in the changed ethos of the new century. He did not make any such hard-and-fast distinction – is it likely that he could have done? – but it may perhaps be granted that his self-critical sense was no more highly developed than that of most composers, who regularly think their latest work their best but still do not like their past achievements belittled; perhaps he was less self-critical than some. But a composer is entitled to be judged by posterity for his best work. On that computation Elgar is historically important for giving to English music a sense of the orchestra, for expressing what it felt like to be alive in the Edwardian age, for conferring on the world at least four unqualified masterpieces, and for thereby restoring England to the comity of musical nations.

from THE ENGLISH MUSICAL RENAISSANCE *1966*

"My dear Shaw: I am recording the violin concerto tomorrow and Friday with Yehudi Menuhin – wonderful boy. Can't you engineer that I sit with you for the first performance of *Too true to be good*? I remember the glory of being with you for *The Apple Cart*." *Edward Elgar*. – A letter dated 13 July 1932.

Aesthetics of the Mahler Ballet

DESMOND SHAWE-TAYLOR

Some ten years ago the news that Kenneth MacMillan proposed to make a ballet out of *Das Lied von der Erde* dismayed some of those who cared most deeply about Mahler's supreme masterpiece, and the project was vetoed by the Covent Garden board. This setback must have greatly distressed the gifted young choreographer; but he had set his heart on the idea, and in due course he carried it through triumphantly at Stuttgart. Now that his *Song of the Earth* has reached Covent Garden, and has again been rapturously received by press and public, it is natural to regard our previous apprehensions as ungenerous and narrow-minded, and to see the brilliant and imaginative choreographer in the light of a Walther von Stolzing whose positive achievement has routed the pedantic Beckmessers and stupid Kothners.

But the case is more complex than that. What MacMillan has achieved in this ballet is indeed extraordinary, and at times very moving. As Andrew Porter, an unqualified admirer, puts it in the current number of *About the House* (the Covent Garden magazine), 'It is precisely because there is no *detailed* attempt at illustration that the ballet is successful in a way that strict musicians might hardly believe possible.' MacMillan has judged and held his distance from the subject-matter of Mahler and his Chinese poets with marvellous skill and sensibility; what he has given us is a poetical paraphrase, never a literal translation.

For example, the merest hint of chinoiserie appears in his treatment of a single number, *Of Youth* (the one about the party of friends in the porcelain pavilion reflected in the water), to just the same limited degree that we feel a pentatonic tinge in the music. The suggestion of drunken movements in the fifth song (and, to a lesser degree, in the first) is so stylized as to be entirely free from vulgarity; the encounter of flower-gathering girls and handsome young horsemen in the fourth song (*Of Beauty*), though a shade more representational than usual, is conceived in a wholly lyrical spirit; and the very end of the long final song (*The Farewell*), in which the three leading dancers (Haydée, MacLeary, Dowell: exquisite creatures all) advance towards us – when it would have been the obvious solution to make them retreat and vanish – with wave-like gestures of eternal renewal, provides a climax of piercing loveliness that seems exactly true to Mahler's vision. (Alas, that the audience should burst in with applause before the music has faded into silence!)

Why then is my surrender incomplete? Why have I any reservations whatsoever about this poetical ballet which I am so glad to have seen and so eager to see again? Mainly because, well as I know and deeply as I love Mahler's score, I cannot possibly take in, with all my faculties at full stretch, the whole complex multi-layered audio-visual experience that is being so lavishly unfolded

When I listened to the music even half as attentively as I would have done at a concert, my visual focus blurred for the moment, and I found that I had missed as striking a balletic event as an entrance of the Messenger of Death; conversely, when I concentrated on the ballet (which was of course more often, this being the new feature), I found that the music had slipped past beautifully but insubstantially, like a dream, seeming incomprehensibly brief. I felt as though confronted by a huge club-sandwich, of which every layer was excellent but the whole too tall for the mouth to bite.

I have asked other musicians whether they found that Mahler's music had made anything like its full musical impact on them under these conditions, and they mostly admitted that it hadn't – tending to attribute the fact to the shortcomings of the conductor, Hans Swarowsky. Mr Swarowsky's handling was indeed somewhat rigid: but I do not really believe that the result could have been wholly satisfactory under any conductor. The singers who stood one on either side of the stage (the tenor's white tie and tails striking an oddly incongruous note) were two of the most promising of the younger generation, Yvonne Minton and Vilem Pribyl; but, whether intentionally or not, their delivery of line and text was cool and self-effacing to a degree that would be inconceivable in a concert performance. They were being used in a subordinate capacity that is aesthetically indefensible.

Imagine a Bruno Walter, a Kathleen Ferrier and a Julius Patzak to have been involved in the proceedings . . . but at once the mind recoils, and we perceive that artists of such a calibre could not possibly have been involved. I don't mean simply that their *amour propre* would have forbidden it, but that if they had performed in Covent Garden at the maximum intensity of which they were capable, they would have provided (at any rate for the really musical people in the audience) an impossibly vivid counter-attraction to the doings on the stage, as well as a degree of rhythmic subtlety and rubato which would have made some of those doings distinctly hazardous; while conversely, if they can be imagined as giving for the occasion some such adaptable performance as we heard at Covent Garden, we should then have been outraged by the waste of their interpretative genius.

There lies the aesthetic dilemma as I see it: we cannot have

Mahler's glorious music under ballet conditions at anything like the necessary imaginative heat; and we can attend fully to Mac-Millan's intrinsically beautiful and relevant dance-poem only while half-hearing a musical accompaniment that is likely to be under-nourished and not of the finest quality. Though frequent repetition will undoubtedly make the music go more smoothly and efficiently at Covent Garden, it will also tend to iron out such individual turns of phrasing and touches of colour (from the two singers above all, but also from the orchestral players) as are indispensable in this ultra-refined and richly woven texture. There is simply too much going on for such matters to be completely attended to, whether by performers or by listeners.

I think I can see why those who apprehend the art of ballet more vividly than I, and feel its emotional impact more deeply, should in their enthusiasm salute *Song of the Earth* as one of the great ballets of the century. But the other ballets that come into the highest category were composed either to music written specifically for dancing or to music markedly less elaborate and self-sufficient than Mahler's great score. MacMillan's work displays rare apprehensions of beauty and a high degree of imaginative sympathy; but not even he can weld all this over-rich matter into such an aesthetic whole as we admire in *Petrushka* or *Les Noces* or *The Three-Cornered Hat*.

from The Sunday Times

A Centenary Evaluation of Delius

DERYCK COOKE

Although Frederic Delius lived most of his life on the Continent, his music has never gained the slightest footing in any continental country, except for a short-lived popularity in Germany before and just after the First World War, which has long since died out. Only in this country has it won any kind of lasting recognition; and it is a truism to say that this has been almost entirely due to the advocacy of Sir Thomas Beecham, who for half a century, from 1909 until his death pursued a consistent policy of thrusting Delius' music on the attention of the British public.

But I am convinced that Delius' popularity in this country has been a factitious, ephemeral affair. It only really began with the 1929 Delius Festival, when it was given a great send-off by the presence of the heroic figure of the blind and paralysed composer himself, who had emerged from comparative obscurity; and afterwards it was sustained by the magnetic personality of Beecham. At other concerts, I have never noticed any tumultuous applause after a Delius work, though the performances were often good enough to elicit enthusiasm from an audience of genuine Delius lovers. The wave of popularity began to dwindle after the Festival of 1946, with the progressive decrease in Beecham's performances of the music, and it has reached a very low ebb in the last few years. It seems certain to me that only a minority of the English musical public has ever really loved Delius.

The same is true of the musical profession, whose attitude tends to create the general climate of opinion; I have met far more English musicians who disliked Delius' music than who admired it. It is significant that there has been no thorough and comprehensive study of his music. Consider the main literature on this composer – only four books in all, and only one of them is a critical study of the complex style and form of the music. Eric Fenby's moving account of how he worked as amanuensis to the stricken composer threw invaluable light on Delius' personality and his method of working, but it naturally was not concerned with a critical examination of his output.

Compare with this the extensive list of books on Elgar, several of which are detailed critical studies, and one of which is a volume in the 'Master Musicians' series – an honour significantly denied to Delius.

29 January [1962] will be the hundredth anniversary of Delius' birth, and a concert of his music is being given in the Royal Festival Hall, but of the two popular London music magazines, neither carries a centenary article: there is little doubt that the press mainly regard the Delius centenary as a tiresome obligation, and once this year is over they are hoping to drop Delius like a hot coal.

My own explanation of this general unpopularity is that Delius is a peculiarly individual, isolated composer – a composer *sui generis* – whose style is incomprehensible to most people, because they expect it to conform to certain traditional standards which are outside its terms of reference. And the cause of this isolation was the anomalous social position of Delius himself. Alone among composers of any standing, except perhaps Busoni, he had no roots in any single national culture. His Dutch–German ancestry; the English environment of his childhood and youth; his years of wandering in Scandinavia, the United States, and Germany; his final settling in France for the main part of his life – all this made him into a stateless artist. He was technically an Englishman; he was born in Bradford and spent the formative years of his life, until the age of nineteen, entirely in England; he spoke with a Yorkshire accent, and was even a cricket enthusiast; but he was never at home in this country. And despite his German blood, and the fact that he called himself Fritz Delius till he was forty, he was not at home in Germany either; he preferred to make his home in France. Yet he never became the slightest bit gallicized, for after a few years in Paris, spent mainly with an international artistic group, he retired to the country, and lived more or less as a recluse at Grez-sur-Loing, cut off from French life.

Not unnaturally, this isolated, cosmopolitan existence produced an isolated, cosmopolitan musical style. The normal composer is a national composer, in the most fundamental sense: whether he uses the folk-music of his race as Janáček did, or only its traditional classical style, as did Brahms, he expresses the spirit of his people; and he bases himself primarily on an appeal to his compatriots – his reputation begins at home. Then, by a seeming paradox, this national quality enables him to appeal to groups in other countries, as a recognizable representative of his own race.

But Delius' style is a non-national amalgam of influences from the various countries with which he had connections. It blends together Scandinavian elements from Grieg, features of the Negro music of Florida, aspects of the German style of Wagner, procedures from French impressionism, and has at times a strong English pastoral idiom which Delius may possibly have originated. None of these predominates as a main stream, on to which the others have been grafted; and in consequence, Delius has fallen between all the national stools, particularly those of Germany, France and England. His rich Wagnerian harmonic texture appealed for a time in Germany, when his music was still 'modern' and 'difficult'; but when it lost its newness, the presence of strong elements of French impressionism became apparent, and the Germans, who have never appreciated Debussy, judged it vague and amorphous. In France, Delius' impressionistic elusiveness might have appealed if it had not been weighted down with a particularly rich German texture; the French found his music heavy and woolly, on the few occasions when they had a chance to hear it. In England, the English pastoral element was the main reason for the temporary response to Beecham's advocacy; real Delius lovers in this country have been chiefly attracted by the music's power to evoke the open air and the English countryside; but the equally strong German and French elements always made him an exotic for the majority. This is one reason why the English have never taken Delius to their hearts, as they have the truly English Elgar and Vaughan Williams.

Three other points are worth mentioning in connection with England. In the first place, sensuous and emotional chromaticism, which plays such a large part in Delius' music, has been regarded by the majority of English musicians as something unmanly, morbid, almost sinful – surprising though that may be in a people which produced Purcell. Then there was Delius' entirely un-English attitude to life – his hedonistic, Nietzschean, anti-Christian self-centredness – which can be felt in his music; this even upset some of his warmest admirers, such as Fenby and Hutchings. Lastly, in regard to the present, there is the unfortunate legacy of the false identification of Delius with the English pastoral school in the 1930s and 1940s. The young musicians of today, who hardly know Delius' music, see him as belonging to the orbit of Vaughan Williams, Bax and Ireland, which, with the unkindness always shown by the English to their leading composers, they are busy debunking as hard as they can.

Like other composers, Delius wrote a number of inferior works, and some of the out-and-out Delius worshippers have not made a clear distinction between good and bad. Beecham, for example, sang the praises of the early Piano Concerto, which Delius himself regarded as a poor work; he also dug out the quite immature opera

Irmelin, and in his biography of Delius he advocated more performances of the early works in general.

If we want to take the best of Delius, we have to agree with
Eric Fenby, and reject all the music he wrote up to 1899, before
the age of thirty-seven, and I would say most of the music he
composed after 1916, from the age of fifty-four onwards. His main
claim to an abiding place in musical history lies in some fourteen
works, almost all written between these two dates. These are the
large-scale *Mass of Life*; two shorter choral works, the *Songs of
Sunset* and the *Songs of Farewell*; the opera *A Village Romeo and
Juliet*; three tone-poems involving voices – *Appalachia*, *Sea-Drift*,
and *The Song of the High Hills*; four purely orchestral tone-poems –
Brigg Fair, *In a Summer Garden*, *Eventyr*, and *Song of Summer*; the
suite of *North Country Sketches*; two orchestral miniatures – *On
Hearing the First Cuckoo in Spring* and *Summer Night on the River*;
and a single one of his four concertos – the one for violin.

Taking these works as a basis, the first positive quality of Delius'
music is surely the intense individuality of his style; and this is in
itself a token of genius – for I agree with what Mosco Carner has
said of Puccini: 'It is a sign of genius if an artist has been able
to create a world which, by the force of his imagination and gifts,
he compels us to recognize as peculiarly his own.' Second, and
hand in hand with this originality goes an ecstatic sensuous
beauty. Such a remark may seem naïve in an age which has explained beauty away in terms of 'significance'; but in music,
sensuous beauty is an irreducible quality – a great quality, which
some composers have pursued more avidly than others; Mozart,
for example, more than Haydn, as we realize if we think of the
Clarinet Concerto and Quintet.

It was by absorbing the influence of Wagner that Delius first
found himself. We can hear this clearly in one of the few places in
his first really mature work where the influence has not been quite
fully absorbed: in *A Village Romeo and Juliet*, of 1901, the 'dawn'
music is unmistakably Delius, but it betrays a debt to the 'dawn'
music in *The Twilight of the Gods*. The second main influence was
the impressionism of Debussy. This is rather more elusive and
difficult to pin down; but the opening of *Brigg Fair*, for example,
with its flute arabesques, its impressionistic string, harp and horn
texture, and its free progressions of dominant sevenths and ninths,

is obviously unthinkable without the example of *L'Après-midi d'un faune.*

Wagner's romantic melodic and chromatic harmony, and Debussy's arabesques and sensuous progressions of dominant sevenths and ninths – absorbing those of Grieg – might seem to account for Delius' mature style, allowing that he made something very individual out of his sources. But there was another, equally strong influence – the Negro plantation songs which he heard in Florida in the 1880s; he was fascinated, not only by their melodic style but by the original type of harmony which the Negroes used to improvise when they sang them. His tone-poem *Appalachia* is based on an old Negro slave melody, and the final slow choral statement of the tune is a stylization of the Negro harmony which Delius heard. In places it strikingly anticipates the use of such harmony by jazz composers like Gershwin, many years later, showing that Negro jazz originated its own harmonic style, and did not derive its dominant ninths from Debussy, as is generally assumed.

Delius' style is a peculiarly limited one: he confined himself largely to a very personal harmonic basis, and to a slow or slowish tempo, to express a particular aspect of human feeling, concerned with the beauty of nature and the transience of human life. This means that he lacked the wide expressive range characteristic of the very great composer; but we need not criticize him for that. The wise composer confines himself to expressing only what he is fitted to express, and if he does this with mastery, he can claim his own place in musical history. In any case, Delius' expressive range is often declared to be much narrower than it really is. The aspect of human feeling which he dealt with has itself many aspects; and the third positive quality of his music is his amazing variety within his limited range.

It is often said that there is a lack of rhythmic interest in Delius' music, and a lack of formal grasp, which place him on the level of a mere amateur, who is only successful on a miniature scale. It cannot be denied that there is some truth in this accusation, when applied to all but his best music; but when it is directed against that, it is carried to such lengths as to be a particularly flagrant example of the general incomprehension of Delius.

Delius' rhythm and form, like his melody and harmony, are

isolated, cosmopolitan products, which have no national home. He followed the same iconoclastic path as Debussy, rejecting traditional rhythmic and formal methods, and evolving new procedures of his own; but he mainly retained the slow, fluid rhythmic style of Wagner's *Tristan*, which was unacceptable for new music in France after Debussy. On the other hand, he largely rejected in Wagner the traditional method of rigorous thematic development, in favour of Debussy's mosaic-like type of construction; and this made him unacceptable to the symphonically-minded Germans – and to the English too, since most English musicians regard the symphonic tradition as the ultimate yardstick for measuring everything.

In evolving his own rhythmic style and formal method, Delius presented further difficulties to his hearers by limiting himself far more than Debussy. Intent on expressing his own inner world, he largely rejected the more extrovert, incisive aspects of rhythm and form as useless for his purpose. This means that there are none of those clear-cut rhythmic shapes, exciting thematic-rhythmic developments, and sharp contrasts of conflicting themes and keys which we find in the work of almost every other tonal composer. Delius softened the edges of rhythm and form, within the general orbit of a slow tempo, until his music took on all the aspects of a stream of pure rhapsody. And it is this illusion of rhapsody that has given rise to the general misunderstanding.

For the sense of rhapsody *is* an illusion. Pure rhapsody – in the sense of a continuous stream of ideas which have no thematic, rhythmic or formal connection – is a myth. The truth is that Delius pursued as close a thematic, rhythmic and formal logic as Debussy. I believe that if any of Delius' propagandists had taken the trouble to make and publish meticulous analyses of his best works, it would have been realized that he had, as Eric Fenby has said, 'a well-nigh perfect sense of form for what he wanted to say'.

The further positive quality of Delius' music – a most unexpected one – is the fascination of his original thematic, rhythmic and formal methods, within his limited range. Again, there is a remarkable variety, for these methods are used in a different way in each work. I have spent a good deal of time analysing his finest works, and I have been amazed at his endless resource within such a restricted orbit. But this very fluidity makes it ou of fashion amid the mechanized rhythms and forms of the new music.

Delius was the creator of a highly individual and beautiful art, which is limited to exploring a single area of the human spirit, but does so with comprehensiveness and mastery. It may be a narrow art, but it goes very deep; it says many things that no one else has said; and there is no case for neglecting it except that of passing fashion. A just treatment of Delius' music, after this centenary year, would be to go on performing the best of it, but not whole concerts and festivals of good and bad alike, as in the 1930s and 1940s. To hear too much of any composer can deaden his impact, but Delius, with his confined expressive range, cloys the appetite sooner than most. Only two of his outstanding works occupy a whole evening – *A Mass of Life* and *A Village Romeo and Juliet* – and these do possess sufficient variety to prevent any sense of satiation. The others are normal-size concert-works; and the best way to feature them would be to set them between works by other composers of the most extrovert character, from the classical and modern periods. In this way, their special character would be set in high relief as one of the finest manifestations of late-romantic music.

from The Listener *25–1–1962*

Sibelius and Nielsen

JOHN HORTON

With the appearance of two composers of the calibre of Sibelius and Carl Nielsen, both of whom were born in 1865, the Scandinavian lands can be said to approach the status, musically speaking, of Great Powers. No longer is it a question of admitting the worth of lyric miniatures, but of reckoning with symphonic structures impressive in dimensions and rugged of aspect, presenting a defiant challenge to the musical experience of audiences and critics whose own native traditions may be far more continuous than those of Finland or Denmark. The challenge has not gone unanswered, and controversy over the relative and absolute merits of the two protagonists still flourishes, especially in the English-speaking countries where interest in both, but particularly in Sibelius, has always been stronger than anywhere outside Scandinavia itself. In Britain there has been a falling-off in the enthusiasm that accompanied Beecham's sponsorship of the works of Sibelius in the 1930s, followed by a reaction, during the middle years of the century, in favour of Nielsen; recent changes of fashion, and a renewed admiration for the late nineteenth-century Viennese symphonists, have given rise to further questionings which clearly will not be resolved until both the northeners can be seen further off in the perspective of history. . . .

Though comparable in stature and reputation – and, it must be repeated, in the vicissitudes and local limitations of their fame – the two composers show profound differences of musical temperament arising partly from the natural and cultural environments in which they grew to maturity. Sibelius belonged to the Finnish race with its twin cultures, the Swedish and the Ugrian-Finnish, with yet a third in the background, that of European Russia, whose own origins were partly in Scandinavian lands. As the years went on Sibelius seems to have encouraged the popular view of his personality as enigmatic, lonely and introverted, drawing inspiration from nature, both directly and through the poetic medium of *Kalevala* with its mythology and nature symbolism. His tone-poems, and perhaps his symphonies also, belong to that superhuman, or sub-human, universe rather than to the life-size world of ordinary humanity.

Carl Nielsen, on the other hand, identifies himself with human comedy and tragedy, and is characteristically Danish in his frank enjoyment of the kindlier and warmer aspects of nature and humanity, in his mercurial temperament, and in the prolixity of his fancy. But it may prove fallacious to carry too far an examination of his music from a psychological standpoint. His main interest seems, after all, to be in the qualities of vocal and instrumental sound and in exploring fresh possibilities of combining them. 'The glutted must be taught to regard a melodic third as a gift of God, a fourth as an experience, and a fifth as the supreme bliss' this observation of Carl Nielsen recalls the well-known remark by Sibelius about the glass of cold water. Both aphorisms are sympto matic of a revulsion against the later developments of German romanticism.

The musical structures of Sibelius have often been analysed and described. They involve great economy of material, with the creation of apparently undistinguished ideas which gradually reveal powers of inner development and outer coherence under the stress of an intense rhythmic drive and sense of climax. The time-span is made to appear all the greater through the tension of organic growth upon a foundation of slow but inevitable harmonic movement. Subordinate devices strengthen the feeling of progression over a huge time-scale: the long-drawn monotone that focuses attention on the moment and the means of its own release, the splendidly graduated crescendos. Carl Nielsen often displays no less ability to pile up tensions and climax; but he is more generous, even prodigal, with his ideas, not all of which he necessarily carries on to the later stages of development. Much has been made of his treatment of key systems; they are as firmly grounded in tonal harmony as those of Sibelius, but there are frequent and unpredictable deviations and often a gradual change of key-centre in the course of a lengthy movement without an eventual return to the starting-point. Whereas with Sibelius every note contributes towards a unified drive on an ultimate goal, in Carl Nielsen's major works there are diversions and interruptions, humorous or petulant according to the prevailing aspect of his musical temperament.

from SCANDINAVIAN MUSIC *1963*

Falla and Spanish Tradition

ATES ORGA

Manuel de Falla (1876–1946), in common with most nationalist composers enjoys today rather dubious favour. On the one hand is argued that his nationalism is a weak pastiche of an idiom already effectively exploited by non-Spanish composers. Cecil Gray did much to promote this view in his book, *A Survey of*

Contemporary Music (1924). As far as he was concerned the music of Albéniz, Granados and Falla 'is always pleasant to listen to, but reveals no distinctive personality. Spanish national music has so far produced no Borodin or Mussorgsky, but only three Rimsky-Korsakovs – which is three too many.' Gray, usually a perceptive writer, was occasionally prone to such over-simplified generalization, and in the case of Falla such remarks have been the source of much casual dismissal.

On the other hand there is the view that, as a nationalist, Falla in any case was already doomed to failure when such mid-European contemporaries as Schoenberg and his disciples were forging ahead into a new world of revolutionary theories and innovations. Their language was closely involved with the emergence, in the first two decades of this century, of several progressive artistic movements: surrealism, expressionism, cubism, and to a lesser degree – since this was dependant to some extent on the two former trends – dadaism. Klee, Kokoschka, Tzara and Arp were the spiritual leaders of the creative arts, but while many adhered sometimes slavishly, to their philosophies and aesthetic, Falla remained uninfluenced and unimpressed. Curiously even such protagonists of cubism as Falla's friend, Picasso (who designed the sets for the first performance of *The Three Cornered Hat* in London in 1919), and his compatriot, Gris – with whom one might have reasonably expected a national affinity and sympathy on Falla's part – remain unidentified with the nature and character of his music.

This argument, a *fait accompli*, ignores the possibility of nationalism – as developed by Falla, Stravinsky, Bartók and other – assuming a role in twentieth-century music as important and necessary as serialism and neo-classicism. This is particularly true of Falla's maturity. Gray's view stems from various sources: one of these was inadequate knowledge of Falla's later works. His assumption is often supported with the excuses afforded through Falla's small output of music, and his nationality, factors which do not stand up to analysis. It is true that over a period of some forty years he produced only eight principal works which were completed. Since these finished compositions date from between 1904 and 1926, it may at first seem justifiable to level the criticism that it is difficult to grasp the development and maturing of creative talent in a comparatively limited period of time and on the basis of such few works. How, it is asked, could a composer of such small output assume any importance? Familiarity shows that such an opinion has little foundation, for in these works Falla expressed more than many composers do in a lifetime of industrious effort. Through his deliberate exploitation and study of Spanish tradition, his music and theories become very important, and particularly significant when considered historically. He was in fact an evolutionary nationalist, comparable to only a few other musicians; the richness and variety of his scores is an eloquent testimony of his gifts.

As a Spanish composer, it is certainly unfortunate that the impact of Falla's music – as with his immediate contemporaries – is weakened through the extensive use of Spanish folk-music by too many indiscriminate foreign composers, often in search of local atmosphere rather than in any genuine artistic stylization. This brings us to the roots of Gray's comments, for particularly during the nineteenth century the national identity of any Spanish composer was obliterated through the application of Spanish colour (limited to a few melodic phrases, and instrumental characteristics) by such influential cosmopolitans as Glinka and the Russian school, Liszt, and – among the French – Bizet, Chabrier, Debussy and Ravel. They were clever in their use of this music, but they invariably copied an idiom of which their knowledge was largely superficial. By contrast Falla realized the essence of national music by going to its elemental sources. The dominance of foreign composers at the expense of the Spaniards makes this situation extraordinary and unique among the nationalist schools but that is no ground for criticizing Spanish composers. Others have suffered a good deal less in this respect, either setting a precedent or developing from their predecessors, and unencumbered by the marauding ravishes of outsiders. Consider for instance the positions of composers like Smetana, Dvořák, Grieg, and the Russians.

In any work of art, progression, not regression, must be the governing factor in evaluation. In the post-1900 Russian nationalist school, for example, Stravinsky's music developed, while the subsequent nationalism of the Communist period is largely unsuccessful because it lacks this quality, and tends to

regress. By this token it is possible to place Falla. Set against the
background and confines of a Spanish tradition, his work is
clearly progressive. He looks to, rather than takes from, the past:
the core of his art lies in its relation to this past, and that is really
the only basis on which we can successfully discuss and appraise
Falla's contribution to music.

It is convenient to divide his development into four periods:
the first (to 1907) covers the student years and the emergence of
national feelings; the second (1907–1914) centres around Falla's
stay in Paris; the third (1914–1919) represents the logical climax
of nationalistic tendencies latent in the first period; while the
final period (1920–1946) moves away from obvious nationalism
Falla's style gaining a new independence and revealing a search
for new forms of expression with a foundation in Spanish classical
tradition.

Since the first and third periods are related, it is useful briefly
to consider the Paris years. This stay was fruitful in so far as Falla
learnt and observed from established composers like Debussy,
Ravel and Dukas. He also established himself as a pianist of some
note (he had studied with José Tragó at the Madrid Conservatoire
having begun piano lessons with his mother who was Catalan
making his Paris début in October, 1910, in the first complete
concert of Spanish music ever given in France. This was
memorial concert for Albéniz who had died the previous year.

At that time Paris was particularly responsive to Spanish music
which was widely performed and published. Falla appreciated the
atmosphere, but did little creative work. In the main, his Paris
period proved a time of observation and of perfecting the nuance
of his art, as well as strengthening his early Impressionist
tendencies – indebted to the French example, as in *Nights in*
Gardens of Spain (1909–1915), the concerted piano part assuming
a largely colouristic rather than virtuoso prominence. Harmonic-
ally, also, this work shows Impressionist influence, in the first
movement's use of parallel chords, unresolved dissonance, and the
prolonged passages where the middle and higher registers of the
piano provide a timbre and character close to Debussy and Ravel

Falla here fused foreign influences with an idiom – as yet
unperfected – derived from his study of Spanish folk-music.
Nevertheless he had sufficiently absorbed the melodic and h

monic implications of folk-music that the style of many passages in *Nights in the Gardens of Spain* has an already distinctive ethnic character. Professor J. B. Trend has commented that Falla's music in general symbolizes 'a power of what Spaniards call *evocación* – a sense of poetry or suggestiveness . . . something which can be felt rather than explained'.

In many ways the vagueness of this remark is as escapist as Gray's generalizations. Certainly Falla's music has the atmosphere which Trend suggests, but is it sufficient to talk of music in these terms? Part of the fascination of studying a composer and his work is to attempt a definition of the structural and emotional stimuli of his language: analysing the nature and origins of such stimuli can afford penetrating insight into the workings of a composer's mind. Yet too often one reads about the 'feeling' of music, without further clarification. Falla has suffered this treatment quite frequently, yet if his music is related to his regional and cultural environs, several significant pointers to his style emerge. This brings us to the consideration of his first and third periods in particular.

To a large extent he owed his interest in Spanish tradition to his composition teacher, Felipe Pedrell (1841–1922), an influential composer and scholar, with whom he commenced a course of studies in 1902. Pedrell advocated the philosophy of the eighteenth century Jesuit writer, Antonio Eximeno, which was principally one that 'each people should construct its musical system on the basis of its national folk-song'. His contribution towards an authentic, unpopularized image of national music (coinciding with similar movements elsewhere in Europe, although rooted somewhat earlier) did much to establish the influential claim of Spain's cultural heritage. By the time Falla came to study with Pedrell, the latter had published his manifesto on national opera (*Por Nuestra Música*, Barcelona, 1891), and Falla could not have been unaware of its contents. But, unlike Pedrell, he did not make the error of interpreting too literally the ideals of the nationalist school, and in his best work he realizes and surpasses the essence of Pedrell's theories, beginning with *La Vida Breve*. This prize-winning 'lyric drama' was Falla's first success, and resulted from a competition for national opera, organized by the Spanish Royal Academy of Fine Arts in 1904. It had been preceded by a number of prentice works, later discarded, which included at least five *zarzuelas* – a staged divertissement akin to the ballad-opera, *Singspiel* and *opéra comique*, but of earlier origins – as well as chamber works which reveal classically influenced inspiration. The other main work of these years was the Four Spanish Pieces for piano, composed in 1906, and published in 1909.

Another formative factor in Falla's appreciation and realization of Spanish tradition was his family background. Suffice to say that his father was Andalusian: and for most people Spanish music has always been associated with Andalusia, the other four regions of the country having no such immediately recognizable identity for the layman. This is partly due to Moorish influence in Andalusia, which lasted from 712 until 1492, when their political dominance in their last stronghold, Granada, was routed by the armies of Ferdinand of Aragon and Isabella of Castille. They were finally expelled in 1610.

While it is inaccurate to say that Moorish music directly influenced or altered the growth of indigenous music in the area, it is nevertheless true that characteristics of instrumental and vocal performance were integrated, and the Spaniards were attracted to the basic qualities of the idiom. This is not altogether surprising since it is probable that both cultures stemmed from the same source in the theory and practice of ancient Greece.

I think it may be useful to digress here on the nature of Moorish music in Spain, which remains a debatable point, and Falla's own attitude towards its influence. A distinctive but not always acceptable argument has been made by Henry George Farmer who maintains that Moorish influence on Spanish music was an all important formative factor, and remains clearly definable. Car Engel had made a similar claim as long ago as 1866, when hi *Introduction to the Study of National Music* was first published, an Spanish writers such as Menéndez y Pelayo and Mitjana y Gorda share the same opinion. Falla, however, put forward differer theories in his pamphlet *El Cante Jondo (Canto Primitivo Andaluz* published in Granada in 1922, as an introduction to a festival o *cante jondo* organized in June of the same year by Falla and Garc Lorca.

Falla categorized the emergence of Andalusian folk-song three stages. The first gave priority to the development and ado tion of Byzantine chant by the primitive Church in Spain during the fourth and fifth centuries. This composite language admitted an early oriental influence in idioms adopted from the Greeks, Hebrew chant, and possibly later mannerisms, from the music of the Levant. Falla's second category concerned itself with the Moorish invasion of the Iberian peninsula, while the third considered the influence of nomadic gipsies who migrated to Spain in 1447-9.

The theory of Byzantine influence suggests that the basic essentials of Andalusian music were established *before* the Moors arrived, thus weakening the arguments of scholars such as Farmer. This coincides with, and probably stems from, Pedrell's similar view put forward in his important collection, *Cancionero musical popular español* (four volumes, 1918-22), as well as in earlier books. The theory may have some substance: for example, seven of the original eight Moorish modes were identical with the already established sacred Iberian modes, and therefore introduced little that was new. This fact, coupled with both modal systems adhering to the Pythagorean scalic theory, seems to substantiate a common root which admitted the fusion of these apparently different cultures without distortion, a point I made in passing a few paragraphs above.

Falla's belief in the gipsy influence is somewhat questionable, since their nomadic music has been largely coloured by the traditions of the lands they passed through; if the gipsies had a distinctive aboriginal culture it has long since vanished, although remnants may survive in the music of the genuine Hungarian rural gipsies, as distinct from Magyar and so-called 'gipsy' music. In Andalusian music, the gipsy influence might have strengthened the oriental element for originally the gipsies came from northern India and the Indus basin. In their mass migration in about 1000 A.D., one group passed through Persia, possibly picking up certain types of Seljuk music, which in itself may have developed from Greek or Byzantine chant.

From Persia, the gipsies wandered across Syria and North Africa and on to Spain. Allowing for the infiltration of alien influences, a tradition with origins in some corrupt form of Indian or Himalayan music – and which had for several centuries been subjected to Islamic idioms – could have been quite easily integrated into the existing cultural life of fifteenth-century Spain, but is unlikely to have introduced anything new. With Moorish domination on the wane, any gipsy overtones passed into the vocabulary of the peasantry. At this time and subsequently after 1492, the notated music of the Church shows heavily Euro-peanized traits and marks the beginning of Spain's renaissance school. There is no inflexion of Moorish or gipsy tradition in this music.

The most frequently popularized view of gipsy influence in Andalusian music is the emergence of the word *flamenco*, a term of doubtful meaning and scarcely a century old. The gipsies have always had the reputation of ornamenting and bringing their own personality to bear on any native music (the Balkans are a good case in point), and in fact *flamenco* is no more than a highly coloured stylization and re-interpretation of the Spanish national spirit and of *cante jondo* (another fairly recent term). Medina Azara put forward the theory that *cante jondo* was influenced by the Hebraic synagogue chant of the Sephardic Jews (expelled from Spain in 1492 as part of the fanatic onslaught against non-Chris-tians), thereby introducing yet another possible influence, again oriental in origin. Their rituals and music have been faithfully preserved to this day in the Sephardic colonies of the Near East.

There is no circumstantial evidence in this hypothesis, but *cante jondo* was nevertheless a very early form of national music. It is imbued with a 'tragic sense of life' (as Miguel de Unamuno so aptly phrased it), and during the nineteenth century it was taken up by the gipsies, and became closely associated with prisons. In both instances it was, no doubt, some deep-rooted affinity with the impassioned sentiments of the music and words which provided the main attraction.

At this moment of time it is largely futile to argue as to the priority of primary influences in Spanish music. It is, however, obvious that from the earliest a basic *oriental* derivation was a principal quality. It is impossible now – as it was for Falla and Farmer, and indeed for any folk-lorist or musicologist – to provide conclusive evidence, since practically no manuscripts have sur-vived and few textbooks of the period are explicit on this question. Any view must be largely conjectural.

from Music and Musicians *August 196*

Schoenberg

DONALD MITCHELL

I think one may claim that one of the main tasks that faced the creators of the New Music was reintegration. Perhaps it may be expressed thus, this seeking after new means of composing, of putting together:

> to obtain the status of a rule; to uncover the principle capable of serving as a rule.

Those words are not mine. They are not even the words of a musician. They comprise, in fact, the definition of 'standardization' by the architect Le Corbusier, a figure in modern culture of the greatest importance, not only for what he had done, for what he has built, but for what, as a creator, he stood and stands. He may be compared, not vaguely, but in close detail, with Schoenberg, with whose career and personality Le Corbusier shares an astonishing amount of common ground. (An ironic parallel resides in the sharp resistances each of these remarkable men has aroused, with the result that some of Le Corbusier's most significant and influential buildings have never risen beyond the drawing-board, while much of the music of the most influential composer of the twentieth century was for years scarcely heard in the concert hall.) Le Corbusier, out of the experience of his practice as an artist – I used the word advisedly: our ignorance of the *art* of architecture is shameful – evolved his Modulor: 'A Harmonious Measure to the Human Scale Universally applicable to Architecture and Mechanics'. Schoenberg, likewise, out of the practical business of composing, evolved his 'Method of Composing with Twelve Tones Which Are Related Only with One Another'. It is amusing to compare the reception of Le Corbusier's Modulor with the reception of Schoenberg's Method, not because the world of architecture offers a salutary contrast to that of music, but because the resistances to, the criticisms of, the Modulor – of course, one has to take into account the impact of the whole man, the total personality, just as one must with Schoenberg – are couched in the very same terms, the very language, in which the latter's

Method was assaulted. We find, moreover, Le Corbusier fighting on those two fronts with which students of Schoenberg's art are so richly familiar (incidentally Schoenberg himself tells us that he was called an architect, not to flatter him, but to deny his serial music spontaneity); on the one hand Le Corbusier has had to insist that 'Science, method . . . the ART of doing things: never has it shackled talent or imprisoned the muse', on the other, to defend the Modulor from some of its indiscriminating disciples:

I have devoted watchful attention to the use of the 'Modulor' and to the supervision of its use. Sometimes I have seen on the drawing-boards designs that were displeasing, badly put together: "But it was done with the 'Modulor'." "Well then, forget about the 'Modulor'. Do you imagine that the 'Modulor' is a panacea for clumsiness or carelessness? Scrap it. If all you can do with the 'Modulor' is to produce such horrors as these, drop it. Your eyes are your judges, the only ones you should know. Judge with your eyes, gentlemen. Let us repeat together, in simple good faith, that the 'Modulor' is a working tool, a precision instrument; a keyboard shall we say, a piano, a *tuned* piano. The piano has been tuned: it is up to you to play it well. The 'Modulor' does not confer talent, still less genius. It does not make the dull subtle: it only offers them the facility of a sure measure. But out of the unlimited choice of combinations of the 'Modulor', the *choice* is yours."

Substitute 'ears' for 'eyes', 'Method' for 'Modulor', and that brilliant passage might well have been written by the musician, not by the architect. Consider these passages from Schoenberg:

The introduction of my method of composing with twelve tones does not facilitate composing; on the contrary, it makes it more difficult. Modernistically-minded beginners often think they should try it before having acquired the necessary technical equipment. This is a great mistake. The restrictions imposed on a composer by the obligation to use only one set in a composition are so severe that they can only be overcome by an imagination which has survived a tremendous number of adventures. Nothing is given by this method: but much is taken away.

The possibilities of evolving the formal elements of music –
melodies, themes, phrases, motives, figures, and chords – out
of a basic set are unlimited.

One has to follow the basic set; but, nevertheless, one composes
as freely as before.

It would hardly be necessary to recite these well-known quo-
tations were it not for a still-widespread belief that Schoenberg's
Method magically substituted an unnatural and arbitrary set of
rules for what was, hitherto, the unimpeded 'inspiration' of the
composer, rules which either excluded inspiration (so chained and
enslaved becomes the Muse!) or made inspiration simply super-
fluous, i.e. the Method was a convenient recipe for composition,
rather like cooking: Take a Basic Set, warm it gently until it gains
shape, invert it, etc.

Perhaps it was inevitable that the Method itself should become
the centre of attraction. This danger was seen at the outset, when
Schoenberg's 'new formal principles', in an essay of that title by
Erwin Stein, were first set down in print – a most important
paper, first published in 1924, at a time when the Method had only
just reached its final stage, had just, that is, been composed (composed, *not* abstractly constructed outside musical experience).
Stein writes:

> No doubt the chief objection to the new formal principles will
> be: "Why, all this is constructed!" And so it is – not theoret-
> ically, however, but practically, not in terms of intellectual
> concepts but of notes. Let us see a work of man that is not
> constructed! Or is it seriously suggested that fugue or sonata
> have grown like the lilies of the field? That the Ninth 'struck'
> Beethoven, just as a bad joke occurs to a journalist? Why don't
> you have a look at his sketch-books? The constructor of genius
> invents.

And elsewhere he observes:

> The depth and originality of Beethoven's musical ideas cannot
> be adequately described by such words as 'intuition' or 'inspira-
> tion'. Beethoven *worked* – not only with his heart, but also with
> his brain. Why, indeed, should thinking necessarily stupefy?

But despite this very lucidly expressed warning, Schoenberg's Method was talked about, thought about, fought about, as if it were altogether a matter of theory. That it was deduced from his practice as a composer, then demonstrated in his serial compositions, that time and time again he begged for judgement of his work (and that of his pupils) based not upon appraisal of the Method but upon evaluation of the music as music, these facts were lost in a fog of mostly uninformed criticism. Worse still, Schoenberg's music, between the first and second world wars, made the most infrequent appearances in the concert hall, a neglect that was, of course, intensified by the ban on his music imposed by the Nazis. This quite extraordinary and exceptional state of affairs was in no way accompanied by a diminished controversy in respect of the Method. On the contrary, we had the curious situation in which the works of certainly the most influential composer of the twentieth century were hardly to be heard, while the Method – which had first been born of music and afterwards rationalized and adopted as a creative principle in work after work – was as hotly disputed as if the music had, in fact, been ever present in hostile ears. It was not long, indeed, before the merits of serial technique were pronounced upon by those who had had no contact with Schoenberg's music whatsoever; an oddly unreal, artificial and basically unhealthy condition which had tragic consequences for Schoenberg's personality, if not for his art. How conscious he was of the unmusical spirit in which his music was often approached could not be better illustrated than by this letter, written in his own English, which belongs to 1938:

Now one word about your intention to analyse these pieces as regards to the use of basic set of twelve tones. I have to tell you frankly: I could not do this. It would mean that I myself had to work days to find out, how the twelve tones have been used and there are enough places where it will be almost impossible to find the solution. I myself consider this question as unimportant and have always told my pupils the same. I can show you a great number of examples, which explain the *idea* of this manner of composition, but instead of the merely mechanical application I can inform you about the compositional and æsthetic advantage of it. You will accordingly realize why I call it a 'method' and why I consider the term 'system' as incorrect. Of course, you will then understand the technic [*sic*] by which this method is applied. I will give you a general aspect of the possibilities of the application and illustrate as much as possible by examples. As I expect you will acknowledge, that these works are principally works of musical imagination and not, as many suppose, mathematical constructions.

One doubts whether the kind of attitude of which Schoenberg complains could arise except in a period in which, as Sigfried Giedion puts it, 'thinking and feeling proceed on different levels in opposition to each other'; initial resistance to Schoenberg hardened into a purely intellectual reaction to what was considered to be a wholly cerebral invention (the logic of the opposition need not detain us here, though we may savour the familiar irony of the pot calling the kettle black). Thinking excluded feeling, even on the rare occasions when one of Schoenberg's serial works was performed. It has not been so since, that is, after 1945, when many works by Schoenberg, played to a public largely innocent of – perhaps blissfully uninterested in – the Method and the interminable speeches of its opponents (and some of its propagandists), have offered so intense an emotional experience that their audiences have insisted upon an immediate encore.

Where lies the explanation of this phenomenon? No one in his senses can suppose that concert audiences in different countries, listening to different works, will have risen to their feet to celebrate the triumph of a 'system' and demand its repeat. Of course not. What was desired was the chance immediately to renew contact with music that had deeply stirred them. No doubt, had it been possible, Schoenberg's opera, *Moses and Aaron*, would have been encored after its première in Zürich in 1957; the spontaneous storm of applause was so overwhelming, so demonstrative of the profound impact the work had made, that it has lived on in the memory of those who witnessed it almost as an experience in its own right. This posthumous triumph was suggestive of the success his music might have enjoyed if it had been played more and talked about less.

from THE LANGUAGE OF MODERN MUSIC *1963*

"Schoenberg was ignored until he began to smash the furniture and throw bombs, whereupon everybody began to talk about him." *H. T. Finck*

Stravinsky and the Ballet

CONSTANT LAMBERT

When we consider the stuffy and faded academicism of Stravinsky's and Schoenberg's first works, it is impossible not to draw the conclusion that the disruptive element in Debussy's impressionism provided the liberating force that led these composers to their own revolutionary style.

It is strange to think that Stravinsky's ballets were at one time considered to be a healthy and vigorous reaction against the impressionism of Debussy, comparable in force to the reaction of Cézanne against Monet. Novelty of colour alone can be held to explain this confusion of thought. The garish and overloaded orchestration, barbaric rhythms and savagely applied discords of Stravinsky's ballets temporarily numb the critical faculties, and prevent one from realizing that however different the texture may be Stravinsky is using sound in the same way as Debussy. Barbaric impression has taken the place of super-civilized impressionism – that is all.

The difficulty of estimating Debussy's influence on Stravinsky is complicated by their common derivation from the Russian nationalists. A famous instance of this derivation is to be found between the opening of Debussy's *Nuages* and the opening of Stravinsky's *Le Rossignol*. Both passages bear an extraordinary resemblance to one of the songs in Mussorgsky's *Sunless* cycle. It is almost impossible to decide whether Stravinsky, the last of the three, is reacting to Russian nationalism, or to that side of Debussy that reacted to Russian nationalism; and we are faced with the same difficulty when we try to decide whether the oriental arabesques that occur from time to time in Stravinsky's melodic writing are a latter-day continuation of the oriental tradition started by Glinka in *Russlan and Ludmilla*, or whether they are a reflection of the undoubtedly oriental quality in many of Debussy's themes.

We must remember that Russian nationalism is by no means a continuous tradition. The death of Borodin was succeeded by a period of conservatism and academic reaction, in comparison with which the works of Brahms take on an almost Offenbachian quality. It is not too much to say that the vividly picturesque tradition of the Russian nationalists emigrated to France somewhere in the early 'nineties to return home dressed in the latest Paris models, just in time to join in the Diaghileff ballet. In *L'Oiseau de Feu* Stravinsky applied the rejuvenating influence of Debussy's impressionism to the by now, somewhat faded Russian fairy-tale tradition in much the same way that one pours a glass of port into a Stilton, thereby hastening the already present element of mortification. The resultant effect is rich and *faisandé*, but a little over-ripe, with a suggestion of maggots in the offing. The exhilarating and wintry gaiety of the fair in *Petrushka* with its buxom nurses, dancing bears, drunkards, gipsies and barrel-organs, seems at first sight far removed from the ruined temples in the moonlight, the reflections in the water, of Debussy's pictorial world, but the difference between Petrushka and the fair scenes in the early Russian operas lies precisely in the application of Debussy's pictorial methods to a cruder and more vivid tradition.

In *Le Sacre du Printemps*, considered at one time as the outstanding reaction against the invertebrate qualities of the Impressionist school, the influence of Debussy's technical methods is even more marked, though the self-consciously barbaric colour of the ballet may make this influence a little hard to recognize at first sight. The two finest sections in the work, the preludes to either part, are in the direct Impressionist tradition, although one may notice in passing that Stravinsky manages his orchestral texture less skilfully than Debussy; the various threads of *La Nuit Païenne* are less clearly presented than those of *Les Parfums de la Nuit*; the whole effect, in its lack of definition and its reliance on colour alone, being more impressionist than Debussy.

There is an obvious end to the amount of purely physical experiment in music, just as there is an obvious end to geographical exploration. Wyndham Lewis has pointed out that when speed and familiarity have reduced travelling in space to the level of the humdrum, those in search of the exotic will have to travel in time, and this is what has already happened in music. The Impressionist composers vastly speeded up the facilities for space travel in music, exploring the remotest jungles and treating uncharted seas as though they were the Serpentine. Stravinsky, at one time the globe trotter *par excellence,* can no longer thrill us with his traveller's tales of the primitive steppe and has, quite logically, taken to time travelling instead. He reminds one of the character in a play by Evreinoff who lives half in the eighteenth century, half in the present.

The advantages of time travelling are obvious. The pioneer work has been done for you already and, owing to the increased facilities for moving from one century or decade to another, you can always be in the right decade at the right time, whereas in space travelling you may be delayed by a month or two, or even find that the intellectual world has gone on to the next port.

The most successful time traveller of our days was undoubtedly Serge Diaghileff, though it might be more accurate to describe him as a ubiquitous and highly efficient Cook's man to the time travellers, rather than a bona fide voyager. Though he had to the end a congenital, but carefully disguised, dislike of time travelling he was the first to realize the artistic and commercial possibilities of the new device. In his palmy days before the [1914–18] war he was of course, a space traveller, bringing to the Western world a picturesque oriental caravan laden with the rich tapestries and carpets so suited to the taste of an age that was able to combine material prosperity and spiritual preciosity in such nice proportions. He was not only giving the intellectual public what it wanted, he was given them what he liked himself. In music his genuine taste was for the luscious, and in *décor* for the opulent. In spite of all his very successful and convincing toying with post-war intellectuality, his favourite ballet was probably *Scheherazade*.

But an impresario however gifted cannot remain fixed in any particular world of taste whether he finds it sympathetic or no. He depends on surprise and novelty for his *réclame*, and Diaghileff, by appealing to a more intelligent audience than that sought by the ordinary commercial impressario, was, like the composers of the Impressionist period, forced into a policy of novelty and sensationalism that gathered speed as it went. By the time the audience had just caught up with his last creation he must be ready with the cards of the next trick up his sleeve. He thus found himself in something of a dilemma after the war, for although the audiences were fully prepared to go on applauding the old ballets, and to find all the old glamour in an entertainment that now had the added glamour of being 'White Russian', he himself knew that this enthusiasm was in the nature of a 'hangover' from the pre-war period, and that unless he could find a new avenue of taste for exploration he would be as dated as the older dancers whom he had ruthlessly left by the way. But he could never again achieve his earlier triumphs of the exotic period [and] consequently evolved the most typical artistic device of the present age, that is to say, time travelling in more than one century or period at once. It is a device that is peculiarly well adapted to musical expression and in particular to ballet. . . .

By his adoption or even invention of the particular type of present-day pastiche that can be conveniently described as time travelling Diaghileff immediately established a position of mastery again. It was not even necessary that his associates should be time travellers themselves – for by picking on collaborators sufficiently disparate in outlook he could achieve the required effect – but to start with, at least, he required a similar mentality on the part of his associates, and in Stravinsky, whose executive abilities so far outweighed his creative gifts, and who, like himself, was a some-what *déraciné* figure, he found the ideal collaborator. *Pulcinella* was the first example of this movement, and though it may not seem on the face of it a very important piece of work it ranks as an historical date with *Pelléas*. It marks the beginning of the move-ment sometimes dignified with the name of neo-classicism.

Stravinsky was by far the best person for Diaghileff to send time travelling in the eighteenth century because, both temperament-ally and racially, he was out of touch with the whole period. A Frenchman or an Italian might have felt some embarrassment about jazzing up the classics, but Stravinsky is like a child delighted with a book of eighteenth-century engravings, yet not so impressed that it has any twinges of conscience about redden-ing the noses, or adding moustaches and beards in thick black pencil.

Pulcinella combines the chic of today with the chic of the eighteenth century – always a safe period to consider 'good taste'. Yet there is something touchingly naïve about Stravinsky's attitude towards Pergolesi. His thematic material is all there for him, he does not even have to vamp up a pseudo-Russian folk-song, and yet by giving the works a slight jolt, so to speak, he can make the whole thing sound up to date and so enjoy the best of both worlds. The jolt he gives the machine consists, on the whole, in a complete confusion between the expressive and formal content of the eighteenth-century style. In Stravinsky's adaptation the expressive element is treated in a mechanical way, and purely conventional formulae of construction are given pride of place. Like a savage standing in delighted awe before those two symbols of an alien civilization, the top hat and the *pot de chambre*, he is apt to confuse their functions.

from MUSIC HO! *1934*

"Stravinsky's symphony for wind instruments was written in memory of Debussy; if my own memories of a friend were as painful as Stravinsky's seem to be, I would try to forget him.' *Ernest Newman.*

"Ce *Sacre du Printemps* – bien plutôt un massacre du printemps!' *H. Moreno.*

Walton's Viola Concerto

DONALD F. TOVEY

The style of this work is modern in so far as it could hardly have achieved its present consistency before 1920 (the actual date 1929); but it does not consist of negatives. Hence it will arouse the anger of many progressive critics and composers in these days of compulsory liberty. William Walton's music has tonality, form melody, themes, and counterpoint. The counterpoint, and hence the harmony, are not always classical. Classical counterpoint is harmony stated in terms of a combination of melodies: classical harmony is the result of good classical counterpoint where the inner melodic lines are not meant to attract attention. Modern counterpoint tends actually to avoid classical harmony. It prefers that the simultaneous melodies should collide rather than combine; nor does it try to explain away the collisions. It wishes the simultaneous melodies to be heard; and if they harmonize classically the combination will not assert itself as such. Hence modern counterpoint is no longer a technical matter at all; its new hypothesis has annihilated it as a discipline. But this very fact has thrown new responsibilities on the composer's imagination. A technical discipline becomes a set of habits which, like civilization itself, saves the artist from treating each everyday matter as a new and separate fundamental problem. The rule-of-thumb contrapuntist need not trouble to imagine the sound of his combination; his rules and habits assure him that it cannot sound wrong. The composer who has discarded these rules and habits must use his imagination for every passage that he writes without their guidance. It is by no means true that mere haphazard will suit his purpose. Nor, on the other hand, is it true that any great classical master used rules as a substitute for his imagination. One of the first essentials of creative art is the habit of imagining the most familiar things as vividly as the most surprising. The most revolutionary art and the most conservative will, if they are both to live, have this in common, that the artist's imagination shall have penetrated every part of his work. To an experienced musician every score, primitive, classical, or futurist, will almost at a glance reveal the general question whether the composer can or cannot use his imagination. About details I would not be too sure. To the experienced musician Berlioz has no more business to exist than the giraffe; 'there ain't no such animal'.

Walton is no Berlioz: a glance at his score will suffice to show an art that has been learnt as peacefully as any form of scholarship. And it is possible to read the first twelve bars of this Viola Concerto carefully without finding anything irreconcilable to an academic style in the 'nineties. After the twelfth bar the range of style expands. But let us note that it thereby differs from the many

other modern styles which contract. Walton's style is not sentimental; but neither is it anti-romantic.

Similarly, it is neither theatrical nor sensational; and its forms
do not at first seem to have more than a slight external resemblance
to sonata forms. Yet it has essential qualities of sonata style in
its ways of getting from one theme to another and in its capacity
to give dramatic meaning to the establishing of a new key.
Walton's dramatic power has asserted itself in oratorio; but its
unobtrusive presence in this thoughtful piece of purely instrumental music is more significant than any success in an oratorio
on the subject of Belshazzar's feast. The sceptical critic can always
argue that an oratorio, especially on such a subject, can hardly
go wrong unless the librettist's intellect is subnormal. But when a
composer can write an effective concerto for viola (an instrument
with a notorious inferiority complex) and can move in it at something like the pace of a sonata, it is as obvious that he ought to
write an opera as that Bruckner, Wagnerian though he was, ought
not, and fortunately did not. . . .

There are so few concertos for viola that (even if I happened
to know any others) it would be a poor compliment to say this was
the finest. Any concerto for viola must be a *tour de force*; but this
one seems to me to be one of the most important modern concertos for any instrument, and I can see no limits to what may be
expected of the tone-poet who could create it.

from ESSAYS IN MUSICAL ANALYSIS *193*

Shostakovich Without Ideology
the Soviet's most celebrated composer has had his ups and downs but is the Party really to blame?

PETER HEYWORTH

Dmitri Shostakovich is the victim of two myths. In the Soviet
Union, he has been held up as the prime example of how collec-
tive criticism and the guiding hand of the all-knowing Party can

rescue a composer from the barren trammels of modernism and help him to speak in a language intelligible to the people as a whole. In the West, he has generally been regarded as a composer of immense promise whose genius has been stunted and deformed by the obscurantist Communist doctrine of the arts as servants of social ends.

Shostakovich's career offers enough evidence to make either of these views superficially plausible. It is true, in a way, that he was – at a crucial moment in his development – in some degree 'rescued' from modernism. It is most certainly true that he suffered a great deal in the worst days of Stalinism. Yet both theories leave a good deal unexplained. For instance, if Shostakovich's weaknesses as a composer are to be attributed to the stultifying dogmas enforced by Zhadanov, why is his Symphony No. 12, written in the full flood of Khrushchev's thaw, by so far his worst? Conversely, if the Party 'rescued' him from modernism, how is it that his Fourth Symphony, which was banned in 1934 during rehearsals for the first performance, didn't turn out to be particularly 'modern' when it was finally heard a couple of years ago? The fact of the matter is that Shostakovich's evolution as a composer has been too unpredictable to provide useful ammunition for political controversy. It will be many years before we know the full truth, but it certainly won't be as simple as ideological warriors would have us suppose.

In 1917, when the Revolution broke out in his native city of Leningrad, Shostakovich was a mere child of eleven. He is thus the only composer of world repute who has spent his entire working life under Communism, and in the dramatic ups and downs of that life are mirrored much of the stormy history of the arts in the first Marxist state.

Shostakovich was only nineteen when his First Symphony, written in 1925 while he was a student at Leningrad Conservatory, carried his name around the world. Because of this early start and his residence in what was still in some degree the country's cultural capital, he participated directly, as contemporaries like Khachaturian did not, in the extraordinary artistic ferment taking place in those first years of the Union of Soviet Socialist Republics. This was a period when the young revolutionary state took it for granted that one of its functions was to support revolution in the arts; and as a result musicians of radical aesthetic bent – politically naïve, disingenuous, converted, or merely curious – flocked to the new Mecca.

In Leningrad the young Shostakovich was able to see Berg's *Wozzeck* on the stage of his local opera house shortly after its first performance in Berlin in 1925, and almost a generation before he would have seen it had he lived in Paris, London, or New York. There is every reason to suppose that its effect on him was profound. No less crucial to his development were the symphonies of Mahler, which conductors like Bruno Walter and Fritz Stiedry were then making known in the Soviet Union. Although Stravinsky had cut all links with his fatherland, his early neo-classical works were performed there. Bartók came as an interpreter of his own music, and so did Hindemith, Milhaud, and Honegger. Above all, at this time scores were still arriving from the West.

Surrounded by all this revolutionary ferment in the arts, what could have been more natural than that a prodigiously gifted rising composer should have plunged into it with all the abandon of youth? And in doing so was he not helping to overturn the stuffy old idols of the bourgeois world with its plushy, flyblown romanticism? Like young Hindemith and Weill in Berlin, like young Walton in London, like Stravinsky and Les Six in Paris, so Shostakovich threw himself into this new world of anti-romantic modernism. As a result, his music in the late 'twenties is for the most part irreverent, grotesque, leg-pulling, and full of his own special brand of sardonic, parodistic humour. Music of all sorts poured from his pen: a satirical opera called *The Nose*, incidental music to Mayakovsky's *The Bedbug*, the score for a ballet on the adventures of a Soviet football team. These must have been intoxicating years, and, like many young *avant-garde* artists, Shostakovich devoted a lot of his energy to cocking snooks at the past. For the time being all this went down quite well. As long as the Soviet Union still regarded itself as the bridgehead of a world revolution, it had nothing against art that held bourgeois society and its morals up to ridicule.

In 1931 Shostakovich completed the opera that was to mark the turning point in his career: *Lady Macbeth of Mtsensk*. Based on Leskov's short novel, it tells the story of a woman who murder first her rich father-in-law and then her feeble husband in orde to run off with a brutal farm labourer. He of course deserts her, so she murders his new mistress and then drowns herself. The general style of this lurid work is expressionist and there can be little doubt that *Wozzeck* was a considerable influence on its general aesthetic aim, for Shostakovich's intention was to depict the heroine as a pathetic victim of circumstances, rather as Berg seeks our pity for his feeble-minded batman.

At first *Lady Macbeth* was an immense success. Certainly there was no question of banning it. Quite to the contrary, it was staged all over the Soviet Union. But in 1934 something went wrong. It is said that Stalin attended a performance and, sitting directly over the ample and hard-worked brass section, was baffled and enraged by what he heard. Certainly neither in musical style nor in moral outlook was the opera well calculated to appeal to his rather restricted sensibility. True or not, this story is indicative of the fundamental changes that had overcome the Soviet Union since the blithe days of Shostakovich's youth. Stalin had abandoned, for the time being, all hope of world revolution, in order to concentrate on strengthening the Party's grip on Russia itself. Naturally, the arts had a role to play. From underminers of bourgeois life in countries supposedly ripe for revolution they had to be turned into supporters of the *status quo* in the Soviet Union; and clearly an opera written in a style that the Party functionaries couldn't understand, and which in some degree could be said to glorify a murderess, did not serve this purpose. Accordingly, *Lady Macbeth* was attacked in *Pravda* and disappeared from all Soviet stages until the winter of 1962, when a revised version entitled *Katarina Ismailova* was mounted in Moscow. At the same time as *Lady Macbeth* ran into trouble, the Fourth Symphony, which Stiedry was already rehearsing in Leningrad, was withdrawn. At Edinburgh in 1962 Shostakovich claimed that he had himself withdrawn the Symphony as he was 'dissatisfied' with it – and promptly went on to emphasize that not a single change had been made in the score during the intervening years.

Pravda's attack on *Lady Macbeth* was the first of a series of official assaults on artistic independence which did immense damage to the cultural life of the Soviet Union. But it does not follow that everything the Party organ wrote on this occasion was foolish. I was fortunate enough to see the original version of the opera on the last occasion it was given, in Düsseldorf in 1960. *Pravda* was, of course, wrong to assert that an opera on this theme should not have been written, but it is by no means certain that it was wrong to mock the idea of turning such a woman into a heroine. The circumstances in which Shostakovich's Lady Macbeth coldly commits two murders are by no means comparable to those in which poor tormented Wozzeck knifes his mistress. Furthermore – and this is crucial – Shostakovich's music cannot rival the power of Berg's score in compelling acceptance of the composer's point of view. It is a youthful, brilliant score, but in its dramatic effect it does not often rise above the level of *grand guignol*. It totally lacks the tragic dimension of *Wozzeck*.

For over eighteen months after *Pravda*'s rebuke this usually fertile composer wrote nothing. And then in 1937, still only thirty years of age, he produced his Fifth Symphony, obligingly headed 'Creative reply of a Soviet artist to just criticism'. Contrary to everything that a Western liberal might expect, it proved to be Shostakovich's first fully mature work. Naturally enough, the Party's cultural officials were jubilant. Had not their criticism been admitted by its object as deserved? Better still, had it not yielded fruit in the shape of the finest score that Shostakovich had yet written? The precedent was an ugly one. The bureaucrats had demonstrated to their own satisfaction that they could 'improve' an artist, and in the coming years they were not to prove shy in attempting to repeat their success.

So much for the crisis of *Lady Macbeth*. With the Fifth Symphony, Shostakovich redeemed himself; and shortly after came the War, in which he was used as a trump card for Soviet propaganda. After the much publicized *Leningrad* Symphony (1942) there followed the far greater Eighth Symphony (1943), which contains some of the most profoundly disturbing and violent music he has ever written. He followed up this massive score with the lighthearted Symphony No. 9 (1945), in which he seemed to return to the jaunty manner of his mis-spent youth. For a moment it appeared as though Shostakovich had again won the right to a certain degree of creative independence. In fact, of course, the Party had other things to attend to. But once the War and the initial aftermath were over, it set about reasserting its grip on all aspects of Soviet life.

On this occasion the assault on the arts was led by the formidable, catlike figure of Zhadanov, and what happened made the
event of 1934 seem like the merest storm in a teacup. In 1948
Zhadanov himself presided as grand inquisitor over a conference
of musicians. Alexander Werth's fascinating book *Musical Uproar
in Moscow* describes the shameful humiliations inflicted on any
composer who tried to stand up for himself. Backed by nauseating
waves of sycophantic laughter and applause, Zhadanov poured
cheap mockery on contemporary music. Prokofiev had the courage
not to attend – on grounds of ill health. But the more timid
Shostakovich, whose nervousness still makes it an agony for him
even to acknowledge applause on a platform, was obliged to admit
the error of his ways in two pathetically subservient speeches.

If Shostakovich's disgrace in 1934 did not produce the Fifth
Symphony, as Soviet critics would have it, it at least did not deter
the writing of a masterpiece. The infinitely more drastic events
of 1948 were totally destructive in effect. A blight compounded of
bigotry, philistinism, professional envy, chauvinism and sheer
brutish stupidity overnight reduced the whole of Eastern Europe
to a musical desert. The astounding thing is that some of the
musical officials who served as instruments of these outrages still
sit in office in Moscow and greeted Stravinsky on his recent return
to Russia. For a time it was thought that the effects on Shostakovich had been disastrous. For years nothing of importance was
published, and it was not until the death of Stalin in 1953 that he
released first his Tenth Symphony (armed with a curiously self-
deprecatory preference) and then the Violin Concerto. In this same
period he wrote the Fifth String Quartet, which is almost certainly
the best of an uneven but under-rated series. Thus it turns out that
what were apparently the most black and barren years of Shostakovich's life were in fact quite exceptionally fruitful. Once again
the outward political scene offers little explanation for the music.
For public consumption he served up a few trite cantatas on the
approved pattern ('The Sun shines over our Land', and so on), as
well as a certain amount of film music.

When works that Shostakovich had written in the winter of
Stalinism were revealed to the world after the dictator's death and
discovered to be among his best scores, it seemed that Khrushchev's
thaw might well usher in the most splendid and fruitful period of

the composer's checkered career. And indeed the old sources of strife were rapidly disappearing, for as the régime was becoming comparatively more liberal, so Shostakovich was himself growing more conservative in his musical sympathies. In 1958 he turned up at the Warsaw Festival of Contemporary Music and listened attentively to all the advanced products of the West, from Nono to Cage, from Boulez to Stockhausen. On his return to Moscow he wrote an article in which he praised Bartók and Britten, preserved an eloquent silence over Stravinsky (who was and is still a highly controversial figure in the Soviet Union), and dismissed all dodecaphonic music as valueless.

But once again Shostakovich failed to oblige those who would interpret his career in terms of political pressures. The last decade has produced only one really fine score – the terse yet intensely lyrical Cello Concerto. The symphonies of these years have been a particular disappointment. No. 11 (1957), which is based on events of the abortive revolution of 1905, contains some evocative descriptive writing but finally lapses into bathos and monumentality. The Symphony No. 12 (1961) rarely rises above this sorry level. It is a stiff, mechanical affair that at moments sounds like a cruel parody of the composer's symphonic mannerisms. Thus at the crest of his career, at a time when there can have been little grounds for conflict with authority, Shostakovich produced a score that would have given pleasure to Zhadanov himself. Some people argue that its deadly lack of imaginative power stems from the fact that it was written for the twenty-second Party congress of 1961 and deals with the events of the 1917 Revolution. But Shostakovich is not the first composer who has written a score to order (Haydn and Bach, not to mention Verdi, were used to doing so), and there is no more reason to suppose that the subject of the Revolution is antipathetic to him than there is to suppose that the sins of a Renaissance pope render the Resurrection antipathetic to a Christian.

Others will point to the fate of the composer's most recent Symphony, No. 13 (1962), abruptly withdrawn soon after its first performance and as a result yet to be heard in the West, as evidence that even now Shostakovich is not a free agent. But as far as I know no official objection has ever been raised against the music as such. And to judge from an unclear tape of the original performance, I would hazard a rash guess that this work is unlikely to prove one of his more remarkable scores, or even much of an improvement on its disappointing predecessor. Certainly I could distinguish nothing in it that might offend the most exquisite bureaucratic sensibility. In fact the trouble seems to have arisen purely from the fact that the Symphony includes a setting of *Babi Yar*, the anti-anti-Semitic poem which got Yevtushenko into hot water with Mr Khrushchev.

What then accounts for this apparent decline at the very moment when Shostakovich might be expected to be writing his finest music? That is a question we shall not be able to answer for many years, but any attempt to interpret the extraordinary ups and downs of Shostakovich's career in terms of political pressures is too simple by far. Ultimately, the mainsprings of a man's art are to be found in his character, and the music itself offers one or two clues to what may lie buried there.

Shostakovich has himself discussed his failure to write a successful first movement allegro. The essence of sonata form lies, of course, in the resolution of conflict, and, significantly, this is something that Shostakovich has rarely been able to achieve. There is a further feature of his music, perhaps more closely connected with this than may at first appear. The prevalent mood in many of his works is a deep, insatiable melancholy. Set against it are brief outbursts – often in a scherzo – of a hilarity so taut and high-pitched that it could fairly be called manic. The result often comes close to a sort of musical embodiment of a manic-depressive temperament.

We have now approached dangerously close to the treacherous field of psychological speculation – an area in which a music critic loiters at his peril. Criticism cannot be based on personal observation. But anyone who has seen anything of Shostakovich cannot fail to be struck by that strangely twisted face, at once sharp and innocent, like some neurotic yet highly intelligent schoolboy. And just as the face, the jerky, clumsy walk, and abrupt, inhibited and ill-co-ordinated gestures combine to convey the impression of a man profoundly at odds with himself, so does the music, for all its imaginative power, finally make the same impression. In this Shostakovich most resembles Mahler, a composer for whom he has always had a special affection and who has clearly been a potent influence in his stylistic development. One day it may be possible to discuss with more confidence the sources of these inequalities and unresolved tensions, which are at once the source of his music's fascination and of its shortcomings. But that day has not yet come.

from High Fidelity Magazine *1964*

PART III

Opera

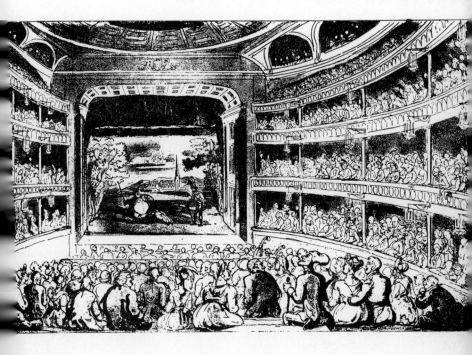

The Mythical World of Opera

W. H. AUDEN

In the primary world we have all experienced cases when, as we say, we 'felt like singing'. We may even sometimes be tempted to sing, but if we do, we are dissatisfied with the results, for two reasons. First, most of us cannot produce pleasing sounds. Secondly, even if we are professional singers, we cannot compose a song expressly for the occasion; we can only sing some song that is already in existence which we happen to know. In the hypothetical case of someone who is both a singer and a composer, he will be equally baffled because music takes time to compose and by the time he has composed something for the occasion, the occasion will be over. However, an examination of the kinds of situations and experiences in the primary world which make us feel like singing offers a clue to the kind of secondary worlds which opera can create.

These are always extraordinary situations or states of violent emotion in which we feel an urgent need for utterance. We cannot remain silent, but we feel that words would be an inadequate medium for such utterance. Why we should feel that song would be adequate where words are not is a difficult question to answer. I think it has something to do with the fact that our use of words is by no means confined to formalized literary forms, like poetry and fiction. Words are a medium for everyday informal communication with other members of our own species concerning practical affairs. And then again most of our normal conversation is addressed to, or elicited by, another individual and thought of as private, that is to say concerning only the speaker and the listener, not an audience.

Furthermore, when our emotional state passes a certain degree of intensity, even when, as in love, another human being seems to be the cause, it seems to be of universal significance. It is no longer sufficient that the girl we love should know that we love her. The whole world must know. The formalized art of poetry goes some way to meet our needs. Adverse drama already involves the audience as well as the protagonists, but music goes much further.

Singing is a form of public outcry. It is, on the voluntary level, what an 'ouch' of pain or the howl of a hungry baby is on the involuntary.

It is possible to speak in two manners, in prose or in verse. But there are no two ways of singing. The only alternative to song is silence. Though few have the talent for composing verses, almost anybody can be taught to speak them – at least adequately. Very few, however, can be taught to sing. To possess the vocal chords which would make sounds other people want to listen to is a gift granted to very few – singing, like classical ballet dancing, is a virtuoso art. A virtuoso art can be tragic or comic, but it has only one style, the high style. A low or humble style and virtuosity are incompatible.

If one listens to a recording of an opera sung in a language that one does not know, one can generally tell what is the particular emotional state – love, rage, grief, joy or so forth – which a singer is expressing at a given time, but one cannot tell whether a singer is a duchess, a chambermaid, a prince or a policeman. All social distinctions and all differences in age are abolished by song. In the case of some operas like *Rosenkavalier* and *Arabella*, one cannot even tell the sex. Nor, I think, on the evidence one hears from them can one tell whether the singer is a noble hero or a wicked villian. When one can guess these things it is because the composer has obeyed certain historical conventions. By convention, for example, the noble hero is a tenor, the wicked villian a baritone. Old men are basses, the voices of servants have a lighter timbre than that of their masters or mistresses. But this is purely a convention which a composer is free to ignore if he wishes.

The job of a librettist is to furnish the composer with a plot of characters and words. Of these the least important so far as the audience is concerned are the words. The opera house is not a *Lieder* recital hall and they will be very fortunate if they hear one word in seven. The verbal text of an opera is to be judged not by the literary quality or lack of it, which it may have when read, but by its success or failure in exciting the musical imagination of the composer. This does not mean of course that its literary quality is of no importance. Most composers will be more stimulated by good verses than by silly ones, provided they are so written as to be acceptable to musical notes and are singable.

Would it not be better, we ask at this point, if all composers wrote their own libretti like Wagner? If most do not, the reason, I think, is not merely that they feel incompetent to write one. However much preliminary discussion may have gone on between composer and librettist, the composer cannot know what the actual text will be until he receives it, and when he does it will certainly present him with problems he had not foreseen. The challenge of solving these is a stimulus to his imagination which would be lacking if he had written the text himself.

Verbal speech and music are two kinds of language, and if they are to be married satisfactorily it is essential to know in what way they differ from each other, and what are the virtues and limitations of each. A verbal statement and a musical phrase are both temporal successions of sounds that take time to say or to play but words, unlike notes, have denotative meanings. Consequently in most verbal statements there is little or no relation between the temporal succession of the words and the thought which they express. When we speak, that is to say, we are usually stopping to think, but music is always going on to 'become'. In verbal speech, I can say "I love you". Music can, I believe, express the equivalent of "I love" but it is incapable of saying who or what I love – you, God or the decimal system. Music, one might say, is always intransitive, and in the first person.

For this reason it makes no sense to ask of a piece of music or a painting: Does the composer or the painter mean what he says or is he just pretending? Lying or self-deception can be expressed by neither. Verbal speech on the other hand has three persons, singular and plural, past, present and future tenses, an active and a passive voice. But in a certain sense one might say that most verbal statements are in the subjunctive rule – verifiable statements are in the subjunctive rule – verifiable that is to say, if at all, by appeal to non-verbal facts. This being so, what elements in verbal speech can most readily be wedded to musical notes, in order to produce song? To begin with, obviously, the more dynamic verbal elements – interjections like Oh, Alas, Hail; verbs of motion like running, flying, swimming; verbs indicating the physical concomitants of emotion like laughing, weeping, sighing; and phrases expressing temporal succession or repetition. Then, because of the essential public nature of music, all nouns which denote beings, motions and concepts which are universally felt, consciously, to be of sacral importance – the sun, the moon, the sea, the four elements, God, death, grief, love, joy and what have you.

To be avoided by a librettist as difficult or impossible to set are, firstly, puns or double meanings. For instance the line, 'Farewell, thou art too dear for my possessing' is unsettable because there is no way of conveying the two meanings of 'dear' as precious and expensive. Verse that relies for its effect on spatial imagery, upon complicated metaphors, is also unsettable. Music cannot imitate visual facts, and the complicated metaphor, like 'the crowd that spanielled him at heels', takes more time to grasp than music can give it even if, as is unlikely, the audience can hear every word. Then it seems to be an empirical fact – I suspect it has something to do with musical tempo being generally slower than speech tempo – that composers find short lines of verse easier to set than long ones. The decasyllabic line of English blank verse in the heroic couplet, for example, appears to be too long to fall easily into natural musical phrases. The question which a librettist must continually ask himself is: "Can I imagine this line I have just written gaining in emotional impact if it is sung instead of being spoken?" If he cannot, then the chances are that his composer will feel the same.

When writing an aria or an ensemble, Chester Kallman and myself always find it helpful to let our choice of words and style be guided by a sort of platonic idea of a suitable melody. Naturally we were not such fools as to breathe a word about this, but to our utmost astonishment and delight, every time both Stravinsky and Henze composed actual music, it corresponded to our platonic ideas.

A secondary world must draw its building materials from the primary world, but it can only take such experiences as its creator is capable of imaginatively transforming and recombining. This seems to mean that in practice no secondary world can have a setting in the immediate present. The factuality of the immediate present is too strong to imagine it other than it is; too strong, at least, whenever strong emotions and suffering are involved. It might be possible to have an *opera buffa* with a contemporary setting but not, I think, an *opera seria*.

At the same time no secondary world can fully hold our attention unless it has something significant to say – we need not necessarily be consciously aware of what it is – about our present life. The most successful heroes and heroines in opera are mythical figures. That is to say, whatever their historical or geographical setting, they embody some element of human nature or some aspect of the human condition which is a permanent concern of human beings irrespective of their time and place. Perhaps I should modify this slightly and say that while no genuine myth is ever totally irrelevant, their rank of importance varies with time and place. To one age and one culture this myth may seem more relevant, to another age and another culture that. Further historical and cultural changes may produce new myths. Kafka was not only a mythopoeic genius but also a twentieth-century one. Nietzsche showed great insight when he wrote of Wagner's libretti:

> Would you believe it that Wagner's heroines one and all, once they have been divested of their heroic husks, are almost indistinguishable from Madame Bovary? Just as one can conceive conversely of Flaubert being well able to transform all his heroines into Scandinavian or Carthaginian women and then offering them to Wagner in their mythologized form as a libretto. Indeed, generally speaking Wagner does not seem to be interested in any problems than those which engross the little Parisian decadence today; always five paces away from the hospital. All very modern problems. All problems which are at home in big cities.

Where Nietzsche was wrong was in imagining that this was a fault. Had Wagner been unable to feel in Norse mythology or the Nibelungen legends any relevance to the moral and social problems of the nineteenth century he could not have made them come alive in his operas.

Because of the dynamic nature of music and the virtuoso nature of singing, opera cannot successfully deal with passive characters or helpless victims of fate. To sing is the most gratuitous of acts, so that the world of opera is a world of personal deeds. Nothing can happen in it which a psychologist could call socially conditioned behaviour. The characters who are naturally suited to inhabit it therefore are not only passionate but wilfully so;

persons who insist on their fate, however terrible or comically absurd. Though some tenors are under the illusion it is permissible, the sorrowing character in opera must never actually sob or weep. He must sing his grief, that is to say, remain his master. So long as the characters in opera remain the master or mistress of their soul they can come from any social class or indeed, as Janáček's excellent opera *The Cunning Little Vixen* demonstrates, they can be animals. Since Mozart's time the librettist has been expected to provide the composer with characters who are interesting as well as capable of singing. Most eighteenth-century *opera seria* before Mozart deserves the epithet 'Canary fodder' which has been unjustly applied to the operas of Bellini and Donizetti. For in this style of opera one operatic element, virtuoso singing, was exalted to the almost total neglect of character and plot interest. A typical opera of this kind consists of a succession of elaborate *da capo* arias preceded by short passages of recitative, an occasional duet but no ensemble, and after each aria the singer left the stage. All that the librettist was expected to do was to provide a few lines of singable verse expressing stereotyped emotions and moral judgements, the words of which could be repeated as often as the composer's musical ideas required.

In consequence very few operas of the period have remained viable as stage works, however beautiful some of their music may be. Mozart broke through the convention with his extended symphonically treated finales; Bellini and Donizetti realized the great dramatic possibilities of the ensemble; and in their very different ways Verdi and Wagner broke up the formal symmetrical aria and at the same time gave the recitative dramatic and lyrical qualities which it had previously lacked. We use the term 'music drama' in a less specialized sense than Wagner did, when we say that every successful opera since Mozart had been a music drama. Since the characters sing they must stand fairly still in order to be heard. And since to sing anything takes much longer than it takes to say it, one of the librettist's headaches is to provide his libretto with a sense of dramatic movement so that it doesn't become static like an *oratorio*.

When one examines successful libretti I think one will find that in them exits and entrances have a much more vital role to play than in the spoken drama. An excellent example of this is the first act of *Tristan*. It lasts one and a half hours and almost the only event in it is the mutual drinking of the love potion. Yet never does one have the sense of that becoming static. When one looks and sees how this is done, one notices the extraordinary skill with which Wagner managed the exits and entrances of his four main characters. Opera, said Goethe, is a succession of significant situations arranged in an artificial sequence. A good opera plot is one that provides as many and as varied situations in which it seems plausible that the characters should sing. This means that no opera plot can be sensible, for in sensible situations people do not sing. An opera plot must be, in both senses of the word, a melodrama.

When sensible or unemotional moments occur in the story, and it is very difficult to eliminate them entirely, then the characters must either speak or employ a musical convention like *recitativo secco*. Of course in tragic opera, as in spoken tragedy, a plausible situation and plausible motive is to be preferred to an implausible. But music can make things credible or at least acceptable which in a spoken play would cause laughter. In a spoken play, for example, I think we should laugh if we were told that a woman had been careless enough to throw her own baby into the fire instead of the child of her enemy, but when this happens in *Il Trovatore* we have little difficulty in swallowing it. Again, the emotional persuasiveness of music is so much greater than that of words. The character in opera can switch from one state of feeling to another with an abruptness which in a spoken drama would be incredible.

from T. S. Eliot Memorial Lecture
printed in SECONDARY WORLDS *1967*

A safe and easy method of properly producing Italian operas according to modern practice[1]

BENEDETTO MARCELLO

The Poet

In the first place the poet will not need to read or ever to have read the ancient authors, because not even the ancients ever read the moderns. Likewise he will not need to profess any understanding of Italian metre or verse. But he will say that he has pursued all the studies of mathematics, painting, chemistry or medicine, protesting finally that his genius has forced him to take up poetry, not meaning by this the method of correctly accenting, rhyming, or the terms of poetry, but rather introducing into his works some terms of the sciences indicated above, or of other sciences which have nothing to do with poetic training. He will accordingly call Dante, Petrarch, Ariosto, etc., obscure, harsh and tedious poets, and therefore of no account or little to be imitated. But he will have by him a stock of various modern poems, from which he will take sentiments, thoughts, and entire lines, in praiseworthy imitation.

Before starting work the poet will seek to obtain from the impresario a precise note of the number and quality of scenes the latter desires, in order to include them all in his drama, even at the risk of intolerably boring the audience. He will then write the whole opera without formulating any plot, simply composing it line by line, in order that the public may remain curious to the very end. He will never inquire into the merits of the actors, but will rather ask whether the impresario will have a good bear, a good lion, good thunderbolts, earthquakes, flashes of lightning, etc. At the end of his opera he will introduce a magnificent scene, of striking appearance, to ensure that the public will not walk out in the middle of the performance, and he will conclude with the customary chorus in honour of either the sun or the moon or else the impresario.

The poet will visit the prima donna frequently, because the

---

[1] I.e. in the early eighteenth century. The text is slightly abbreviated. *Ed*

success or failure of the opera usually depends upon her, and he will adapt the opera to her genius, lengthening or shortening her role or that of the bear or other characters accordingly. He will also call upon the composer and will inform him where the recitative is to proceed *lento*, where *presto* and where *appassionato*, as the modern composer is not expected to perceive anything of that sort for himself. He will be extremely polite to the members of the orchestra, the costumiers, the bear, the supernumaries and the stage hands, commending his opera to them all.

The Composer of the Music

The composer will not need to have any notion of the rules of good composition. He will not understand the numerical proportions of music, or know the names and number of the modes or notes, or how they are classified, or what are their properties. He will have little facility in reading and therefore will not make out the meaning of the speeches; he will not distinguish between the long and short syllables, or the force of the scenes. If he plays the harpsichord he will not observe the special qualities of the stringed or the wind instruments, and if he is a player of stringed instruments he will not take pains to understand the harpsichord, being convinced that he can become a good composer in the modern manner without practical acquaintance with that instrument.

It will do no harm, however, if he should have been copyist for some noted composer, and should have kept the original manuscripts of his operas, stealing from them ideas for arias, recitatives and choruses. On receiving the opera from the poet he will then prescribe to him the metres and the number of lines of the arias, entreating him, further, to provide him with a fair copy of the whole, without omitting any full stops, commas or question marks. He will take care, after that, never to read the entire opera, to avoid getting confused, but will set it line by line, showing no regard for full stops, question marks, or commas.

The composer will arrange that the best arias fall to the prima donna, and if the opera needs cutting he will not permit their removal, but rather of entire scenes of recitative, of the bear, or of earthquakes. If the second lady should complain that she has fewer notes in her part than the prima donna, he will manage to console her by making the number equal with the aid of repetitions, appoggiaturas, and graces in good taste. He will also show the greatest attentions to all the other *virtuose*, saying to each one that the opera owes its success to her talent. The same thing he will say to each man in the cast, to each member of the orchestra, to each supernumerary, bear, earthquake, etc.

Finally, the composer will have the following words placed under the announcement of the cast:

The music is by the ever most archi-celebrated Signor N. N., conductor of the orchestra, of concerts, of chamber concerts, dancing master, fencing master, etc. etc. etc. etc.

from ILTEATRO ALLA MODA *1720*

Overdue Reforms

CHRISTOPH W. GLUCK

When I undertook to write the music for *Alceste*, I resolved to divest it entirely of all those abuses, introduced [into opera] either by the mistaken vanity of singers or by the too great complaisance of composers, which have so long disfigured Italian opera and made of the most splendid and most beautiful of spectacles the most ridiculous and wearisome. I have striven to restrict music to its true office of serving poetry by means of expression and by following the situations of the story, without interrupting the action or stifling it with a useless superfluity of ornaments; and I believe that it should do this in the same way as telling colours affect a correct and well-ordered drawing, by a well assorted contrast of light and shade, which serves to animate the figures without altering the contours. Thus I did not wish to arrest an actor in the greatest heat of dialogue in order to wait for a tiresome *ritornello* (orchestral interlude), nor to hold him up in the middle of a word on a vowel favourable to his voice, nor to make display of the agility of his voice in some long-drawn passage, nor to wait while the orchestra gives him time to recover his breath for a cadenza. I did not think it my duty to pass quickly over the middle section of an aria of which the words are perhaps the most impassioned and important, in order to repeat regularly four times over those of the main part, and to finish the aria where its sense may perhaps not end for the convenience of the singer who wishes to show that he can capriciously vary a passage in a number of guises; in short, I have sought to abolish all the abuses against which good sense and reason have long cried out in vain.

I have felt that the overture ought to appraise the spectators of the nature of the action that is to be represented and to form, so to speak, its argument; that the concerted instruments should be introduced in proportion to the interest and the intensity of the words, and not leave that sharp contrast between the aria and the recitative in the dialogue, so as not to break a period unreasonably nor wantonly disturb the force and heat of the action.

Furthermore, I believed that my greatest labour should be devoted to seeking a beautiful simplicity, and I have avoided making displays of difficulty at the expense of clearness; nor did I judge it desirable to discover novelties if it was not necessarily suggested by the situation and the expression; and there is no rule which I have not thought it right to set aside willingly for the sake of an intended effect.

Such are my principles. By good fortune my designs were wonderfully furthered by the libretto, in which the celebrated author (Raniera da Calzabigi) devised a new dramatic scheme; for florid descriptions, unnatural paragons, and sententious, cold morality, he had substituted heartfelt language, strong passions, interesting situations and an endlessly varied spectacle. The success of the work justified my maxims, and the universal approbation of so enlightened a city (Vienna) has made it clearly evident that simplicity, truth and naturalness are the great principles of beauty in all artistic manifestations.

from DEDICATION TO 'ALCESTE' *1769*

Difficulties in staging 'Don Giovanni'

ANDREW PORTER

At times I have been severe about opera productions which seized on one aspect only of a work and, by ignoring others more obvious, misrepresented the piece as composer and librettist had conceived it. Unless persuaded to the contrary by producers and designers of genius, then of *Lohengrin*, for example, I wanted a staging that recked the historic pageantry and realistic detail over which Wagner took such pains; and of *The Magic Flute* an elaborate fairy pantomime with six lions, and aerial boys, and flames in the helmets of the Armed Men. For the Inner Significances, the Basic Myths, the Profound Psychological Truths, all these things beloved of clever producers emerge more powerfully from truthful stagings. It does not need a Wieland Wagner, or of *The Magic Flute* a dozen different producers whom anyone can name, to sledgehammer them home.

But at a Festival things are different – when it is a question not of a repertory staging that must serve for seasons to come, but of a production which, seen once, illumines a particular point even though it distort others. Moreover, experience brings tolerance – and especially in the field of Mozart performance. After hearing Mozart's four great operas from *Figaro* onwards hundreds of times, in a score or so of different productions, I know that, rich as life itself, they are as little susceptible of being seen steadily, or seen whole. The critic who is satisfied is lost, said Shaw; equally lost the critic who cannot discern, and be enriched by, what may be valuable in even the most oddly wilful presentation. Harry Buckwitz's *Magic Flute* at Munich last summer (1964), and the new Holland *Don Giovanni* here reviewed, were both damned locally. Each departed from tradition to embody a particular statement about the work.

The illusion that there can be an ideal, 'complete' Mozart performance fades. Once to me such a thing seemed approachable in student days by those Vienna versions when Schwarzkopf Seefried, Jurinac and Kunz were in their prime; a little later when in the Glyndebourne *Figaro* Ebert added a social sharpness to the

Austrian comedy of character, and the revolutionary sting made our rapture the keener. Rather similarly, Rennert's *Don Giovanni* for Glyndebourne pierced to darker corners than a purely romantic treatment of work could. The Gui-Ebert-Messel *Magic Flute*, close to Schikaneder, also came closer to Mozart than any totally solemn staging.

Meanwhile there were other things to learn, such as the simple matter of eighteenth-century musical notation, and the intricate matter of adornment and variation. After the Sadler's Wells *Figaro* – a landmark in Mozart performance – Glyndebourne's plain, unidiomatic reading of the 'text' could no longer be accepted. Each version adds something, until it seems that individual performances begin to matter less than the corpus of Mozart experience to which they relate. There is no 'whole truth' about *Don Giovanni*; no pattern or scheme fits more than a part of it. Contraries coexist. When Brigid Brophy discerned in Don and Commendatore a *Hamlet*-like son and father, then a son and a father, then later a homosexual relation between the two, the patterns shifted under her, as in this work (rich as life itself) they always do.

At the base of *Don Giovanni* – though many commentators seem to forget this – there is a familiar tale, and specifically a pre-existing libretto which Da Ponte adapted when the Prague commission turned up. The figures did not spring from Mozart's subconscious. But – need one point out the parallel with Shakespeare and his sources, or that this is a reason for Mozart's greatness? – inspiration (that 'perfectly precise psychological term for an image which visits the artist from a source of which he is unconscious' – Miss Brophy) intervened to make *Don Giovanni* more than a *dramma giocoso*.

So every age finds its own *Don Giovanni*. In Paris the piece was once prized mainly for Rubini's F *in alt* added to 'Il mio tesoro'. During Patti's reign Zerlina was the principal role. For the nineteenth-century Don Giovanni was a rebel hero, splendid as Lucifer, defiant to the last; E. T. A. Hoffman's Anna, the only woman worthy of his mettle, became popular. Then psychology made us wonder about Anna's obsession with her father – her extravagant cries for vengeance, her cradled grief in 'Non mi dir'. For a while a series of vivid Elviras, lustrous in otherwise weak casts, almost turned the opera into *her* tragedy. All partial truths.

We have had Giovannis cruel, reckless and attractive, Giovannis dangerous and evil; all aspired, at the least, to some heroic stature in the final encounter. Virginio Puecher's production for the Holland Festival presents the first Don Giovanni I have seen who is by intention unheroic – a hollow mockery of a satanic hero, a middle-aged undergraduate, his emptiness exposed at the last.

In Puecher's penultimate scene two worn-out faiths confront one another: that of the anti-social(ist) rebel who has gone through life as a parasite on his fellows, and conventional Church morality. Giovanni, who throughout has cut a rather Farouk-like figure, now loses any pretence to chivalric dignity. The Stone Guest is a huge marionette ascending to the flies, arrayed in the panoply of a Spanish Catholic knight, an impressive show – and worked by wires. It is hardly a contest between them; *both* are swept away, obliterated, forgotten, and the real people take the stage for the epilogue. Puecher, however, is too honest to hold *them* up as admirable: Anna and Elvira are both psychological messes; Zerlina's universal panacea is too simple; only the gallant Ottavio has nothing against him. But at least they are living, whole people. And Puecher's production, though it leaves much out of account, triumphantly asserts Mozart's belief in human values, and his uncanny understanding of human nature and its wellsprings.

This conception of the piece, and the scenic form in which Luciano Damiani had clad it, evidently proved too much for the company. A slip in the programme bore an announcement from producer and designer that 'insurmountable problems of a technical nature have prevented them from realizing the performance entirely according to their intentions. They therefore cannot assume artistic responsibility for it'; the Festival meanwhile thanked the director of the theatre and his staff for 'making the performance possible in spite of the difficulties'. Since Puecher and Damiani had put in 'weeks of intensive preparation', we obviously saw something of their ideas, but in an imperfect form.

The first surprise was to see the Don Giovanni stab the Commendatore in the back. There was a lot of naked steel about. In both scenes Anna exacted her promises of vengeance brandishing

Ottavio's sword; Elvira nursed a little dagger which she produced in 'Ah, chi mi dice mai' – and Giovanni's exculpatory phrases had unusual urgency! Masetto drew a knife on him in the garden scene, and again he had to wriggle out of a dangerous situation. (But no producer I know has adequately motivated Masetto's then going to the party after all. At sword's point? To watch over a Zerlina determined to go in any case? Something about his singing of 'Si, si facciamo core' should tell us.)

Puecher notes how Mozart 'resisted' Don Giovanni; allowed him no conquests, only humiliating failures; again and again had him checked by his servant. (Mozart's doing? What we really need, on this as on so many counts, is a socio-psychological study of Da Ponte! Too often is Mozart 'explained' in terms of his libretti). Renato Capecchi, a fine singer of the role and a clever actor, convincingly embodied Puecher's idea. So did Paolo Montarsolo, a superb Leporello, wittier and more natural in his utterance of the Italian word – with what colour and life he invested them – than the famous Austrian and Welsh interpreters.

Living Italian and fine singing also marked the performances of Ilva Ligabue, Graziella Sciutti, Luigi Alva and Leonardo Monreale (Masetto). Ligabue is a passionate, glowing Elvira. Sciutti, in excellent voice, sang both arias entrancingly. Alva was a brave Ottavio. Luisa Bosabalian's Anna, pretty well sung, was in character somewhat indeterminate. A sedate woman shocked by the attempted rape into sudden hysteria? It was hard to be sure. The portrayal seemed unrealized.

The playing of the Hague Residentie Orchestra was poor, but Giulini's handling of the numbers was shapely. He was obviously trying, without fuss, to make the musical best of a performance which had foundered and been patched. (But before exposing his singers to a British public he must teach them about appoggiaturas.) The cast was admirably free from the odious trick of 'beat-watching', a freedom occasionally won at the expense of ensemble. What remained of Luciano Damiani's scenery, even in this imperfect form, was superb, drawn with the cool precision, exquisite proportion and dramatic aptness that distinguished his *Galileo* for the Piccolo Teatro.

Before Edinburgh, one trusts, there will be more weeks of intensive preparation so that Puecher and Damiani can work out their ideas in full. The convenient if somewhat inaccurate epithet Brechtian is bound to crop up. A 'Brechtian' *Don Giovanni* had to come sooner or later. How admirable of the Holland-Edinburgh direction to have engaged for it a first-rate cast and conductor too. Already in The Hague this *Don Giovanni* was immensely rewarding. It left an indelible impression. Fully worked out in Edinburgh, it might prove overwhelming.[1]

from the Financial Times *15-7-1965*

Rossini

H. F. CHORLEY

Here, as belonging to a year of transition [1830] – to the temporary wane of Signor Rossini's popularity, and to his final retirement from composition for the stage – some remarks on the greatest musical genius of southern Europe are not unseasonable.[2]

The world is only beginning to appreciate this genius at its real value. Yet that Signor Rossini, on his first appearance, intoxicated the general public as no other composer, earlier or later, has done, is equally true. The vivacity of his style, the freshness of his melodies, the richness (for an Italian) of his harmony, the room and verge afforded to the singers, make up a whole in comparison with which the brightest splendours of Cimarosa and Paisiello

---

[1] *Author's P.S.* Alas for those hopes. *Don Giovanni* came to the Edinburgh Festival a dull, sorry little substitute for the finished production: 'artistic disagreements' had led to an anonymous non-production in shiny black-and-gold costumes against black flats and a wrinkled sky-cloth. A concert performance would have been preferable: that at least would have left the imagination free. This had just enough of scenic content and conventional acting routines to peg the show to pedestrianism. . . . A lowest common denominator of *Don Giovanni* stagings, flavourless, characterless, meaningless.

[2] Although Rossini did not die until 1868 and was therefore still alive (and in full possession of his faculties) when Chorley's book was published in 1862 his last opera, *Guillaume Tell*, had been composed as long ago as 1829 at the age of thirty-seven. *Ed.*

and Paër (to whom Signor Rossini is indebted for many of his forms) are but so many faded and pale emanations from luminaries of a second order.

There is no such luxury of beauty in any former Italian writer. I have never been able to understand why this should be condemned as necessarily false and meretricious – why the poet may not be allowed the benefit of his own period and his own manner, why a lover of architecture is to be compelled to swear by the Dom at Bamberg, or by the cathedral at Monreale, that he must abhor and denounce Michaelangelo's church on the Baths of Diocletian at Rome, why the person who enjoys *Il Barbiere* is to be denounced as frivolously faithless to Mozart's *Figaro* and as incapable of comprehending *Fidelio*, because the last act of [Rossini's] *Otello* and the second of *Guillaume Tell* transport him into as great an enjoyment (after its kind) as do the duet in the cemetery betwixt Don Juan and Leporello, and the Prisoners' Chorus. How much good genial pleasure has not the world lost in music owing to this pitting of styles one against the other!

To some such unfair construction as that typified in the above paragraph was Rossini subjected by the 'judges' of opinion, so-called, who ruled during the noontide of his popularity. That was held to be a mere passing madness, which could not last. The old amateurs who delighted in the delicate music of Paisiello and the clear merriment of Cimarosa pronounced the works of the young Pesarese master overcharged, out of taste, and were not to be charmed by the fascinations of his melody, which no composer has poured forth in such delicious abundance, or by his exquisite and new concerted effects, as in *Il Turco, Cenerentola, Otello, La Gazza* – in every opera from his pen. They declared, and declared truly, that he had borrowed from other composers largely – from Haydn in his 'Zitti, Zitti' (*Barbiere*), from Paër, from Generali; but what of that? They might just as fairly have railed against Shakespeare because he quoted Plutarch and Hollinshed verbatim; or against Handel, who scrupled not to appropriate any material that suited his purpose for the moment; having forgotten what a gorgeous treasure of originality remains to each of the three when every debt has been paid to the uttermost! We are *now* aware of the glow, the colour, the emotion thrown into Italian opera by Signor Rossini, as compared with his predecessors; but purists, thirty-five years ago, saw none of these things – none of the enrichment and enlargement brought into his art by the master, without any such innovations as imply destruction. They resigned themselves, with a sort of fastidious self-pity, to the enthusiasm of the hour – as wise men will to a passing frenzy – preferred to talk of the composers and singers whom they had thoroughly delighted in when they were young, in the days when Art was Art indeed – quiet and select, however beautiful, – not a delirious orgy, which could only intoxicate those feeble-brained and hot-blooded folk who courted intoxication. In a humour such as this were the operas of Signor Rossini treated by such English amateurs of music as Lord Mount-Edgecumbe and his contemporaries.

They had also to run the gauntlet of criticism totally different in spirit. At the time of their sudden outburst the world of Europe was beginning also to waken to the solid and lasting claims of the great writers of the German school. Mozart was comparatively unhackneyed; Beethoven was just beginning to pierce the sympathies of the imaginative and enterprising (in spite of the imperfect execution of his works). Weber had got hold of a fresher stage than that of Italy by the fascination of a wild and popular nationality. There is more to master in the music of all these three men than in that of Signor Rossini. Germany was newer than Italy. Orchestral art was then in the first freshness of its youth; and hence the sagacious, the scientific, and the sour set their faces against the facile author of *Il Barbiere* as the spoiled idol of fashion, as a mere flimsy tune-spinner whose seductions (supposing anyone willing to be honestly seduced) must prove transient, palling, unreal. When the composer was in England, singing at Marlborough House for H.R.H. the Prince Leopold, or under the wing of the Duke of Wellington (a man as genuine in his musical amateurship as in everything he set himself to study or to do), it was a fashion with the narrow (let me say, the pedantic) members of the English profession – then proud to be able to comprehend German music – to show their pride by deprecating the newest and greatest of the Italians. There were such things as good and cultivated Englishmen who, on principle, when Signor Rossini entered one music shop, repaired to another. So that this unprecedented Italian popularity of his was not without its counter

check, not only in London but in every metropolis on this side
of the Alps. Even when he consented to attach himself to the
Opera of Paris, for a time, he himself (subtlest among the subtle,
most experienced among the experienced) found it well to change
his manner – to be careful, to attend more closely to finish – as his
operas, *La Siége de Corinth, Le Comte Ory, Moïse,* and last, and
greatest of all, *Guillaume Tell,* attest.

Another cause may be ascribed for the pause of Signor Rossini's
popularity besides the newly-acquired importance of what may be
called the scientific school of stage composition. It is wonderful
that one so far in advance of his age as Signor Rossini should have
consented to waste his genius on subjects so utterly unworthy of
it as are the majority of his opera-books. Considered as a series,
their want of dramatic interest is perplexing and remarkable – so
much so as to have suggested to sagacious persons the idea that
the composer of *Tancredi* and *Otello* could not treat dramatic passion
or situation, and was nothing when he was not sensually musical.
No folly more baseless ever presented itself to fantastic spinner of
theories. It would be difficult to name any more forcible example of
musical expression that the third act of *Otello,* than the apparition
scene in *Semiramide,* than the second act of *Guillaume Tell*; or
(to change the humour) than *Il Barbiere,* from its first to its last
note. Then, for colour, what can exceed in freshness certain scenes
of *La Donna del Lago*? – in intensity, the Plague of Darkness in
Moïse?

Evidences of power without limit present themselves in the
music of this great genius. That such power has been, in his case,
not unaccompanied by a self-disregard closely trenching on cyni-
ism, it is unhappily impossible to question; and this may have
been crossed by a vein of self-assertion amounting to arrogance.
Too inattentive to the march of time, the musician may have
fancied that he could retain, after fascinating, his theatrical
audience by the spell of music alone. . . .

Thus an assertion which at first sight may seem a paradox, if
examined will prove to be tenable as a truth. The time on which
Signor Rossini fell was unfortunate to the steady duration of his
popularity – the more so since, owing to his indifference to what
was passing in the world around him, he did not provide for the
exigencies of the hour. The phrase of 'no man's enemy but his

own' applies in fullest force, to the direction given by this man of superb musical genius to his career.

Yet after everything has been admitted and regretted, as a body of imperishable music the operas of Signor Rossini will endure so long as the art of music lasts. Now when the heat of immediate partisanship has died out, musicians of every country can admit his wondrous grace, his fertility of invention, his admirable treatment of the voice, his simple and effective taste in arrangement of the orchestra. He has already lived down some of his rivals and successors. He can never be made a model; neither can any man of spontaneous inspiration who owes so little to rule as he. The day may never come in which commentators will wrangle about his outer forms and inner meanings; but that every year as it flows on will deepen and ripen his fame, I no more doubt than that wood grows and water runs.

from THIRTY YEARS' MUSICAL RECOLLECTIONS *1862*

'Les Huguenots'

PHILIP HOPE-WALLACE

I have not heard *The Huguenots* since I took myself to see the centennial revival in Paris thirty-one years ago. What an experience that was.

Traditionally this opera, which starts with Luther's 'Ein' feste Burg' and ends hours and hours later with a fusilade and general collapse of *all* stout parties, overruns its time. I saw it to the end but all public transport had stopped too, which involved a five mile walk across Paris (I couldn't afford taxis then).

How amazed I was that much of this music had once been *th* star vehicle for the greatest stars of all. Meyerbeer at his wors writes like some gifted piano tuner who thinks up a 'Dans orientale'. Yet what fun it all is. If you have any taste for operati madness indulge it here. "Effects without causes," grumble Wagner. But the cynical Heine raved like Berlioz. I rather fanc an opera with a bathing ballet in it; what it has to do with th

Massacre of Saint Bartholemew you may question but is it not
endearingly French? At any rate I loved that part of it (Act II)
set in the gardens of the Château de Chenonceaux, the one built
half over water, owned by the Chocolat Meunier family, and
faithfully reproduced down to the last details in the mighty Paris
scenery; possibly the original sets in 1936 still – their *Rigoletto* did
100 years' service. Covent Garden please note.

The opera gets better and better. In Act IV the Catholics, backed
up by nuns as well as monks, bless the poignards to be used in the
slaughter ('Conjuration' to outdo Rossini's ditto in *William Tell*).
Protestant Raoul in love with Catholic Valentine overhears. He
wants to warn his co-religionists, Coligny among them. She tries
to stop him getting involved. "The danger presses, no more
caresses," they bawl, but when she bars the door he leaps out of the
window; which, after a high D, can take it out of an amply constructed tenor.

In Paris the lovers were Georges Thill (superb) and Marjorie
Lawrence, in the days before her paralysis. In this role created by
Falcon, who quite literally left her voice in it, Miss L was loud
and generous but she came down the celebrated descending scale
like an elephant coming downstairs on a tea tray. I had been
watching a very old opera buff who might well have been at the
first performance of all. High collar, wrap-around white tie. He
sat in the front row entranced but at this moment he suddenly
buried his frosty brow in his white gloves and veritably I believe
died then and there, with a world he had loved. One knows the
feeling.

from The Guardian *4–1–1968*

Meyerbeer

RICHARD WAGNER

agree with nearly everything you have to say of my opera [*The
Flying Dutchman*]. Only one thing startles me and – I admit it –
incenses me, and that is that you calmly tell me that I often have a

flavour of Meyerbeer! Really, I simply cannot conceive what in this wide world *could* be called 'Meyerbeerish' except, perhaps the artful attempt to win a shallow popularity. If, indeed, there were anything real and self-consistent which could be called the spirit of Meyerbeer, in the sense in which may speak of the spirit of Beethoven – or even, if you like, of the spirit of Rossini – I submit that it could still only be by some amazing freak of nature that I could draw upon a source of which the least whiff wafted from afar nauseates me. It is no more nor less than a death sentence upon my creative power, and the fact that you can pronounce it shows me clearly that you still have no really impartial opinion of me, but only one deduced from the knowledge that circumstances have brought me into certain relations with Meyerbeer the *man* for which I owe him a debt of gratitude.

from a letter to Schumann 1843

'*Maritana*' in *Vienna*

W. V. WALLACE[1]

Vienn

My dear Davison,

I have expressly delayed my letter to you until after the Thir performance of Maritana. You may judge for yourself what th success has been by the following – the Overture was encored, bu I would not play it a second time as the Opera is already too lon for a Viennese audience. 1st act, Staudigl's Duet with Mdl Meyer encored, the Gypsy Chorus applauded tremendously fc the first time, after the Finale the Singers were called out, as als the unworthy composer. 2nd act – the Trio 'From an old tim encored, also Staudigl's Ballad, every number was applaude after the Finale in which the [illegible] was received splendidly, was called before the curtain twice. In the 3rd act the Duet b tween Lazarille and Maritana was encored, the Staudigl nearly s the People Mad with his Grand Air, everybody says, that he nev made such an effect before in Vienna; the New Chorus of Gyps

[1] A hitherto unpublished letter to the editor of *The Musical World*.

which I composed here was also repeated. At the end of the opera, all the artists and myself were call'd several times before the curtain, so much for the Third Performance. I have had much to contend with, the Prima Donna can neither sing nor play, so that the part of Maritana, was a complete Nullity, in Fact, the Opera as it is play'd here, ought to be call'd 'Don José', for Staudigl's part is at present the principal one in the piece. The Tenor sings very well, but he had not the most remote Idea of acting. Nothing would even tempt me to give another Opera at this Theatre under the Present Management, the Imperial Theatre is the only one to look to, and I shall write an Opera express for it, to be produced next Season. All the artists of the Imperial Theatre are delighted with 'Maritana' and I expect it will be Produced there, immediately. In the meantime Jenny Lutzer will study the Part, as the Public is desirous of hearing her in it, this is [a] good thing for the Opera, as she is at Present engaged at the An der Wein. Some of the Papers here have commenced a Crusade against English art and artists, first Hotten then Balfe, who is most unmercifully torn. My turn comes next, I am accused of not being of the English School, they say, I am at one moment German, another Italian, anything but English. Now! as [four words illegible] when I am spoken to about an English Operatic School, never having heard of such a thing, it puts me much in mind of the Fable of the Wolf and the lamb drinking at the stream, for my part, I think that Music is an art that knows not Locality but Heaven, whether one receives its inspiration through an Italian or a German Medium. I can but think, that if the Melody is good, the Accompaniment correct, and the Dramatic Sentiment in accordance with the exigencies of the Scene, that one has attained the end desired, viz to write a good Opera. Nothing can be more evident than that a veritable Panic has taken hold of the Vienna Composers, the dread of a French Invasion in England is not half so great as that which they feel, knowing that Macfarren, Loder and Sterndale Bennet may yet come over and complete the havoc which Balfe has begun. There is not anyone here that can approach Sterndale Bennett as a pianist and composer for his merit. Nobody that can write a Symphony like Macfarren's C # Minor, and as to Operas, I have been Present at the Production of three new Compositions, and only one of them had even a comparative success. The Public of Vienna is perhaps the most Musical in Europe, and while that Public comes in crowds to witness my Opera, I care not what a few envious Professors may say through the Medium of Journals. I shall send you the Papers that most praise the Opera, also the Journal which has spoken most severely against it. Many of the first artists have written to me to say how pleased they were, all these I shall have much pleasure in showing you on my return, in about Twelve Days I hope to have the pleasure of seeing you, with best regards to Desmond Ryan, Rosebury and to White, and all friends,

Believe me
ever yours
W. V. Wallace

N.B. Do something for me in the M[usical] W[orld], you will much oblige me.

1848

Wagner at Bayreuth

GUSTAVE KOBBÉ

Wagner doubtless selected Bayreuth from among those towns which were eager to have his theatre located within their bounds because of its somewhat secluded character. Here he could count upon a reverential spirit, with absolutely no other interest to divert it from its devotion to the Wagner cult. He himself admirably sums up the history of the place. 'If,' he says, 'I made in *The Mastersingers* my Hans Sachs eulogize Nuremberg as lying in the centre of Germany, I thought that the same might be said still more justly of Bayreuth. The immense Hercynian forest, into which the Romans never penetrated, once extended hither. The name Frankenwald still remains, showing that the whole region was once a forest, the gradual clearing away of which is indicated in sundry local names, or made up in part of the syllables "reuth" (*reuten,* to make a clearing). Of the name Bayreuth two differen interpretations are given. According to one account, in early times the land hereabout was given to the Bavarian dukes and the Frankish king, and here the Bavarians cleared away the forest and made a home for themselves. This interpretation of the word flatters a certain historic sense of justice, in that the land, after frequent changes of owners, at last reverts to those to whom it owes a portion of its culture.'

Another and more sceptical explanation would have it that 'Bayreuth' is simply the name of a hamlet built up 'beim Reuth' (in the clearing). However this may be, the 'reuth' remains, indicating a place won from the forest, and made productive; and here we are reminded of the 'Rütli' of old Switzerland, whence the word derives a still more pleasing and more elevated significance. The land became the Frankish frontier of the German empire against the fanatical Czechs, whose more peaceable Slavic brethren had previously settled there, and so far advanced in civilization that to this day many of the names of places bear both the Slavic and the German stamp. Here first did Slavs become Germans without having to renounce their own peculiar characters; and they peacefully share in the fortunes of the common population. This speaks well for the peculiarities of the German mind. After a long continued rule over this frontier, the Burgraves of Nuremberg made their way into the marches of Brandenburg, where they were destined to found the kingdom of Prussia, and finally the empire of Germany. Though the Romans never penetrated hither, still Bayreuth was not uninfluenced by Roman civilization. In ecclesiastical affairs it broke boldly away from Rome. The old city, often reduced to ashes, adopted the French taste under princes with a liking for embellishment; an Italian erected, in the shape of a grand opera house, one of the most famous monuments of the rococo style. Here flourished ballet, opera, comedy. But the Burgomaster of Bayreuth 'affected' (as her ladyship expressed it) – affected to pronounce his speech of welcome to the sister of Frederick the Great in pure German.'

'Wahnfried', Wagner's house, and the grounds in which it stands occupy about 4,500 square feet. A roadway for wagons leads straight from the gate to the front door. Those on foot approach the house through two beautiful arbours. Above the door is the following inscription:

Hier wo mein		Sei dieses haus
wähnen	WAHNFRIED	von mir
Frieden fand—		benannt.

expressive of the repose Wagner found here after his hopes were realized.

Under this inscription is the sgraffito drawing by Robert Krausse. This is an allegorical drawing. Wotan, the principal figure, represents German mythology. To the right is Greek tragedy, to the left music, and to these Siegfried looks up, the embodiment of the 'Art Work of the Future'. As a stranger approached the house at the time the author was at Bayreuth three dogs sprang out of a roomy kennel and began a furious barking. These were the Nibelungen dogs – Wotan and his wives, Freia and Fricka. The house was built according to Wagner's own suggestions. In the basement are the kitchen and servants' rooms; in the cellar a furnace (this mode of heating is rather uncommon in Germany) and a capital wine cellar. I usually dined at the restaurant where Wagner bought his wines, and I soon came to the conclusion that he knew as much about wines as he did about music. The *Leitmotiv* in his wine cellar was a fine array of Johannisberger, but as he was a universal genius he had not confined himself to German vineyards.

On the ground floor you enter a roomy hall which runs clea up to the roof and receives its light from above. There are marbl statues of the heroes of Wagner's operas, by Zumbusch, and twe busts of the Meister by Dr Kietz, of Dresden. The frieze i decorated with frescoes representing scenes from *Der Ring de Nibelungen*. A room of about 1,500 feet square opens into thi hall. The walls are for the most covered with little bric-a-bra shelves and bookcases. The latter contain a great amount c curious literature, mostly folk-lore relating to the subjects o which the Meister has based the plots of his music dramas. The is also a piano in one corner. The room receives light from a larg bay window. In one side of this bay window is a large tropic plant; in the other the plain table at which Wagner sat at wor There was usually nothing on the table except a few sheets music paper and an inkstand, and on the inkstand a penholde which looked as though the Meister had been chewing at it. The back door of this room leads into the garden.

In this room, the hall and the large dining room Frau Cosima usually received her guests. When Liszt stood beside her it was easy to see the resemblance between them. Liszt has on his face a number of huge warts, for each of which his female adorers had some pet name. These warts made his fine, strong head all the stronger looking, and he can hardly be blamed for the fact that a lot of silly women made fools of themselves over him. The same is true of Wagner, upon whom, in 1882, I saw a French authoress and other women attempting to fawn in the most open and disgusting manner. The company at the Wahnfried receptions in 1882 consisted chiefly of the artists and their friends, some German musicians and members of the Patronatsverein. At one reception there were some Englishmen present who had opera glasses through which, as they stood in the middle of the room, they examined the ceiling and walls and the company as well. Some of the pretty 'Blumenmädchen' (the alluring flower girls in the second act of *Parsifal*) came in, and Liszt, whose eye for female beauty seemed undimmed, at once began to chaff them and joke with them. Wagner suddenly rushed in from a side door, threw his arms around Scaria, the basso, exclaiming: "This is for your splendid performance yesterday," kissed him and rushed out of the room again. Nearly an hour afterward he appeared again and was walking towards Liszt, who was in the middle of the room, when one of the Englishmen who had been looking through an opera glass spied him and at once made for him. "Herr Wagner," he said, in broken German, as he got near to him, "I had such a good time listening to *Parsifal*."

Hardly had Wagner heard the words 'had a good time', before he turned and darted from the room, shrieking, as he threw up his hands in dismay: "If you want to have a good time go and hear something of Offenbach's!"

That was the last seen that night of the Meister and – the Englishman.

In the evenings when there was no reception at Wahnfried there were always some of the principal singers to be found in the wine room of the Hotel Sonne. One night Materna would dress the salad and Scaria brew the punch, and the next night the roles would be reversed. The prettiest among the 'Blumenmädchen' looked after the trimmings. One evening Materna told us that Wagner had been in particularly good spirits at the theatre rehearsal that afternoon. While he was singing a certain phrase for her, to show her some particular nuance, his voice broke. Turning to Liszt and bowing apologetically he said: "Excuse me, sir; I have not practiced my solfeggios this morning." This led Scaria to tell us an anecdote which he had from Wagner himself. When Wagner was conductor of the London Philharmonic concerts he rehearsed a Beethoven symphony from memory. As the sainted Mendelssohn, who had dined with the Queen and the Prince Consort, had always led from a score, the directors thought there must be something radically wrong in Wagner's method of procedure and remonstrated with him so strongly that he promised to conduct from the score at the concert. Accordingly that evening he had a music book on his desk and turned the leaves from time to time as he conducted the symphony. After the concert one of the directors came up to him and said: "Now, Herr Wagner, you must admit that the symphony went much better with the score than without it." Wagner calmly pointed to the score he had used. It was that of Rossini's *Barber of Seville*.

This seems to be the proper point at which to introduce some of Wagner's characteristic sayings which have been reported by Von Wolzogen, Dannreuther and others. Speaking of a perfect balance between the means employed and the effects produced he said: "Mozart's music and Mozart's orchestra are a perfect match; an equally perfect balance exists between Palestrina's choir and Palestrina's counterpoint; and I find a similar correspondence between Chopin's piano and some of his études and preludes. I do not care for the 'ladies' Chopin', there is too much of the Parisian salon in that. But he has given us many things that are above the salon."

Few musical people – in this country at least – will agree with his opinion of Schumann, though Wagner on Schumann is less intolerant than Schumann on Wagner. "Schumann's peculiar treatment of the pianoforte," he said, "grates on my ear; there is too much blur; you cannot produce his pieces unless it be with obligato pedal. What a relief to hear a sonata of Beethoven's! It early days I thought more would come of Schumann. His *Zeit-schrift* was brilliant and his pianoforte works showed great originality. There was much ferment, but also much real power, and many bits are quite unique and perfect. I think highly, too, of many of his songs, though they are not quite as great as Schubert's. He took pains with his declamation – no small merit a generation ago. Later on I saw a good deal of him at Dresden, but then already his head was tired, his powers on the wane. He consulted me about the text to *Genoveva*, which he was arranging from Tieck's and Hebbe's plays; yet he would not take my advice – he seemed to fear some trick."

Wagner was much censured for what were considered his bitter attacks upon Mendelssohn, yet he expressed unreserved admiration for several of Mendelssohn's compositions. He was especially fond of the *Hebrides* overture, calls Mendelssohn a musical landscape painter of the first order and speaks of this overture as his masterpiece. "Wonderful imagination and delicate feeling are here presented with consummate art," he said. "Note the extraordinary beauty of the passage where the oboe rises above the other instruments with a plaintive wail like sea winds over the seas! *Calm Sea and Prosperous Voyage* also is beautiful, and I am very fond of the first movement of the Scotch symphony. No one can blame a composer for using national melodies when he treats them so artistically as Mendelssohn has done in the scherzo of this symphony. His second themes, his slow movements generally, where the human element comes in, are weaker. As regards the overture to *A Midsummer Night's Dream*, it must be taken into account that he wrote it at seventeen, and how finished the form is already!"

Schubert's songs he rated, as noted before, very high; but this admiration did not extend to Schubert's other works. Nevertheless his opinion will be interesting, even to Schubert's most ardent admirers, among whom the author is happy to count himself.

"Schubert," said Wagner, "has produced model songs, but that is no reason for us to accept his pianoforte sonatas or his ensemble pieces as really solid work, not more than we need accept Weber's songs, his pianoforte quartet, or the trio with a flute, because of his wonderful operas. Schumann's enthusiasm for Schubert's trios and the like was a mystery to Mendelssohn. I remember Mendelssohn speaking to me of the note of Viennese *bonhomie* (*bürgerlieche Behabligkeit*) which runs through some things of Schubert's. Curiously enough, Liszt still likes to play Schubert. I cannot account for it; that 'Divertissement à la Hongroise' verges on triviality, no matter how it is played."

Speaking of *pièces d'occasion* and with special reference to the 'Centennial March', he said: "I am not a learned musician; I never had occasion to pursue antiquarian researches, and periods of transition did not interest me much. I went straight from Palestrina to Bach, from Bach to Gluck and Mozart – or, if you choose, along the same path backward. It suited me personally to rest content with the acquaintance of the principal men, the heroes and their main works. For aught I know this may have had its drawbacks; anyway, my mind has never been stuffed with 'music in general'. Being no learned person I have not been able to write to order. Unless the subject absorbs me completely I cannot produce twenty bars worth listening to."

To those young musicians who think they follow Wagner by devising eccentric instrumental effects the following remark will be of value:

"In instrumental music I am a *réactionnaire*, a conservative. I dislike everything that requires a verbal explanation beyond the actual sounds. For instance, the middle of Berlioz's touching 'scène d'amour', in his *Romeo and Juliet*, is meant by him to reproduce in musical phrases the lines about the lark and the nightingale in Shakespeare's balcony scene, but it does nothing of the sort; it is not intelligible as music. Berlioz added to, altered and spoiled his work. This so-called symphony of Berlioz as it now stands is neither fish nor flesh; strictly speaking it is no symphony at all. There is no unity of matter, no unity of style. The choral recitatives, the songs and other vocal pieces have little to do with the instrumental movements. The operatic finale, 'Père Laurent' especially, is a failure. Yet there are beautiful things right and left. The 'Convoi Funèbre' is very touching and a masterly piece. So, by the way, is the Offertoire of the Requiem. The opening theme of the 'scène d'amour' is heavenly; the garden scene and the fête at the Capulets' enormously clever; indeed, Berlioz was diabolically clever (*verflucht pfiffig*). I made minute study of his instrumentation as early as 1840 at Paris, and have often taken up his scores since. I profited greatly, both as regards what to do and what to leave undone."

Regarding the efforts made to introduce his music into France, Wagner said: "Pasdeloup made every effort to acclimatize me in France and I thank him. But no one can become acquainted with me through concerts. I must be introduced at the theatre, for, to appear properly, I need not only singers but scenic effects and the entire dramatic apparatus. In my compositions all the parts are closely related, one conditioned by the others; and if one of these is omitted the unity of my work suffers. My works, however, will never receive recognition in your country. My music is too German. I strive, with all the power given me, to be the child of my fatherland. It is also dangerous to listen to my musical declamation without the use of a text, for they are reciprocal. Why have you not in Paris an international stage, where celebrated foreign compositions can be given in the original language? Composers would then be happy to appear before a Parisian public, which is the most intelligent in the world. I know my music is not played in Paris for other deplorably absurd reasons. Of these, however, I will no longer speak; they belong to the past. I am supposed to be bitterly disposed towards the French. And why? Because they hissed my *Tannhäuser*? Is it certain that it was heard correctly? Auber could answer for me; into his ear I whispered my woes. The moment for earnest music had not then arrived. As regards the journalists, I cannot complain of them all. I did not visit them as did Meyerbeer; yet Baudelaire, Champfleury and Schuré have written the best articles on my works that have appeared. I am not as dissatisfied with Paris as report says."

The best view I had of Wagner was at a dinner given by him to his artists and a few friends at the restaurant near the Wagner Theatre. At one end of this restaurant the floor was sunk considerably and steps led down to it. In this space was the table for the composer and his guests. A dinner was served on the upper portion to which, on payment, anyone was admitted, so that whoever chose to pay for the dinner could also have the pleasure of watching the proceedings in the pit. Wagner and his guests dined to a full house. The composer was the last to appear on the scene, entering hastily. This was the first time I saw him and I must own I was greatly disappointed in his looks. He was in spick and span clothes – something unpardonable in a genius. A light overcoat, grey trousers and lavender gloves were the most conspicuous details of his costume. He was undersized and walked with short, quick steps. Altogether he looked like a little dandy. But when he took off his hat and revealed his grand forehead his genius was impressively apparent. Looking up from the elect to where the spectators sat he exclaimed, somewhat contemptuously: "Da is ja auch das Publikum" ("There are also the lookers on"). Wagner treated his audiences, and even admirers who were nearer to him, pretty much as a father would his bad children.

After dinner there were speeches. Some local dignitaries made long and uninteresting remarks. Wagner's address was brief, but snappy and to the point. In its course he said some nice things about father-in-law Liszt. Wagner sat between his wife and Liszt, and concluded with a fine tribute to his artists. "I am," he said, "under deep obligations to all who have contributed to the fund for the *Parsifal* performances, but I am under deeper obligations to my artists; for, after all, art is not created by money but by artists."

I saw Wagner again after the first and last acts of *Parsifal*. After the curtains closed on the first act the audience broke into loud applause and called for Wagner. The enthusiasm not subsiding, he came out and scolded 'das Publikum' roundly, saying that this was not a theatrical performance and that they ought to be ashamed of themselves for thinking of recalls before the end of the last act. 'Das Publikum' forthwith meekly subsided, and during the rest of the performance was decorously *weihevoll* and *verklärt*. After the last act, however, the artists and Wagner were called before the curtain, the composer thanking his artists much in the same language which he had employed at the dinner. 'Das Publikum' however, which had contributed the shekels, was not thanked. Aside from the performances at Bayreuth, there was something about the Wagner cult as practised there which struck a cool headed American newspaper man – even if he was a Wagnerite as very funny.

from WAGNER'S LIFE AND WORKS *189*

"After *Lohengrin* I dreamt all night about a goose." *M. A. Balakirev.*

"Monsieur Wagner a de beaux moments, mais de mauvais quart-d'heures." *Gioacchino Rossini.*

"Since last night they no longer write Götterdämmerung but Goddamerung." *Newyorker Staatszeitung.*

"I like Wagner's music better than anybody's. It is so loud that one can talk the whole time without people hearing what one says." *Oscar Wilde.*

The First Performance of 'Carmen' in London

HERMAN KLEIN

Until the spring of 1878 very few Londoners had heard of an opera called *Carmen*. Then suddenly the title appeared at the head of the list of Covent Garden novelties: 'To be given for the first time in England; the principal role by Madame Adelina Patti.' Questions were asked. Had not *Carmen* been a complete failure in Paris when brought out at the Opéra-Comique in March 1875; and had not the composer, Georges Bizet, died of a broken heart three months later? Besides, was not the title-role written for a mezzo-soprano (Mme Galli-Marié) and therefore quite unfitted to show off the resources of even so versatile a singer as Patti. Quite true, was the answer on most of these points. On the other hand, it could be argued that Paris had revised its verdict after Bizet had died (though not of a broken heart); that the opera had met with decided success when mounted at Vienna; and that it had been drawing crowded houses at the Brussels Monnaie for a couple of years, with an American soprano, Miss Minnie Hauk, in the part of Carmen.

But Covent Garden was not to land the prize this time. Frederic Gye was no longer in control there, and his sons Ernest and

Herbert, who reigned in his stead, owned not a tithe of the father's tactical skill. Their season was to begin on 2 April and their prospectus was out by the middle of March. Somehow an early copy of it got into the hands of James Henry Mapleson, whose own season at Her Majesty's Theatre was not to start until 20 April. He studied the document with eager eyes, and doubtless felt annoyed as well as startled when he came across the announcement of *Carmen*. Why, he was wanting that opera for himself alone! For months and months his best friend (now that Tietjens was gone), the 'enchanting' Zelia Trebelli, had been imploring him to go and hear this delicious Spanish opera of Bizet's, from which she had already culled Carmen's fatal flower, the ambrosial 'Habañera', and had been singing it with invariable success at all her concerts. He had heard the opera both at Vienna and Brussels, and had determined to produce it as quickly as possible; which, for Mapleson, meant as soon as the right artist to carry it to victory was free to come. He had lost no time. His contract with Minnie Hauk lay in his desk.

So when Mapleson's prospectus came out in due course it announced that in addition to a new version of Verdi's *La Forza del Destino*, a revival of Gounod's *Mireille*, and Marchetti's *Ruy Blas* (performed the previous November), there would be an early production, 'for the first time in this country, of an opera by M. Georges Bizet, entitled *Carmen*, of which connoisseurs in all parts of Europe have spoken in the highest possible terms.' Here was an interesting situation for the London critics to ponder: both impresarios were promising the same new opera. Had both, then, been able to secure the London rights of performance? It looked very much like it. Either that, or one of them was taking 'French leave' in the matter. For my own part, I was ready to back Mapleson, inasmuch as he had made sure of a first rate Carmen in Minnie Hauk, whereas it was extremely doubtful whether Ernest Gye had succeeded in obtaining Patti's consent to undertake the role or even whether he had asked her to do so. (A a matter of fact she was not then to essay it, nor achieve therewith the sole rank failure of her career, until seven years later.) One thing however, was certain – neither impresario had secured the *exclusive* rights of performance in England. These were still available when Augustus Harris purchased them from M. Choudens in 1888.

Only a mild sort of interest was taken by the general run of opera-goers in the first representation of *Carmen* on 22 June. The crowd that filled the house was of the artistic rather than the 'paying' order. (Indeed, Mapleson complained in his *Memoirs* that 'the receipts for the first two or three performances were most miserable'.) My seats were in the dress-circle, and very proud I felt that evening, for my companion was my illustrious teacher, Manuel Garcia. A Spaniard by birth and a friend of Prosper Mérimée, on whose story Bizet's opera was founded, he was enormously interested in the whole production. Sir Michael Costa was the conductor and Trebelli sat with friends in a pit-tier box. The *claqueurs* were still looking for Campanini, to greet him with a round of applause, when they discovered too late that Don José was already on the stage as brigadier of the relieving guard. Similarly, they had contrived to miss Alwina Valleria, when Micaela had modestly crept down the steps leading from the bridge to the Square where the guard-room and the cigar factory stood on either hand. Indescribably quaint and striking as was this new picture of Sevillian life, it only served to enhance our impatience for the entry of the central figure. Everyone was waiting to see Minnie Hauk, the famous Carmen.

Nothing intrigues like the unknown; and I confess that, of the many dozens of Carmens I have seen since that night, I have not awaited one with the same palpitating thrill of excitement and expectation, nor felt a fuller sense of satisfaction when at last the gipsy appeared, strutting forward with hand on hip and flowers to mouth. I heard Garcia's whisper, "She looks the character well!" I felt how right he was when he noisily clapped his hands after her piquant 'Habañera'; a rendering naturally much more effective than Trebelli's on the concert platform, because here vividly and suggestively acted as well as sung. The voice itself was not remarkable for sweetness or sympathetic charm, though strong and full enough in the medium register; but somehow its rather thin, penetrating timbre sounded just right in a character whose music called for the expression of heartless sensuality, caprice, cruelty, and fatalistic defiance.

We felt all this, and more, as the opera proceeded and the gipsy's ardent and impulsive (yet repulsive) nature continued to unfold itself. Her dances in the Lillas Pastia scene, like the chorus and the music generally, struck my master as being eminently Spanish. We generously applauded the Toreador's song – mannificently sung by Del Puente, first and *facile princeps* of bull-fighters – and we admired no less Campanini's beautiful tone and phrasing in the 'Flower Song'. The audience, too, was now growing enthusiastic, and, from anyone but Costa, would have extracted a repetition of the smugglers' quintet. In the scene with Don José, Minnie Hauk struck her first harsh note – that strange mocking note, strident and vicious, that distinguished her angry Carmen from all other's save Calvé's; and we were to hear it again in the climax of the mountain scene and the final meeting with José. Meantime Bizet's marvellous sense of contrast had afforded her a rare opportunity in the Card scene, and also, through Alwina Valleria, our finest glimpse of the graceful suavity and tender sentiment of Micaela's song.

After this, the bull-fight procession and the short Spanish ballet in the last act completed the conquest of my excited old master. He insisted that nothing so realistic had been seen on the operatic stage; that no composer since Mozart had penned a lovelier strain of diatonic melody than the brief duet in which Carmen and Escamillo unite their voices. And I must admit that, as poured forth by Minnie Hauk and Del Puente, it sounded as inspired as it was original. "What a pity!" I muttered, as we left the theatre; "just as she really had fallen in love at last she had to die!" Garcia heard me and remarked, speaking to me as usual in French, "Oui; mais n'oubliez pas, mon cher, que c'était une très mauvaise femme." So much for *Carmen* on its first night in London. Before the end of the season it was acknowledged to be as big a hit as *Faust*; and that was saying a great deal.

from THE GOLDEN AGE OF OPERA *1933*

"If it were possible to imagine His Satanic Majesty writing an opera, *Carmen* would be the sort of work he might be expected to turn out." *Music Trade Review*.

'Otello'

F. BONAVIA

Otello was given for the first time at the Scala, Milan, on 5 February 1887, and its success was immediate and unanimous. The opera represents the goal of a lifetime of great endeavours; ideals and technique have reached the point where they work in perfect harmony together, where theory and practice are one. The theory remains essentially the same. The singer, the visible hero of the drama, still retains the first place, but with this important qualification, that his pre-eminence is not that of a virtuoso but that of the protagonist in a drama. No opportunity is given him for a display of virtuosity; no arias or cabalettas are assigned to him. He takes his place in the play and claims our interest only because the play depends for its development on his action. The style of the music remains essentially melodic – that is to say, the greatest burden of the expression falls on one line of music – but the melody is no longer of formal design. It has acquired greater subtlety, greater power of expression and adaptablity; the music is not joined to the words but lies at their very core. Poetry and music are inseparable, and when we substitute any other text – as must happen when Boito's words are translated – that union is severed. The English translator who adapted Shakespeare's own words to Verdi's music did his work with ingenuity: yet he was unfair both to Shakespeare and Verdi, for the accent of the music is distorted out of love for Shakespeare, while Shakespeare's verse not seldom fits the music as a mangled body fits the rack. . . .

The libretto of *Otello* is easily the best in all Italian opera present and past. Its literary merit – which is great – and the skill and ingenuity of the translation are less our concern than Boito's treatment of the Shakespearean text. The adaptation of any drama or music is a difficult task of condensation, excision, reconstruction, but Boito's was the more exacting since *Othello* is vigorously logical ('a simple situation worked out step by step'); with an action that is continuous, and an interest that is cumulative. Any excision in the hands of less able artists might have meant irreparable loss.

With exceptional skill Boito possessed also exceptional courage, and he showed it by the omission of a first act which might almost have been written with an eye to musical composition. Only a few phrases are incorporated in the love duet. Yet, in the opera, each act is complete within its framework, each takes us a step nearer the catastrophe.

There are themes, but no 'leading themes', in the music. Even the plan of a theme connected with the chief character, as used in *Aïda*, has been abandoned. The motif system suited Wagner well, in the first place because he was by instinct a symphonic writer, for whom variation (the presentation of a theme in different guises) is an essential element of form; in the second place, because his action, centring generally round a few motifs which reappear under different aspects, fits perfectly his musical form. Verdi's acts never exceed a determined period of time and they contain many incidents. In *Otello*, an opera of rapid action and tempestuous passions, there is little opportunity and no necessity for leading themes.

In the great love duet which closes the first act Othello and Desdemona have not one but a dozen phrases of great beauty, every one as different as the thoughts that pass through their mind as they recall the beginning and the progress of their love. Only at the end, as Othello kisses Desdemona, the one theme is heard which will be heard again at the end of the opera when Othello dies 'upon a kiss'. The phrase which accompanies Iago's 'Beware, my Lord, of jealousy' reappears in the prelude to the third act as if to intimate that the 'green-ey'd monster' is at work and Othello in its toils.

But there is no systematic exploitation of motifs. The psychology of the characters does not rest on system, but on the aptitude and efficacy of the musical expression. Desdemona's innocence, Othello's noble simplicity, Iago's crookedness – these are made as plain in every note of the music as in every line of Shakespeare. Not a bar but reveals the felicity of a musical treatment in which melody is still supreme as it was in the operas which delighted Soffredini. Verdi was never more melodious than *Otello*; but this time in a way that fits perfectly a simple or a complex situation, and portrays with equal force and truth innocence and villainy, love and hatred.

Let us glance for a moment at one of the best known pages of the opera – Iago's dream. No oddity of rhythm breaks the course of the melody, no exotic harmony stresses its salient points. Yet it follows every inflexion, every accent, every suggestion of the narrative as closely as the river follows its bank. It represents the dreamer's murmurs as clearly as his imagined ecstasy; it stresses the word 'Moor' which hurts Othello most deeply; it marks the end of the vision with a sudden jerk like the stirring of a sleeper; it melts away finally as dreams melt and Othello's first words are soft as if he himself were still under the spell of the awful dream. Only after Iago has produced the handkerchief does Othello's anger break out with full force.

In the last act the need for psychological development no longer exists. Othello is in grip of a passion as untamable as the sea, and the other characters have reached the point when they are ripe for the last tragic deed. Desdemona stands condemned after Othello has gathered his proofs, to be crushed under the weight of his anger. But the poetry needed to temper the horror of the whole of the last act wells up in the 'Willow Song' as in the last scene of death and sorrow – more briefly but not with less dramatic point than in Isolde's closing song – the last as characteristic of the German as *Otello* is of the Italian genius. That ending to the opera I hold to be even more moving, if less terrible, than that to the play. It recalls the end of the love scene, and brings together the two great mysteries of existence, love and death.

from VERDI *1930*

A Letter to Verdi (1889)

ARRIGO BOITO

Before answering your questions I have been thinking much and now my mind is clear. The fact is that when I speak, write or think of you no notion of your age ever occurs to me. The fault is yours. I know that *Otello* is two years old and is now being performed by Shakespeare's own countrymen. But there is one

consideration more important than your age and it is this: after
Otello it has been said that it would be impossible to end your
career better. This is a truth which implies great and rare praise.
This is the only serious consideration – serious for your contemporaries, but not for history, which judges men according to their
essential worth. It is a rare thing to crown the work of a life-time
with a great victory such as *Otello*. All the other arguments –
strength, age, labour – have no weight whatsoever, and are mere
obstacles to new enterprise. As far as I am concerned, I will assure
you that if I were to undertake the libretto of *Falstaff* I should hand
it to you on the date agreed upon. Of this I am certain.

Now for your doubts. I do not believe that the writing of a
comic opera would prove too heavy a task. Tragedy causes real
suffering in its author, as the brain feels the suggestion of pain
which irritates the nerves. The jest and the smile of comedy
exhilarate mind and body. 'A smile adds one thread to the web of
life.' I do not know whether I am quoting Foscolo correctly, but
I do know this to be true. You have a great desire to work, this
is the real proof of your health and your powers. Ave Marias are
not enough – you need much more. All your life you have wanted
a good subject for a comic opera; it shows that the vein of art at
once refined and gay is in your temperament; instinct is a good
councillor. There is only one better way of concluding a career
than with *Otello* – with the victory of *Falstaff*. After having
sounded every note of human sorrow to end with a magnificent
outburst of merriment – that would indeed be astounding!

I beg you hence, dear Maestro, to think again about the sketch
I sent you. If it has the germ of a masterpiece, the miracle is
accomplished. Meanwhile we must keep it secret. I have spoken
to no one. If we work in secret, we work in peace. I await your
decision which, as usual, will be free and final. I must not influence
you in any way. Your decision will be wise, be it 'yea' or 'nay'.

quoted by F. BONAVIA *in* MUSICIANS ON MUSIC *195*

Massenet

MARTIN COOPER

Massenet's music has suffered from its fashionableness. No composer has been more whole-heartedly despised by one section of
his contemporaries nor more popular with the general public. His
whole nature was centred in the desire to please, and this has been
enough to damn him in the eyes of intellectuals who, in every
generation, provide a strong – and generally wholesome – puritan
element in matters of taste. The desire to please creates prettiness,
that facile and doubtfully-bred poor relation of beauty. The appeal
of the pretty is directly to the untrained senses and, through them,
to the surface emotion. Massenet's music resembles the pretty,
superficial and sentimental type of woman who relies on her
charm, her dressmaker and her hairdresser to carry her through
life. It is an eternal feminine type and, like all such types, it has its
biological and social justification; not certainly as the highest nor
– as misogynists would say – as even the basic type of women, but
simply as *a* type, despised by intellectuals and adored by the
public, which has an unreasoning instinct for what *is* and remains
indifferent to what ought to be. Massenet's operas, something like
twenty of them, are a portrait-gallery of women, most of whom
conform to this type. Each new work after *Hérodiade* (1881) is a
variation on the same theme – the feminine character in the most
striking points in which it differs from the masculine. Manon,
Esclarmonde, Thaïs, La Navarraise, Sappho, Cinderella, Griselda,
Ariadne, Thérèse are all *grandes dames* and they all, in different
ways, conform to the feminine type, accepted in Latin countries
until recently, for whom sexual love provides the central, and
often the only meaning of existence. Long before Massenet died
in 1912 this type had fallen into disrepute in England (largely
owing to the violent protests of the women themselves), and since
then the reaction has spread over the whole world. Beneath a new
form of puritanism the love-obsessed woman has been progressively degraded. We find her in Strauss's *Salome* and again in
Elektra, where Chrysothemis is the mere woman and the foil to
her virile sister: and she has sunk as low as it is possible to sink in

Alban Berg's *Lulu*. In *Turandot*, again, a woman's obsession with love has turned sour and taken the form of cruelty and a craving for power: the wheel has gone full circle from the healthy, instinctive passion of Massenet's heroines with their clinging caresses and their simple philosophy of the world well lost for love. Love has been stripped of its idealistic glamour and reduced to sex alone. . . .

Both Massenet and his contemporary Saint-Saëns were out of sympathy with the developments of French music after 1890, but whereas Saint-Saëns became personally embittered and intransigently hostile to the younger generation, Massenet was both more generous and by nature more easy-going. The testimonies of his pupils – they range from Debussy, Bruneau and Koechlin to Charpentier and Laparra – bear witness to his purely musical gifts, his keen dramatic sense and his personal charm and affability. If he was not much more than the *homme moyen sensuel* writing for his spiritual peers, he was a good craftsman and an excellent man of the theatre. His detractors have mostly been men of higher ideals and sometimes of greater potentialities, but few of them have in practice achieved anything so near perfection in any genre however humble, as Massenet achieved in his best works. He was one of the last of the purely operatic composers in France, certainly overrated by the contemporary public but as certainly underrated by his detractors and their modern descendants.

from FRENCH MUSIC *195*

Sullivan

THOMAS F. DUNHILL

Sullivan was, quite frankly, a tantalizing mixture of talent and genius. His talent has dated: his genius is for all time. His talent concerned itself with the making of serious music in which – as a leader in his profession – he was naturally anxious to prove efficiency: his genius took wing and lightly skimmed on the surface of the waters into which his talent plunged. In serious music-making, despite skill and sincerity, he was not strong enough to break away from the fashions of a peculiarly narrow age in our English art – the age of cumbersome oratorios, sugary anthems and hymns, and a species of domestic music which hovered between flowery elegance and insipid pathos.

Even the comic operas, which are the fruits of his genius, did not wholly emancipate themselves from the sentimentalities which so many people, in those days, craved for; but in spite of occasional lapses they most assuredly possess a spark of independent life, a spark kindled anew every time they are performed. . . .

No fair-minded appreciation of Sullivan need seek to disregard his shortcomings, or neglect to point out passages in his works which are momentarily trivial, inadequate or unoriginal. G. K. Chesterton it was who said, tersely and wisely, 'you never discover who is an inspired poet until the inspiration goes'; there are plenty of opportunities of discovering that Sullivan is an inspired musician by a similar circumstance. But, unlike so many of his contemporaries, he never 'manufactured' music. If a lyric or situation appealed to him his setting had the inevitable charm and fitness that obviously came to him in a flash: if not he apparently took little trouble and, choosing the line of least resistance, just set the words simply in a trite and commonplace way. This accounts for the fact that while there is plenty of poor music to be found in his operas (some of it very poor indeed), there is practically nothing that is laboured or strained. He was always quick to see where the words were all that mattered, and when such was the case he deliberately gave them the most elementary and obvious setting – perhaps because he did not want to waste his energies.

Sullivan certainly believed in economy of effort. Dame Ethel Smyth has recorded (in her *Impressions that Remained*) that when, on one occasion, she showed him some of her work in which he thought there was too great a prodigality of ideas, he said, "An artist has got to make a shillingsworth of good out of a penn'orth of material, and here you go chucking away sovereigns for nothing" – which is, as Dame Ethel says, a sound statement on Art.

Sullivan's music is so entirely devoid of pretentiousness that many people, while recognizing its individuality, have failed to perceive the very marked quality of its style. Style in music, as in literature, does not consist of a studied display of skill or the exploitation of rare artificialities. On the contrary, the real secret of style, as Matthew Arnold declared (and he surely knew a good deal about it), is 'to have something to say and to say it as clearly as you can'. In this sense Sullivan was a greater stylist than any of his more serious contemporaries. Even those among them who counted for most, progressively, were all – one realizes it on looking back as one did not at the time – a little too conscious of their art. The responsibility of living in an age of complex music seemed to sit rather heavily upon them. They did not dare to take things too easily, for the elaborate achievements of the continental giants were a challenge that could not be ignored. Coming after a spell of inefficiency and dullness in English music they probably felt it was their mission to do things thoroughly, and to strive to keep their music alert and moving. This resulted in improved technique plus a great deal of what now seems mere fussy energy. Hundreds of pages of Parry's music, for instance (eager, characteristic and high-minded as it undoubtedly was) suffered from this restless disease.

Sullivan, on the other hand, at least knew the value of repose. He appeared to care nothing for art as such; he did not bother to acquire the newer technique upon which the serious men set such store; he was content to give forth what was in him simply, gladly and with straightforward efficiency. He glanced at the complexities of music, no doubt, but passed them by on the other side, and went his way unconcerned. His easy aptitude had its dangers. He formulated definite ways of doing certain things, and did them in the same ways over and over again. Occasionally, too, he stumbled into vulgarity. But his energy was never spurious or simulated; it was always boyish and high-spirited. In his quieter moments he was hardly ever dull.

In a word Sullivan called upon his listeners to enjoy what he had to say, not to admire it. This faculty of thinking with his audience rather than for them was, indeed, what chiefly endeared him to the world. The very greatest composers, perhaps, are priests of the public, the lesser composers are its servants. Sullivan was not quite in either class. He was rather the companion of the public.

from SULLIVAN'S COMIC OPERAS *192*